Peace after the Final Battle

PEACE
AFTER THE FINAL
BATTLE

THE STORY OF THE
IRISH REVOLUTION 1912-1924

JOHN DORNEY

NEW ISLAND

PEACE AFTER THE FINAL BATTLE
First published 2014
by New Island
2 Brookside
Dundrum Road
Dublin 14
www.newisland.ie

PRINT ISBN: 978-1-84840-272-0
EPUB ISBN: 978-1-84840-273-7
MOBI ISBN: 978-1-84840-274-4

British Library Cataloguing Data. A CIP catalogue record for this
book is available from the British Library

Typeset by JVR Creative India
Cover design by Mariel Deegan/New Island Books
Printed by ScandBook AB, Sweden

the arts council funding
chomhairle literature
ealaíon artscouncil.ie

10 9 8 7 6 5 4 3 2 1

'The Irish attitude to England is, "War yesterday, war today, war tomorrow. Peace after the final battle."'
Irish Freedom, Irish Republican Brotherhood newspaper, November 1910.

Contents

Introduction

The germ of this book started some time back in the mid-2000s when I noticed a date on a memorial. The memorial was on Orwell Road in south Dublin, to one Frank Lawlor, and the date was 29 December 1922. As I was growing up, my father had often referred to this memorial and how the man it commemorated had died there fighting the British for Irish independence. When I was a child he used to call the spot 'ambush corner', and speculated that the IRA had chosen the site as it was on a tight bend, where a truck carrying British soldiers or Auxiliaries would have had to slow down.

The date, which I noticed purely by chance, immediately changed the story. December 1922 was well into the Irish Civil War, when Irish nationalists turned their guns on each other over whether to accept the Anglo-Irish Treaty. Looked at even more closely, the Irish language memorial gave up some more secrets. It read, *'Francis O Labhlar, An Cead Ranga Comhlucht, An trear Cath, Briogaid Atha Cliath, d'Airm na Phoblachta, a dunmaruscaid ar an laithir seo'*. (Frank Lawlor, 1st Company, 3rd Dublin Brigade of the Army of the Republic, was murdered on this spot.)

Not only was Frank Lawlor not killed fighting the British, he was not killed in combat at all, but 'murdered' by fellow Irishmen in the pay of the new Irish Free

State. As it happens, Lawlor was picked up at his home in Ranelagh by undercover pro-Treaty soldiers or police and, apparently in revenge for the recent assassination of pro-Treaty politician Seamus Dwyer, was shot by the roadside, just outside the city boundaries. If my family had got the story of Frank Lawlor so wrong, I pondered, what did this mean for the story of the Irish struggle for independence as a whole?

This book is essentially an effort to ensure that the Frank Lawlors and what happened to them can be understood. The struggle for independence became the founding myth of the Irish state – a status that did nothing to encourage objective study. Such studies as there have been have all too often fallen into one of two traps. One was to glorify it, splitting the story up into various segments – the Easter Rising, the War of Independence and then, as quickly as possible, or perhaps not at all, the Civil War. In 1966, for instance, Roibeárd Ó Faracháin, in charge of marking the 1916 Rising on Irish state television, stated that 'While still seeking historical truth, the emphasis will be on homage, on salutation'.

The second trap was to use the upheaval of 1912–24 as a polemical way of arguing about contemporary issues – particularly the use of violence in the conflict in Northern Ireland that ground dismally on throughout the 1970s, 1980s and early 1990s. To some extent in academic history, but especially in the media and in popular histories, the problem with these debates was that they were not primarily interested in the historical event at all, except as a way of either justifying political violence or condemning it, raging against the revolution betrayed in 1922 or giving thanks for the saving of Irish democracy, showing the illegitimacy of British rule or showing how a peaceful, liberal settlement of Irish grievances was foiled by irrational ultranationalists. None of which helped at all to explain how Frank Lawlor ended up dying on Orwell Road, shortly after the Christmas of 1922.

A great deal of the story of Ireland's nationalist revolution remains basically untold. However, in recent years groundbreaking new research has opened up such topics as what guerrilla warfare really meant, how Northern Ireland became established and how the Irish Civil War was actually fought. This book is not chiefly a work of original primary research (though it does incorporate elements thereof), but a synthesis of the research of historians, Irish and otherwise, in recent decades. It has benefited hugely from the opening of archives such as the Bureau of Military History in 2003, which gives us an unprecedented view of events in those years. It hopes to take the reader though all of the events that led to the partition of Ireland and the substantial independence of two-thirds of the island in 1922. It is not principally a book about high politics, but rather about how the revolution was experienced by people on the ground.

At the same time, such a book cannot avoid engaging with some of the main arguments that have raged, and to some extent continue to rage, about the Irish revolution. The first of these was whether it was revolution at all. This book hopes to show that the struggle for Irish independence was indeed a popular mass movement, far beyond simply young men with guns; it incorporated those who marched against conscription, those who participated in general strikes, those who occupied land they believed belonged to 'the people' (or even themselves), those who campaigned for Sinn Féin (and against them), those who held torch-lit parades for returning prisoners. It will argue that social and economic factors, often dismissed as irrelevant to the nationalist struggle, were, unavoidably, at the heart of events as they progressed. In particular, the land question and its settlement punctuated the progress of the revolution at every step.

The British administration in Ireland before the First World War was not democratic as we would understand the term, nor was the limited autonomy known as Home Rule the same thing as Irish independence. Armed revolt was not inevitable – in large part it was a result of the frustrations caused by the First World War among Irish separatists – but nor was a militant challenge to the old order unforeseeable. While legitimate debates will continue as to whether violence was necessary to gain a significant measure of Irish independence, the argument that the upheaval of 1916–23 changed nothing is, this book will argue, false.

Another vexed question is to what extent the Irish revolution was a sectarian one, pitting Catholic against Protestant. This is a question that contemporaries never adequately answered, and here I have tried to show the complexities involved. Irish Republicanism itself was a specifically non-sectarian ideology, insisting that there was no difference between Irish Catholics and Irish Protestants. And yet Irish history and society meant that inevitably most separatists were Catholics, and that (not all, but a significant number of) Irish Protestants were ardent Unionists. At the same time, the creation of Northern Ireland saw openly sectarian violence between the Protestant majority, now with their own autonomous government, and the Catholic minority.

Finally, this book hopes to show that the Irish Civil War of 1922–23, often dealt with either on its own or as a tragic afterthought to the revolution, was in fact central to its conclusion and to its results. The disillusion and disappointment felt in the early years of Irish independence cannot be explained without a serious look at the intra-nationalist conflict, how it came about and how it was actually fought. It might have been that the partition of Ireland, which was mooted first in 1912, would have been confirmed in 1922 in any case. The independent Irish state might have emerged from the revolution conservative, hardened and suspicious of its own people. It might have been most concerned in its early years with avoiding bankruptcy rather than trying to tackle its social ills without the Civil War. But that it did emerge in this way was due in large part to the conflict of 1922–23.

It is hoped also that this book will show that the contemporary rhetoric of democratic pro-Treatyites against militaristic anti-Treatyites is a poor guide to explaining the chaos and muddle on both sides that characterised the outbreak of fighting over the Treaty.

Finally, this book tries to show how the participants, particularly the nationalist or Republican revolutionaries in organisations such as the Irish Republican Brotherhood (IRB), saw themselves and what they were engaged in. The title of this book, '*Peace After the Final Battle*', is taken from an article in the IRB newspaper *Irish Freedom* in 1910. From this perspective, the events of 1912 to 1924 represented a struggle between good and evil, 'the final battle' to right the wrongs of Irish history, to reverse the process of colonisation and to forge a new Irish nation. Whether they succeeded, and whether the effort was worth the cost, this book will leave readers to judge for themselves.

Chapter 1

Before the Revolution

King George V of Great Britain and Ireland visited Dublin in July 1911. He attended horse races in nearby County Kildare and donated £1,000 to the poor of the city, before proceeding back through the southern thoroughfare of Dame Street to the royal yacht moored at Kingstown. *The Irish Times* reported that enthusiastic crowds had to be restrained by troops of the Irish Guards, while a band played 'Come ye back to Erin'. The paper reported that 'the cheering was sustained with enthusiasm and yet through it all there seemed an undertone of regret that a memorable visit, heartily appreciated by the citizens of every creed and class, had come to a close... "Long life to you" and "Come again soon" could be heard amidst the rounds of cheering'.[1]

Not everyone was so pleased to see the newly crowned monarch in Ireland, of course. The separatist newspaper *Irish Freedom* declared, under the headline 'The English King and Irish Serfs', 'we owe him or his people or Empire no gratitude or hospitality'. He had been 'guarded by spies and mercenaries and welcomed by helots [slaves]'.[2] The Dublin Metropolitan Police (DMP) used batons on small knots of nationalist protesters at the visit.

Nevertheless, the dominant symbolism of the day was unequivocally that of the British establishment. Dublin was draped in Union flags, and crowds (though perhaps not quite of 'every class and creed', as *The Times* liked to imagine) did indeed cheer the king. Dublin Corporation, dominated by moderate nationalists of the Home Rule Party of John Redmond, boycotted the official reception, but the Lord Mayor did attend, while a committee of 'Dublin Citizens' issued a 'loyal welcome'.

Twelve years later, on 11 August 1923, outside the new Irish Dáil or Parliament, green-uniformed Irish soldiers presided over another kind of pageant. They and another 2,000 guests (there by invitation only) saw the unveiling of a monument to two dead heroes, Michael Collins and Arthur Griffith. The President of the Executive Council of the Irish Free State, W. T. Cosgrave, paid tribute to them: 'Scornful alike of glorification and obloquy, [they], following the path of duty, led forth their people from the land of bondage'.

They had, in other words, broken British rule over Ireland; a rule that had apparently been accepted and even welcomed by all but a minority in 1911. But Collins and Griffith died not in the struggle against the British, but in the fight against other Irish nationalists who would not accept the compromises they had made over the question of Irish independence. And according to Cosgrave, 'the tragedy of the deaths of Michael Collins and Arthur Griffith lies in the blindness of the living who do not see, or who refuse to see the stupendous fact of liberation these men brought about'.[3]

Different countries

Ireland in 1911 was a very different place from Ireland in 1923. The years in between had witnessed a host of dramatic and often bloody events: the Home Rule crisis of 1912–14, the First World War, the Easter Rising of 1916, and intermittent guerrilla warfare across virtually the entire country during the period 1920–23.

In 1911 Ireland had been an integral part of the United Kingdom of Great Britain and Ireland. But by 1923 Ireland was divided into two new jurisdictions: the Irish Free State and Northern Ireland. The Free State covered two-thirds of the island and was effectively independent of Britain, though it was officially a dominion within the British Empire. Northern Ireland was an autonomous part of the United Kingdom. A new border divided the two, running in some cases through rural towns and villages. Partition constituted a major rupture in Irish society, but it was not the only significant change.

In 1912, Ireland was not a democracy by any twenty-first-century understanding of that term; only around 15 per cent of the adult population (and no women) had the vote.[4] In 1923, both Irish states had universal adult suffrage. In the Free State, the police, Army and civil administrations of 1912 had largely been replaced by new institutions. The remnants of the old Anglo-Irish landowning elite, who had still constituted a sort of ruling class even as late as 1912, were now a small and powerless minority. Their remaining estates were in the process of being compulsorily purchased and subdivided. In the Free State they had been replaced as the ruling class, in political terms, by a new nationalist and predominantly Catholic political elite.

Even nationalist politics looked very different in 1923 from 1912. What the Home Rulers of 1912 had sought was an autonomous Irish Parliament within the United Kingdom. Some of them envisaged home government as Ireland taking its rightful place within the British Empire. On this basis, at the outbreak of the Great War in 1914, they enthusiastically encouraged their followers to enlist in the British Army. By 1923, a very different vision of what Irish independence meant had taken root. One that excoriated 'imperialism', and any connection at all with Britain, in pursuit of 'the Republic'; an idea viewed as an impossibility, even an absurdity, by most nationalists in 1912. This 'Republic' was an ideal vague enough to mean almost anything in terms of what an independent Ireland would look like, but was concrete enough in the sense of rejecting all ties whatsoever with Britain.

So potent was this idea that Irish nationalists tore each other apart in 1922–23 over whether there could even be a temporary and symbolic acceptance of British sovereignty over a self-ruled Ireland – a distinction that would have seemed a ridiculous abstraction ten years earlier. In this decade in Ireland, therefore, there were dramatic shifts in the state, in politics, in power and in culture; enough, perhaps, to call this period of violent upheaval a revolution.

But there is another way to look at these events. For one thing, all of these processes – universal franchise, Irish self-government, land reform, the rise of a separate national identity buttressed by cultural nationalism – were happening anyway. In the end the British negotiated their withdrawal, securing, at least for the time being, their vital interests in Ireland before disengaging in 1922. For another, the period of 1912–23, though it did see the social and economic elite of Ireland challenged, did not in the end see it replaced or dispossessed. There was no social revolution. Indeed, both the Irish Free State and Northern Ireland emerged as rather socially conservative entities. By this reading, the armed struggle waged by Irish nationalists achieved not a revolution, but merely a speeding up of history, and got many more people (in the region of five thousand) killed in the process.

From these ambiguous results many different interpretations have been drawn. One, the mainstream nationalist one, states that Irish independence and national liberation, while not wholly achieved, were essentially secured by the struggle of 1919–21. According to taste, this can also be joined by the celebration of the securing of democracy against the most radical Republicans in the Civil War of 1922–23.

As against that, the Republican (and sometimes socialist) reading has it that the revolution was betrayed in 1922 – both by the acceptance of the partition of Ireland and by the crushing of political and social radicals in the Civil War that followed. A third, Unionist viewpoint sees the creation of Northern Ireland as a providential escape from ruinous Republican 'terror', and from the subsequent slide of southern Ireland into supposedly priest-ridden and economically backward stagnation.

Though it may show some strengths and weaknesses in the rival versions, this telling of 'the Irish Revolution' will not try to argue for any one of these interpretations. It hopes simply to tell its story.

The roots of conquest

If we are to judge whether Ireland experienced a revolution in these years, why it happened, how necessary it was and what it changed, we must look first at the *ancien régime* – Ireland under British rule.

Ireland had never been an independent unitary state. Before its partial conquest by Anglo-Norman barons in the late twelfth century, after which King Henry II of England claimed the title of Lord of Ireland, Ireland had been a patchwork of quarrelling Gaelic kingdoms. For around 250 years thereafter, the Irish and English lords had sometimes fought, sometimes allied with each other and rarely paid much attention to the small enclave around

11

Dublin – named 'the English Pale' in the 1400s – that was governed by English law.

In 1541 Henry VIII, concerned about a rebellion of the Kildare dynasty and the possibility of Ireland being used by European powers to invade England, declared himself King of Ireland and embarked on a project to extend the power of his state over all of the island for the first time. It took the better part of a century of both fighting and negotiating to accomplish this. The resistance of both Gaelic and Old English lords (the latter the descendants of medieval colonists) was not quashed until 1603, and the process proved a bloody business. Indigenous Gaelic Irish culture, language and law were sidelined and replaced with English models. Large amounts of land were seized, most comprehensively in the northern province of Ulster, and granted to English, and later Scottish, settlers.

English authority also arrived with a new religion: the 'reformed', or Protestant, faith. The role of religious conflict in Ireland is complex, but by and large the population – both Gaelic and Old English – that had lived in Ireland before the Tudor conquest remained (or perhaps became, under the influence of the Counter-Reformation) Catholic – a status that both popular and elite accounts often confused with 'Irish'. Like many early expressions of nationality, the Catholic Irish of the seventeenth century were an ethnic and linguistic mixture, defined largely by what they were not: Protestant, English, newcomers. It would be religion, not language or ethnicity, in the final analysis, that marked the boundaries of national identity in early modern Ireland – a fact that was still largely true by the early twentieth century.

It is not at all clear how well or how widely the doctrines of either the Catholic or Protestant religion were understood by the bulk of the population in seventeenth-century Ireland, but what is clear is that by the middle of that century most of the Irish population were, in their own understanding, committed Catholics. To what degree this was a straightforward response to colonisation and hostility to English rule is by now difficult to judge. Some, mostly Gaelic Irish people, certainly interpreted it in that way. Others, mostly Old English, maintained that they were loyal subjects of the Crown and merely wanted religious freedom. Nevertheless, the results of the religious split between Catholic and Protestant were momentous. For refusing to conform to the state religion, and for backing the pro-Catholic Stuart monarchs in two civil wars (1641–52 and 1689–91) the indigenous Irish upper classes lost virtually all their land and political power by the end of the seventeenth century, leaving both in the hands of a settler, mostly English, Protestant elite.

What this meant was that Ireland by the eighteenth century – though officially a kingdom in its own right, subject to the same king as England, Wales and Scotland (which after 1707 constituted Britain), but with its own parliament and laws – was in many respects a typical colony. The ruling elite was formed by a semi-closed group – foreign in religion, initially in language and in culture, from about 80 per cent of the population – the defence of whose position relied in the final instance on force from Britain itself. The Catholic religion and its adherents were excluded from landed, political and military power by a series of laws, known as the Penal Laws, which prevented them from holding public office, owning land valued over a certain amount and either voting for or serving in the Irish Parliament.

Conceivably, the Irish Parliament might have reformed itself into something more representative and autonomous had it lasted longer – indeed, it made attempts to do so towards the end of the eighteenth century, as well as softening legal discrimination against Catholics, who for instance received the right to vote in 1793. However, liberal Protestant reformism and Catholic discontent – which coalesced in the liberal Republican movement The Society of United Irishmen, founded in 1791 and inspired by the French Revolution – coincided with the Age of Revolution in Europe. The prospect of reform in Ireland ran into a wall of resistance fortified by the fears of more militant Protestants, or 'Ultra-Protestant' factions, and British fears of French invasion through Ireland. The subsequent repression of the United Irishmen led to their radicalisation and eventually to Republican insurrection in 1798 – the suppression of which convinced the London Government that rule of Ireland could no longer be left in Ireland. The Protestant elite, frightened by the rebellion and cajoled by bribery of various kinds, voted its Parliament in Dublin out of existence in 1800, and by the Act of Union of that year, Ireland became an integral part of the United Kingdom of Great Britain and Ireland.

Ireland under the Union

For the next century and a quarter, up to 1922, Ireland was governed at any one time by three administrators, only one of them elected and none of them Irish. The first was the Lord Lieutenant, the representative of the British monarchy in Ireland, who was usually an English aristocrat and who was based in the Viceregal Lodge in Dublin's Phoenix Park. His position was increasingly symbolic, but like the king or queen he had the right delay laws for up to a year and to advise the executive branch of government.

Executive power lay in the hands of the Chief Secretary for Ireland, who was a Member of Parliament

(MP) appointed by the incumbent government in Britain. Increasingly, the Chief Secretary took precedence in practical terms. When in 1905 a dispute arose between the Chief Secretary, Walter Long, and Lord Dudley the Lord Lieutenant, Prime Minister Arthur Balfour intervened, writing, 'If you ask me whether in the case of differences in views the Chief Secretary should prevail, I can only answer yes. There can be but one head of the Irish Administration'.[5] The Chief Secretary from 1907 to 1916 was Augustine Birrell.

The third prong of this trident was the Undersecretary for Ireland. This, unlike the Chief Secretary, was a permanent position held by a senior civil servant and based in Dublin Castle – the centre of English rule in Ireland for over 700 years and, in the minds of Irish nationalists, the dark Bastille of British rule in Ireland. The Undersecretary was responsible for the day-to-day running of the country. In 1912 the position was held by Sir James Brown Dougherty, who was succeeded by Matthew Nathan from 1914.

The personnel in the higher levels of the Irish administration were, moreover, almost all British and Protestant. The last Irish-born Chief Secretary was Chichester Samuel Parkinson-Fortescue, 2nd Baron Clermont and 1st Baron Carlingford (himself hardly representative of anyone beyond his own Anglo-Irish landed class), who had held the position from 1865–66, then again from 1868–71.

'The Castle' administration was disliked across the board among Irish nationalists, even the most moderate. For some of the more extreme: 'Our country is run by a set of insolent officials, to whom we are nothing but a lot of people to be exploited and kept in subjection. The executive power rests on armed force that preys on the people with batons if they have the gall to say they do not like it'.[6]

A French observer living in Dublin thought the British regime in Ireland was underlain by deep-rooted prejudice that the Irish were simply not capable of governing their own affairs; what he called, 'a gentle, quiet, well-meaning, established, unconscious, inborn contempt'.[7]

But in their own minds, most of the administrators of the Union in Ireland saw themselves as reformers, bringing good government and progress. This was particularly so in the case of Augustine Birrell and Matthew Nathan, liberals who saw their role as preparing Ireland gradually for self-government. So how had the British administration performed in its role as reformer of Irish ills, especially sectarian inequality and economic stasis, in the nineteenth century?

A century of reform?

Britain's story in the nineteenth century was of industrialisation and gradual democratisation. In Ireland both of these processes — the creation of an industrial economy advancing political equality — were far from straightforward. Ireland began the nineteenth century not only with effectively a colonial administration, but with the great preponderance of political power and wealth held by Protestants. The roughly 800,000 members of the established Church of Ireland owned the vast bulk of the land. Of the 3,033 government jobs in Ireland, the Catholic population of perhaps six million held just 134.[8]

Order was still maintained by the largely Protestant landlords acting as magistrates and the largely Protestant Yeomanry militia carrying out their orders, which sometimes included the suppression of a state of low-level insurrection. When landlords attempted to raise rents during an economic slump after the Napoleonic Wars, it provoked an agrarian rebellion in Munster from 1821 to 1824 by the 'Rockite' movement (led by local figures in each district, who were each known as 'Captain Rock'), in which over 200 people were killed and 600 'transported' to Australia.[9] Paying tithes to the Anglican Protestant Church of Ireland (the 'established' Church until 1869) was compulsory, and resistance to their collection led to another rural uprising, 'the Tithe War', from 1832 to 1834, in which the authorities recorded 242 murders in rural Ireland, along with 300 attempted murders and 568 cases of arson.[10]

Against this background, giving legal and political equality to Catholics in Ireland without disturbing the Protestant elite too much was a difficult task for London governments and one that advanced only in fits and starts. Penal legislation against Catholics (and some Protestants, such as Presbyterians) had been gradually repealed from the late eighteenth century onward, but it was not until a formidable mass mobilisation under Catholic lawyer and demagogic politician Daniel O'Connell that Catholics were granted full equality, with the right to hold public office being granted in 1829. However, to avoid Catholics having too large a majority in subsequent elections, in return for Catholic emancipation the electorate in Ireland was reduced sharply from 216,000 to 37,000 men as the property qualification for voting was raised from 40 shillings to £10 per year.[11]

Even after the 1850 Reform Act, which broadened the electorate to every man with property worth over £12, only one-sixth of adult Irishmen had the vote as opposed to one-third of Englishmen (women of course were excluded altogether until 1918). Voting also had to be conducted in public until 1872, meaning that a tenant who voted against his landlord could expect to feel the consequences. So it was not necessarily affection that ensured that landlords made up some 50–70 per cent of Irish MPs up to 1883.[12]

Nevertheless, despite the halting nature of progress towards political equality, by the end of the century Catholics did enjoy electoral dominance, where they were a majority. In 1840, when the Liberal Undersecretary for Ireland, Thomas Drummond, reformed Dublin Corporation so that it was elected on on the basis of property ownership (of over £10 per year) rather than religion, Catholic voters immediately outnumbered Protestants by over two to one. Daniel O'Connell became Lord Mayor of the city in 1841, the first Catholic to hold the position since 1689.[13] Thereafter, until the 1860s, in order to avoid sectarian animosity, the office of Lord Mayor was alternated every term between Catholic and Protestant. After the 1880s, however, the city government became solidly nationalist – to such a degree that mostly Protestant Unionists in Dublin deserted the city centre and founded their own 'townships', such as Rathmines, outside the city boundaries. By the 1900s, Dublin, a city with a population of over 300,000 within municipal boundaries, had an electorate of 38,000, including some women.[14]

In 1898, the British extended the powers of local government in Ireland, effectively devolving local power to nationalist and Catholic representatives where they were a majority, meaning that Dublin Corporation in particular became a stronghold of constitutional nationalists, who viewed it as an Irish parliament-in-waiting.[15]

Rural County Cavan, located at the southern rim of the northern province of Ulster, provides a clear example of how the extension of the right to vote gradually undermined the political power of the old Anglo-Irish landed class. Prior to the expansion of the franchise in 1868, three landowning families (the Farnhams, the Saundersons and the Annesleys, all traditional Anglo-Irish landlord clans) controlled politics in the county, keeping its three seats in Westminster safe for the Conservative Party.

However, the introduction of the secret ballot in 1872 meant that they could no longer control how their tenants voted, immediately loosening their grip. The 1884 Act made Catholics (who made up 80 per cent of Cavan's population) an electoral majority for the first time, and despite one Saunderson's exhortation to local Orangemen to 'drill, arm and don uniforms' to resist Home Rule in 1886, political power in the county passed with little violence to nationalists.[16] Still, despite being much more democratic at the close of the nineteenth century than at its start, by 1910 only about 15 per cent of the adult population of Ireland, or about 30 per cent of adult males, had the vote.[17]

Other features of Protestant domination were also gradually but slowly dismantled as the nineteenth century went on. In the 1820s, magistrates started to be appointed by central government rather than being automatically drawn from among the landlords in a given locality. In 1835 the Yeomanry militia was disbanded and disarmed, and power over law and order transferred completely to the new Irish Constabulary (which had been founded in 1822 and after 1867 was named the Royal Irish Constabulary, or RIC). The RIC alone among the police forces of the United Kingdom was armed, with carbines and revolvers, and was taught military drill.[18]

Moreover, unlike other police forces in the United Kingdom, it was responsible directly to the Irish executive, that is, the Chief Secretary for Ireland — and not, as in England, to locally elected representatives.[19] Many Irish rural communities experienced violent confrontation with the forces of law and order in the formative years of the latter during the nineteenth century, especially during clashes between tenants and landlords (RIC officers were advised to 'cultivate a friendly discourse' with landlords).[20] The novelist George Birmingham wrote in 1913, 'In Ireland we are not supposed to love the law, it was made for us not by us. It is only desirable that we fear it'.[21]

In one respect, therefore, the RIC was as nationalists often complained: an example of colonial rule. But equally, unlike its predecessor the Yeomanry, the RIC was a law-bound organisation, responsible to central government – not the all-Protestant tool of the local landowner. By 1910, the great majority of RIC constables (81 per cent) were Catholics, as were 51 per cent of mid-ranking officers such as district inspectors. The ranks of senior RIC officers (often recruited from the military), however, remained dominated by British and Irish Protestants, who formed over 80 per cent of its top command.[22]

Though constables were still trained in firearms and military drill in 1912, by that time their carbines and revolvers were generally left in the barracks unless violence was specifically anticipated. The police, in short, were becoming more 'civilian' and more representative of the population they policed as the twentieth century dawned.

By that time, the state in Ireland was no longer officially Protestant. In 1869 the Church of Ireland was disestablished, meaning that other religions no longer had to pay tithes to it. The Catholic Church, after a long and drawn-out battle both with the state and with secular-minded Irishmen, was granted *de facto* control over the primary education of Catholics in the 1830s and its own university in the 1880s. Straightforward religious conflict was, however, still present in Irish society in the early twentieth century. In Dublin, for example, the Catholic Church and Protestant evangelical societies – notably the Irish Church Mission, founded in the early nineteenth century to convert Catholics to

Protestantism – competed fiercely for converts in the inner-city slums[23]. Similar evangelisation battles took place in the remote west. In 1907 the Catholic Church decreed, in a bull known as *Ne Temere*, that all children of mixed marriages must be brought up as Catholics. In a highly publicised case in 1908, a Belfast Catholic, Alexander McCann, was pressurised by his local priest to take his two children away from his Presbyterian wife when she refused to convert.[24]

By 1910, a considerable number of Irish Catholics were quite integrated into British-ruled Ireland. Some 61 per cent of the 26,000 public employees in the civil service were Catholics and another 9,000 or so served as constables in the police.[25] As many as 50,000 more served in the British armed forces or reserves at any one time. To take three prominent Republican fighters and memoirists of 1919–23; Ernie O'Malley's father had worked in the Congested Districts Board, Tom Barry's was a policeman and Michael O'Donovan's (better known by his pen-name Frank O'Connor) was a soldier. Some future rebels recorded that in their youth they had been rather proud of the British Empire. Seán O'Faoláin, another policeman's son who went on to be a Republican activist, wrote that on Sundays in Cork as a boy he would watch the church parade of the British regiments based there, and when 'God Save the King' was played, 'I would whip off my cap, throw out my chest, glare and almost feel choked with emotion'.[26]

However, despite all the reforms of the preceding century, by the early twentieth century the economic, political and social elite in Ireland remained disproportionately Protestant or British or both. Todd Andrews, a youthful rebel in 1916, and later a senior Irish civil servant, recalled, 'We Catholics varied socially among ourselves, but we all

had a common bond, whatever our economic condition, of being second-class citizens'.[27]

Land

Aside from religious discrimination, the other legacy of colonial domination in Ireland was the land system, by which the landed class (not entirely Protestant, but dominated at the upper level by Anglo-Irish Protestants) owned very large estates and were paid rent by a largely, though again not solely, Catholic tenantry.

This too was undermined by reform from London and a series of Land Acts from 1870 to 1908. The first of these established that tenants could not be evicted without notice. Under the last, the 1903 Wyndham Act, and its extension in 1908, Irish tenants bought their land from their landlords with British Government loans, to be repaid over 70 years at 3 per cent interest. Nationalist and agrarian activist Michael Davitt heralded the results as 'the fall of feudalism in Ireland'. Although the Land Purchase Acts depended on the landlord in question being willing to sell, the results were certainly dramatic. Whereas in 1870 97 per cent of land was owned by landlords and 50 per cent by just 750 families, in 1916 70 per cent of Irish farmers owned their own land. The Irish export trade in cattle and dairy products was also booming, and much of rural Ireland had never been better off. Incomes had increased every year since 1841 by an average of 1.6 per cent per annum, and agricultural wages had gone up 200 per cent.[28] A Congested Districts Board supervised further land redistribution and, through improving farming methods and encouraging local industries, tried to relieve poverty in rural areas.

But like political reform, land reform in Ireland was granted only after bitter struggles. The 1820s and 1830s were marked by bouts of rural insurrection, and when the potato crop, on which the rural poor depended, failed due to blight in 1845, it triggered a catastrophic famine in which over one million died and another million fled the country. It has been debated to what degree the British Government was responsible for this disaster. According to Young Ireland revolutionary John Mitchel, '[A] million and a half of men, women and children, were carefully, prudently, and peacefully slain by the English government. They died of hunger in the midst of abundance, which their own hands created'.[29] The nationalist charge that troops and police guarded food exports while people starved has been somewhat undermined by research that shows that British Government food aid was greater than food being exported.[30]

But the fact remained that direct British rule presided over a mass mortality famine in a country that was not at war, had not suffered a natural disaster such as flood or a drought, in which a functioning state was present and in which the means existed, through food aid from Britain, to feed all the people affected. Some £8 million was spent on famine relief, a figure which looks impressive until judged against the £69 million that the British Government spent on the Crimean War just five years later. In particular, the decision at the height of the famine to shift the burden of relief from government food aid to reliance on private charity undoubtedly cost many lives.

What left the greatest mark of all, however, was that – as tenant farmers could no longer pay rent, having sold everything to feed themselves – troops and police were used to evict some 70,000 families, or perhaps half a million people, from their homes, condemning many to death or destitution.[31] Though mass emigration had already started from Ireland in the first half of the nineteenth century, the calamity of the 1840s turned a migration into an exodus. The Irish population in 1841 was approximately 8,200,000 people. By 1911 it stood at just 4,390,219.

In 1879, with an international slump in agricultural prices, there was again the prospect of mass evictions due to unpaid rent. That this did not happen on the scale of the Famine years was due to the formation of the Irish National Land League for tenant farmers, designed to prevent evictions and to negotiate collectively for 'fair rents'. (Despite their efforts, though, as many as 30,000 families were still forcibly removed from their homes in three years). The Land League's militant methods led to another bout of low-level conflict between Irish tenant farmers, the largely Anglo-Irish landed class and the state. From 1879 to 1882, some 12,000 agrarian 'outrages' – which could vary from burning hay to murders (about 60 of which took place) – were recorded.[32] It was this agitation, known in Irish history as the 'Land War', that prompted the British programme of land reform in Ireland. As a result, most of its beneficiaries viewed the Land Acts not with gratitude, but as a partial reversal, won after a hard fight, of historic injustices. One Cavan IRA veteran, Seán Sheridan, remembered, 'There always had been a void between the people and the RIC... The people had never forgotten the actions of the RIC during the Land League days'.[33]

The other problem with land reform – working on the premise that its goal was to pacify agrarian conflict – was that it did not actually change the structure of the Irish economy, which remained geared to the export of agricultural products to Britain itself. The large farmers who led the export trade (especially in cattle) and who availed of the Land Purchase Acts were simply freed from having to pay rents to landlords. Small farmers and agricultural labourers benefited little. In short, the Irish rural economy of the early twentieth century produced enough wealth, but not for enough people, and as a result emigration from rural areas remained high. The Irish Republican Brotherhood newspaper *Irish Freedom* complained in 1911, 'Our land might be a garden for 20 million people, they [The British] have made of it a cattle ranch, supporting one-fifth of its rightful population'.[34]

The land question was not, as is often maintained, settled by the early twentieth century. It retained the potential for violent conflict. Famine was still not altogether a thing of the past in parts of Ireland, though government responses to it were now much better than they had been in the 1840s. There had been localised famines in, for instance, Kerry in 1898[35] and in Leitrim in 1908 – where local government had to supply emergency food aid to one thousand families to prevent starvation.[36] Fear of famine, if not the absolute reality, remained a concern of Irish governments until the 1940s. At the turn of the twentieth century some 100,000 tenant families still lived on lands owned by traditional landlords, particularly in the west. Elsewhere it was cattle exporters, often the beneficiaries of the Land War, who tried to clear small famers off grazing land, leading to another bout of agrarian agitation known as the 'Ranch War' between 1906 and 1909. Conflict over who owned the soil of Ireland was still an issue. It would emerge again in the revolutionary period.

Industry

It is a truism of nineteenth-century Irish history that Ireland, with the exception of north-east Ulster, did not have an industrial revolution. Traditionally, nationalists blamed this on the British stifling of Irish trade by swamping it with cheap imports. Some northern Protestants attributed it to thrifty Protestant industry versus Catholic indolence. Others have pointed to the fact that most capital in southern Ireland in the early twentieth century was still in the hands of the Protestant upper class, that Irish banks all had their headquarters in London and that profits, largely made from agriculture, were rarely reinvested in Ireland itself. This, more than Catholic sloth, might explain the relative backwardness of much of the south of Ireland.[37]

Certainly though, Belfast (a city of nearly 400,000 at the turn of the century) fit the model of a British industrial city much better than Dublin did. The northern city had its shipbuilding and textile factories and row upon row of red-bricked terraced houses that surrounded them, giving homes to the working-class communities that sustained the industries. The fact that northern Unionists such as James Craig, the son of a distiller, felt that they had prospered under the Union, while southern nationalists felt their development had been stymied by it, contributed as much to the political divisions on the island over independence as did religion or ethnicity.

However, it is wholly misleading to see southern Ireland as a pre-industrial and unchanging backwater. Its main export – cattle – had to be brought to the ports and there loaded onto ships. Dublin manufactured Guinness beer and Jameson whiskey. The country was criss-crossed with railways by 1910, many owned by Unionist politician and railway magnate William Goulding. The south of Ireland was as capitalist as the north; the difference was that it was dominated by the export of agricultural products, especially cattle, rather than labour-intensive manufacturing products.

As was the case in public office and land ownership, the old Protestant elite still largely dominated the highest echelons of industry. But as in those other fields, this was slowly changing by the early twentieth century. William Martin Murphy – a farmer's son from County Cork – became Ireland's first high-profile Catholic and nationalist (he once held a seat for Dublin as a nationalist MP) millionaire. By 1910 he owned the Dublin United Tramway Company, giving him a near-monopoly on public transport in the city and a media empire that included newspapers such as the *Irish Independent* and *Freeman's Journal,* and several other titles.

In the years leading up the First World War, Ireland, in common with many countries in Europe, saw the formation of modern trade unions by a new generation of socialist and labour activists (notably James Larkin and James Connolly) and experienced a wave of strikes. In 1907, a strike on the docks in Belfast briefly united Catholic and Protestant workers and even led to a strike among the police. In 1911, a nationwide strike on the railways was routed, with the owner of the Great Southern line, William Goulding, taking the opportunity to sack 10 per cent of the strikers as a lesson to the others.[38]

In 1913, Dublin was convulsed by a nine-month dispute known as 'the Lockout', which pitted some 20,000 workers against a cartel of Dublin employers led by William Martin Murphy, who 'locked out' their workers who refused to resign from Larkin's Irish Transport and General Workers' Union (ITGWU). The workers, after a bloody and bitter struggle, eventually caved in. There were also mini 'lockouts' in Wexford and Sligo in the pre-1914 years.

Such disputes heightened the confrontation between rulers and ruled in Ireland. The business elite were often Unionists, and the police and troops used to protect their interests wore the uniform of the Crown, but by themselves such strikes were not revolutionary. For one thing they were essentially disputes over non-revolutionary matters such as wages and union recognition. For another, moderate nationalists in the Irish Parliamentary Party generally also disapproved of militant trade unionism. Labour would play a role in the Irish revolution, but not the central one. The main driver of political conflict in Ireland was the question of Irish independence.

Freedom for Ireland?

If the majority of the Irish population was being gradually enfranchised and given a stake in the system of British rule in Ireland in the nineteenth century, the question arose, throughout the century: might not the majority actually govern the country? With the political system reformed, might Ireland not be granted the return of the Parliament that had been abolished in 1801, or failing that, some other form of self-government?

On this point, however, Irish aspirations consistently ran up against two immovable forces. One was the 'Protestant interest', as it was known – an alliance of the Anglo-Irish upper class and working-class Protestants (mainly, but not only in Ulster) – both of whom feared for their position in an Ireland run by the Catholic majority. The other was the imperial British Parliament, which throughout the century remained opposed to Irish self-government.

Daniel O'Connell, having mobilised the Catholic masses to achieve Catholic emancipation in 1829, tried in the 1840s to mobilise them again for the 'Repeal of the Union' – that is, the reconstitution of the old Irish Parliament. His campaign drew crowds hundreds of thousands strong, but fell apart in 1843 after a planned mass meeting in Clontarf in Dublin was banned by a government that said it would be 'an attempt to overthrow the constitution of the British Empire as by law established'.[39] Two regiments of troops and a warship were drafted in to make sure it did not go ahead. There were two insurrections by radical nationalist groups in the mid nineteenth century, one in 1848 and the other in 1867, with the goal not just of self-government but of the establishment of an independent Irish republic. Neither really got off the ground in military terms, but as social movements were much more significant than they are often given credit for.

The first, in 1848, was led by the Young Irelanders, a splinter group of both Protestant and Catholic intellectuals from O'Connell's Repeal movement who disagreed with his conciliatory tactics. Coming during the Famine, it achieved little, but the Young Irelanders' Irish Confederation had some 45,000 members across Ireland, and well-worked-out plans for rebellion.

The Fenians, or Irish Republican Brotherhood (IRB), founded in Paris in 1858 by refugees from the Young Ireland movement, also attempted an insurrection in 1867. As many as 8,000 men marched from Dublin out to Tallaght Hill in March of that year, as a prelude to a rising in the city itself, and several thousand more mustered in Cork, Limerick and Drogheda. But without a clear plan, and with much of their leadership already imprisoned, they dispersed after some isolated skirmishes. The British Government in Ireland suspended *habeas corpus* (the right not to be detained without evidence) for several years as a result of the Fenian threat. Three Fenians arrested for their part in killing a prison guard in Manchester were hanged – entering Irish nationalist legend as the 'Manchester Martyrs' – and over one hundred more were sentenced to death but reprieved after a popular campaign for amnesty.

Thereafter, most Irish nationalists reverted to the more moderate demand of 'Home Rule', or autonomy within the United Kingdom. In 1870, the Home Government Association was founded by a Protestant lawyer named Isaac Butt seeking a new Irish Parliament. By linking up with land agitation pioneered by former Fenians such as Michael Davitt, the association became a social movement and then a powerful political party under a liberal Protestant landlord named Charles Stewart Parnell in the 1880s.

Parnell's party, the Irish Parliamentary Party (also known as the Home Rule Party, the IPP or simply the Irish Party or 'the Party'), effectively monopolised politics in southern Ireland for the following fifty years. At Westminster it agitated for Home Rule, generally in alliance with the Liberal Party, while in Ireland itself it built up a formidable political base, based on the Catholic parish and in close collaboration with local priests.

In 1886 the first Home Rule Bill was drafted by William Gladstone but defeated in the British House of Commons, as 'Liberal Imperialists', loath to see the break-up of the Empire in any form, voted against their own party. Bloody rioting also broke out in Belfast, before and after the Westminster ballot, between Catholics and Protestants against the background of the vote, at a cost of about fifty lives. Northern Protestants had also been against Repeal in the 1840s, but it was in the 1880s that Ulster Unionism was born as a political movement, closely allied with the Conservative Party in Britain.

In 1891 Irish Party leader Charles Stewart Parnell became embroiled in a divorce scandal and was denounced by the Catholic hierarchy. The Party split acrimoniously between 'Parnellites' and 'anti-Parnellites' (or 'clericalists', due to their following the Catholic Church *diktat* in denouncing Parnell). Nevertheless, in 1893 a second

Home Rule Bill came before the British Parliament and passed the House of Commons, but was defeated in the House of Lords. In 1900, the Irish Party reunited under the leadership of John Redmond and by 1912 it had again leveraged the Liberals into drafting a Home Rule Bill, the Third, and putting it once again before the House of Commons. This provoked muted celebrations among nationalists and furious opposition from Unionists, especially in the north-east.

Home Rule could not be confused with Irish independence, or even with O'Connell's demand for 'Repeal of the Union', which would have reconstituted the Kingdom of Ireland as it existed prior to 1800. Home Rule envisaged the creation of an Irish Parliament, subsidiary to the one at Westminster. It would have no control over collecting taxes, over the police or military, over foreign relations or even over the postal service. The final realisation of dreams of Irish freedom it was not.

There the question of Irish self-government stood on the eve of the First World War. Home Rule appeared on the face of it to be a fairly innocuous degree of Irish self-government. But, as we will see, its implementation – and resistance to it – was the spark that set off armed revolution in Ireland.

The Party

The Irish Parliamentary Party was the institution that had made the issue of Irish autonomy its own. In 1912, it was still all but completely dominant in southern Irish political life and among Catholics in the north of Ireland also.

The IPP had a presence in every parish through its subsidiary organisation, the United Irish League. It held 70 Westminster seats out of 103 in Ireland and controlled virtually every corporation, town and county council of note outside Ulster. Its only serious nationalist electoral competitor was the All For Ireland League; a mostly Cork-based nationalist rival led by disaffected IPP members William O'Brien and Tim Healy, which in the election of 1910 took eight parliamentary seats.

The Party had also absorbed the Ancient Order of Hibernians around the turn of the century, a shadowy group that emerged out of Ulster secret societies in the late nineteenth century. Although disliked by the actual hierarchy of the Catholic Church (Cardinal Michael Logue of Armagh described them as 'bullies' and 'a cruel tyranny'), the Hibernians had become a formidable Catholic-only nationalist fraternity and had also become, under the tutelage of Belfast MP Joe Devlin, the strong arm of the Irish Parliamentary Party.

It must have seemed, in 1912, as if the IPP would lead Ireland – gradually, legally – into Home Rule, and into what one of its leading thinkers, Tom Kettle, called 'a union of equals', but this would not happen. A decade of strife and revolution would sweep away the IPP, leaving barely a trace of its existence in much of Ireland.

Conventionally, the Party has been seen as simply unlucky; it was on the verge of triumph in 1912 before it was overtaken by a hurricane of events and buried by more radical rivals, who profited from a series of crises that began with the First World War.

Looked at a little more closely, though, the dominance of the Home Rulers in 1912 over Irish politics looks a little more tenuous. For one thing, the electorate in Ireland in the pre–First World War era was nearly three times smaller than after near-universal adult suffrage was granted in 1918. Furthermore, such was the dominance of the Party over Irish life in this era that many constituencies were not contested at all before 1918. The West Cavan constituency, for instance, where Sinn Féin scored a crucial by-election victory in 1917, had been represented at Westminster since 1904 by Vincent Kennedy of the IPP – who was returned, unopposed, in 1904, 1906 and 1910.[40]

The majority of the electorate that came to repudiate the Party in 1989, therefore, had never had a chance to vote for or against them before. If they were poor or women, it was because they did not have the franchise; if they lived in one of the many uncontested constituencies, it was because the Party's internal selection had previously decided matters for them.

Secondly, the IPP's nationalist credentials were becoming somewhat vulnerable by 1912. The Irish Party had been founded with a fair degree of influence from Fenians. Its founder, Isaac Butt, had campaigned for an amnesty for the insurgent prisoners of the abortive 1867 rebellion. The Party's members annually commemorated, along with separatists, the anniversary of the execution of the 'Manchester Martyrs' – hanged in that same year. In the land agitation of the late nineteenth century, IPP MPs (including at one stage party leaders such as Parnell, and later John Redmond) had been imprisoned by the British authorities. In 1898 the Party had been to the forefront in organising centenary commemorations for the rebellion of 1798. During the Boer War (1899–1901), Irish nationalist MPs had often supported the Boers, or at least shown them sympathy. Some Irishmen in South Africa itself had even fought on their side against the British Empire.[41]

The Party's base, therefore, still celebrated 'fighting for Ireland' and the idea that Irish nationalism was in a long struggle for 'freedom'. But the Party itself had become almost part of the establishment of British-ruled Ireland.

True, its members were still not allowed to join the more exclusive clubs that so influenced the informal exercise of power, both in Dublin and in London, but the Party's leadership was routinely consulted about the British Government's choice of appointee for the post of Chief Secretary and Undersecretary for Ireland. Most of its MPs were from the elite of Catholic society, and by the 1910s had settled into British political life quite well, and viewed Home Rule, or autonomy within the United Kingdom and the Empire, as a sufficient measure of Irish independence.

Dramatic and violent events that exposed the contradictions between loyalties to the British political system and to Irish nationalist aspirations, such as the demands of total war and nationalist insurrection, would therefore expose also the contradictions within constitutional nationalism.

Thirdly, its long hegemony over much of Ireland had made the IPP somewhat arrogant, a little authoritarian and more than a little corrupt. In dealing with political rivals, the Party was not above using violence and chicanery. When in 1909 William O'Brien tried to launch his new party, the All For Ireland League, he was met with a considerable degree of violence from the strong arm of the IPP in the Ancient Order of Hibernians, whose members attacked rallies in County Cork and even fired revolver shots at a meeting trying to launch the new party in Mayo.[42] In Dublin, where the challenge in municipal elections was from the radical nationalists of Sinn Féin and the socialists of various labour groupings, the IPP approach was less violent, but no more noble – using regulations to disqualify voters who might vote for their rivals.[43]

Nor was their exercise of power untainted. County Councils run by the Party were notorious for 'jobbery', nepotism and graft, while in some cases political power appeared simply a useful cloak for protecting economic interests. In Dublin, for instance, where overcrowding and shortage of decent housing for the poor had become critical issues by 1914, an inquiry into the collapse of two tenement buildings found that the Corporation, which had neglected to act on the issue, was dominated by slum landlords, most of whom were IPP members.[44]

In short, though the IPP appeared to be all-powerful in Irish politics in 1912, even had it not been for the eruption of war and rebellion, the expansion of the franchise would have left it vulnerable in the coming years to rivals who could portray it as corrupt, authoritarian and weak-willed with regard to Irish freedom.

Ripe for revolution?

In 1912, Ireland was neither entirely a colony – since it had its own elected representatives – nor entirely democratic, even by pre-First World War standards, since the real power lay with the London Government and with their appointees in Dublin. The large majority of Irish MPs (84 of 103 in 1910) were nationalists of one form or another, seeking self-government for Ireland.[45] And Irish nationalism, even when expressed in constitutional terms, was not entirely loyal to the status quo. Irish nationalists and Catholics had been integrated to some degree into the British state, but this integration was still far from complete in 1912. This was the fundamental contradiction of British rule in Ireland by the early twentieth century and the one that left it vulnerable to revolt.

The United Kingdom was increasingly democratic as voting rights were extended to the working classes. The superiority of the elected House of Commons over the House of Lords was asserted by Liberal governments in disputes over the introduction of social insurance in the budgets of 1909–11. Government in Britain was dependent on a broadly based agreement that those in power were there by the will of the majority (though as yet not all) of the governed. In Ireland, this consensus just did not exist. Had progress towards Irish self-government, land reform and social welfare continued unabated, this might have changed, but raising nationalist expectations left the British state in Ireland in a most dangerous situation if they were not met. And meeting them risked provoking resistance from the still-powerful Unionist elite. All of these contradictions would come to a head with the Home Rule crisis of 1912–14 and the outbreak of the Great War.

Nevertheless, Ireland in 1912 was not in a revolutionary situation. The organs of state were still functioning normally and were not collapsing from defeat in war or economic crisis. No political rival had yet threatened the mainstream nationalists of the IPP. Social discontent, though it existed, did not threaten the state's security. The Irish revolution, therefore, though in some ways the culmination of a long process, was born out of a series of unpredictable crises.

But revolutionary violence, when it came, was not carried out by a Catholic nationalist mass movement, nor agrarian or labour radicals, nor by frustrated Home Rulers, nor sectarian opposition to the Ulster Unionists. The revolution was willed into being by a smaller but altogether more committed world – that of radical Irish separatism. Before plunging into the crises that derailed Home Rule, it is necessary to look first at these men and women and their world.

Chapter 2:

Revolutionaries

In 1905, a 16-year-old County Down Protestant named Ernest Blythe came to Dublin to work as a clerk in the Irish civil service. The young man was shy and no doubt lonely in the new city. By chance, loafing around the Gaelic League bookshop, he heard three people speaking Irish and was intrigued. Although he feared at first that 'if it were discovered that I was a Protestant, I would be put out', he ended up joining the Gaelic League to learn the language. Being a voracious reader and encouraged by his classmates, he soon also started to read *United Irishman*, a newspaper started by a separatist political party, Sinn Féin.

Not too long afterwards, Blythe was taking the tram home from hurling practice with fellow sportsman, Gaelic League activist, Dublin Protestant and future playwright Seán O'Casey (though they 'were both very bad hurlers', Blythe recalled, they 'practiced zealously') when they fell into conversation about nationalist politics. O'Casey brought up the Fenians of the 1860s and how it was a great shame their organisation no longer existed. Blythe agreed, whereupon O'Casey told him that the Fenian, or Irish Republican Brotherhood indeed still existed and that he was a member. Several months later, Blythe was sworn in.[46]

About four years afterwards another Ulsterman also arrived in Dublin looking for work, this one a 19-year-old Catholic farmer's son from Cavan, Paul Galligan. His older brother stood to inherit the family farm near Ballinagh, meaning that Paul had to look elsewhere to make something of himself. The young country boy was devoutly religious and did not drink or smoke, but was a keen footballer. Shortly after coming to Dublin, he joined Kickham's Gaelic Football Club, whose president, James 'Buller' Ryan, was an IRB 'centre', or cell leader. Galligan came from a nationalist family – his mother had been the secretary of the Land League in Carrigallen – and was probably outspoken on issues of Irish independence. 'Buller' Ryan kept his eye on young Galligan for some time before, in 1910 or 1911 – Galligan could not remember the exact date – he proposed that Galligan join the Irish Republican Brotherhood. Galligan duly joined the Henry Joy McCracken Circle, of which Ryan was 'centre', at 41 Parnell Square, a five-minute walk from his workplace in a warehouse on Henry Street.[47]

In Craughwell, County Galway, in about 1916, a man named Thomas Kenny swore another 19-year-old, Gilbert Morrissey, into the Brotherhood, as he had his two older brothers before him. Here in rural east Galway, it was not so much cultural nationalism as the old fights on the land that brought in recruits. Morrissey recalled, 'I think Kenny's main concern was to keep the spark of nationality alive in us until the opportunity came. This was not so difficult in County Galway because, in a sense, arms were never put away. If the people were not fighting against the British forces proper, they were making a fair stand against its henchmen, the tyrant landlord class, their agents and bailiffs, who were backed up and protected by the Royal Irish Constabulary'.[48]

All three of them swore the following oath:

> In the presence of God, I, _____, do solemnly swear that I will do my utmost to establish the independence of Ireland, and that I will bear true allegiance to the Supreme Council of the Irish Republican Brotherhood and the Government of the Irish Republic and implicitly obey the constitution of the Irish Republican Brotherhood and all my superior officers and that I will preserve inviolable the secrets of the organisation.

Ernest Blythe went on to become a leading separatist activist, the first Minister for Trade and Commerce in the revolutionary government of 1919–21, and later, Minister for Finance in the first Free State Government in 1922. Galligan was to lead an insurrection in County Wexford in 1916, before doing several stints of solitary confinement in prisons, getting himself elected as MP for Cavan in the interim. Morrissey, like Galligan, was a rural insurgent in 1916 and became a full-time guerrilla fighter in 1920 and 1921.

In or around the same time, and in similar circumstances, other future leaders of the Irish revolution were entering militant separatist politics. A young Corkman called Michael Collins was sworn into the IRB in London, having been introduced to it by fellow Corkman Sam Maguire. In Ireland, such figures as Thomas Ashe, Richard Mulcahy and others were being sworn in.

If revolutions are mass, popular affairs by definition, they are nevertheless often brought into being by small, determined and organised minorities. So it was in Ireland. Blythe, Galligan and Morrissey, and men and women like them, were relatively few in number in Ireland before the

First World War, but their ideas and actions would do much to shape the future of the country.

'Extreme National Views': the Irish Republican Brotherhood

The common thread that linked these three men, and most other dedicated nationalist revolutionaries, was the Irish Republican Brotherhood, or IRB. In the second half of the nineteenth century, the IRB or Fenians had built up a substantial underground organisation with up to 40-50,000 members, mostly among the Catholic labouring class, dedicated to open insurrection to topple British rule.[49] By 1916, though, it had only 1,300 members in Ireland. The IRB also had a powerful presence in America through its sister organisation, Clan na Gael. The Clan was a valuable source of funds and arms, and valuable too as a place of refuge if Ireland became too uncomfortable. In 1867 the IRB had their first shot at rebellion, but it collapsed through poor organisation and government infiltration.

The 1867 insurgents were influenced by French and American Republicanism and demanded universal suffrage, 'which shall secure to all the intrinsic value of their labour', and the 'absolute liberty of conscience and the separation of Church and State'. With a nod to English democratic radicalism, they declared that 'we intend no war against the people of England', and with reference to the agrarian struggle in Ireland, stated, 'our war is against the aristocratic locusts, whether English or Irish, who have eaten the verdure of our fields'. The Brotherhood marched several thousand men out to Tallaght Hill near Dublin and proclaimed an Irish Republic to be in existence.[50] It lasted less than a day.

Ideological Republicanism was more in evidence in the late nineteenth-century Brotherhood than in its early twentieth-century incarnation, whose members were as likely to call themselves 'separatists' as 'Republicans'. However, it is probably a mistake to think that the Fenian who marched out to Tallaght Hill in 1867 was more politically sophisticated than his counterpart who manned the rebel barricades in Dublin in 1916. *Irish Freedom*, the IRB newspaper founded in 1910, complained that 'our Republican principles' ('a free and independent republic on a broad and democratic basis') were not widely understood among separatists, either in the past or at that date. The editorial was 'amazed to find so many nationalists with a leaning towards monarchical ideas' ... 'The absence of deeper Republican thought was the reason for the "fading away" after 1867', they complained. 'Fenian propagandist work in the 1860s was entirely separatist with no reference to Republicanism'. The modern IRB man had to be 'a disciplined soldier for Ireland' but also 'a true and staunch Republican', which meant subscribing to 'personal liberty, equality of all men in the eyes of the state and denial of rights unless they are accompanied by an acceptance of duties'.[51]

This entailed a somewhat complex relationship with democracy. The IRB envisaged a democratic Irish republic and all of the most radical nationalist organisations supported universal suffrage as a demand, but they also regarded themselves as an elite vanguard who may have to push the passive majority in the right directions. According to *Irish Freedom*, 'He is called to a brave charge who is called to resist the majority, but resist he will knowing that he will lead them to a dearer dream than they have ever known'.[52]

While the ideology sketched above did in some ways underpin early twentieth-century Irish Republicanism, it is most unlikely that the average IRB member, let alone the tens of thousands who later passed through the Irish

Volunteers and Irish Republican Army, attained this level of ideological sophistication.

More generally, what the IRB represented was an uncompromising attitude towards Irish independence and a willingness to use force to get it. 'The issue', the first edition of *Irish Freedom* (November 1910) told its readers, 'is Irish Independence'. 'We have been told to forget history, to become practical people like the Scots and the Welsh'. The compromises of the constitutional nationalists in the Irish Parliamentary Party, aimed at securing Home Rule within the United Kingdom, were 'rotten and immoral'. 'The Irish attitude to England is war yesterday, war today, war tomorrow. Peace after the final battle'.[53]

In practice, therefore, Irish Republicanism meant not necessarily a commitment to a particular political philosophy, but to extreme methods. In Wexford there was a strong IRB presence (100 sworn-in members) in the town of Enniscorthy, where 'the Organisation' was revitalised after 1907 by a man named Larry De Lacey. With the aid of old Fenians of the 1867 generation (one of whom, Charlie Farrell, was known to say, 'Ireland will never be free until Enniscorthy and every other Irish town runs red with blood'), they recruited men carefully in the years leading up to the First World War, selecting only those, 'we knew held extreme national views'.[54]

These views may have included many different tendencies but they were united by a rejection of British rule and its implicit assumption that the Irish were unfit, or at best 'not ready', for self-government. The collective separatist attitude also consisted in large part of contempt for the Irish Parliamentary Party and moderate Irish nationalists, who were characterised as either simple careerists, unwilling to upset their British paymasters, or worse, as willing collaborators in 'English tyranny'. IRB activist Seán MacDermott, for instance, derided the IPP in a public speech as 'place hunters', 'dastards, cowards and slaves',[55] while Paul Galligan called them 'the old gang of selfish imperial crawlers'. The IPP were engaged in 'slavish grovelling at the feet of England' – whereas the separatists would 'stand out before the world like men and wring full liberty from England'.[56] The Party and its affiliates in the Ancient Order of Hibernians were simply, for the separatists, 'job-getting and job-cornering' organisations.

Catholics and nationalists

Seán MacDermott wrote in 1913 that the major obstacles in the way of Irish independence were not necessarily the British, who would simply have to be fought, but 'the Hibernians, the IPP, the [Catholic] clergy and the spy system'.[57] Fenianism had always had a slightly anti-clerical flavour. The Catholic Church had denounced it in the nineteenth century as a 'lawless' and 'godless' secret society. The Fenians, in response, though overwhelmingly Catholic in origin, had always asserted their right to separate politics and religion, and this was still true in the early twentieth century. The Catholic Church was, by and large, most hostile to secret oath-bound groups, whose rhetoric smacked of continental atheistic Republicanism. As a result, much is often made of the IRB's anti-clericalism.

Certainly, Republicans throughout the coming years were prepared to ignore Church condemnations of revolutionary violence where they felt it was necessary. And equally, the fact that they subscribed to Republican concepts such as liberty of religion and the separation of Church and State encouraged some Protestants such as Ernest Blythe and Seán O'Casey to get involved in the organisation. But most separatists, Republican or otherwise, were Catholics and also believers. At one point concern arose amongst the IRB circle in Wexford as to whether the Brotherhood's secret oath was irreligious. An IRB man had to be brought by the leadership to a meeting in Dublin where a Father Sheehy told the Republicans that 'the IRB oath was not contrary to the teachings of the Church' in order to assuage their fears. 'When we returned to Wexford we explained the position to our members and they all appeared to be satisfied'.[58]

Similarly, Ernest Blythe recalled:

> Several members of the organisation apparently had had conscientious scruples and had mentioned the fact of their membership in Confession, with the result that the priests had told them they must get out. Consequently a number of members were lost. The authorities of the organisation in Dublin thought of a way to stop the rot ... I was told that it was to hear a statement by a priest who was himself a member of the organisation ... The priest was a Father O'Sullivan ... He was a member, I gathered afterwards, of Clan na Gael and not exactly a member of the IRB. I looked forward with some interest to hearing why he felt that the IRB did not come under the classification of a condemned secret society. He did not touch on the point at all, but merely said he was a member, that he had no conscientious troubles, and proceeded to make a patriotic speech. The meeting, however, was quite effective, because we heard nothing more of members leaving for some time.[59]

Irish nationalism, therefore, including separatism and despite the secular rhetoric of Irish Republicanism, was an intensely Catholic phenomenon. One Volunteer fighter during the 1916 Easter Rising found himself 'thinking of my school days, the lectures the Christian Brothers had gave us ... about the Mass Rock and the Famine and blessed Oliver Plunkett and of Emmet and Tone, McCracken and Sheares'.[60] The rebels of Easter 1916 blessed the flag of the Irish Republic with holy water before going into battle and said the rosary before and during the fighting. On the first day of the rebellion, Joseph Plunkett, one of the Rising's leaders, paid a visit to the Catholic archbishop's palace in Drumcondra to inform him of the impending insurrection. A few weeks before, his father, a Papal Count, had visited the Pope himself to tell him of his son's plans.[61]

But what made separatism and Republicanism distinctive was the insistence that Catholicism was not a necessary condition of being Irish. The despised IPP and the Hibernians were after all Catholics – indeed in the case of the latter, exclusively so. It was activist zeal, not 'ethnic' or religious origin, that made the true nationalist in separatist eyes. At the same time, however, the history of the oppression of Ireland to which they subscribed was essentially Catholic history and drew principally on the collective memories of that community. This contradiction between, on one hand, principled anti-sectarianism, and on the other, the championing of the Catholic communal cause would run through the Irish revolutionary period.

'War yesterday, today and tomorrow'

The IRB had lapsed into something of a debating club in the early years of the twentieth century, but was revived as a militant force by the efforts of a small number of energetic activists. Starting from Belfast, Dennis McCullough (a Belfast Catholic) and Bulmer Hobson (a County Down Quaker) had reinvigorated the Organisation – forming fronts such as the Dungannon Clubs and the Wolfe Tone Clubs and sending activists across the country to organise cells, or 'circles' in IRB terminology. By 1916, the IRB had 1,300 members in Ireland, with a 'Supreme Council' at its head.[62] It was not a guerrilla Army, rather something resembling a secret revolutionary vanguard. Nevertheless, its 'circles' did have guns and sometimes used them. In Clare and Galway, for example, local IRB men fired shots in local land agitation in the years up to the First World War.[63]

The state kept an eye on the IRB; its organisers were routinely followed by the RIC and their speeches taken down as evidence. *Irish Freedom* reported that its copies were being confiscated and destroyed by the Constabulary.[64] One IRB activist, Hugh Holohan, died in 1911 reportedly as a result of being beaten by the batons of the Dublin Metropolitan Police at protests during the visit of King George V, 'a victim of police brutality during and prior to the visit of his Britannic majesty', according to the separatists.[65] However, by the second decade of the twentieth century, such repression was rather half-hearted, as the British authorities simply no longer considered the Fenians a serious security threat. A mere twelve detectives in the DMP's 'G' Division were assigned to political work in the Irish capital, with only another three attached to the RIC Special Branch covering the rest of the country. No funds were released to recruit informers and no long-term spies had been planted within the Brotherhood since the 1890s.[66] Considering that the organisation's members felt themselves to be already engaged in clandestine war on the state, this, in the long term, proved to be a serious error on the part of the authorities.

But if there was really to be 'war yesterday, today and tomorrow', what kind of war would it be? The Rising of 1867 envisaged open, 'honourable' warfare under the leadership of Irish veterans of the American Civil War. Yet after the failed insurrection of 1867, other tactics had also been used. A 'shooting circle' was formed in Dublin to kill police informers and had shot four men dead in the city by the end of that year. A bomb aimed at freeing Fenians imprisoned at Clerkenwell Gaol in London killed twelve local civilians later that same year.

Even at this early stage, there was a tension between violence that was considered honourable and and what was termed 'terrorism'. 'Honourable warfare' meant that fighters would openly carry their arms, fight only against other armed men and give enemies a chance to surrender. Not only was this moral, but also, in contemporary western European culture, 'manly'. Anonymous attacks on unarmed targets were considered, by contrast, to be cowardly and unmanly. A Fenian 'centre' (cell leader) named Patrick Lennon, charged with the assassination of two policemen in Dublin in 1867, openly admitted to leading attacks on Royal Irish Constabulary barracks during the March rebellion ('and if another insurrection broke out, I would lead another party'), but condemned both the shootings of policemen and the Clerkenwell explosion – neither of which, he maintained, had anything to do with the IRB.[67]

In 1879, the leaders of 'the Organisation' decided on a 'New Departure', eschewing for now physical force in favour of adopting the land question as a means of agitation and building a broad nationalist movement.[68] Official IRB policy (indeed, its constitution) now stated that armed rebellion would not be pursued again until it had mass backing from the people – a fact that Bulmer Hobson, one of the leading lights of the IRB in the early 1900s, often pointed out to his more impatient comrades. Nevertheless, the 1880s saw two 'ginger groups' within the Brotherhood launching what they themselves called 'terrorist' campaigns – that is, attacks on civilian targets with the aim of spreading fear among their enemies.

The first was a bombing campaign from 1881 to 1885, during which a faction of Fenians, funded by elements of Irish-American Republicanism, detonated a series of bombs in British cities. Patrick J. Tynan, the head of the conspiracy, believed that only the threat of force caused 'terror and panic to the British heart', and that the Irish question 'must be decided by force, or else there is the certainty of national death'. At the high point of their campaign the group successfully caused near-simultaneous explosions in the Tower of London, Westminster Crypt and the chamber of the House of Commons on 24 January 1885, before mass arrests of the conspirators ended the campaign.[69] Similarly, in May 1882 a Fenian group named 'The Invincibles', in reprisal for the use of Coercion Acts against the Land League, brutally assassinated with surgical knives the two leading British administrators in Ireland, Chief Secretary for Ireland Frederick Cavendish and Undersecretary Thomas Henry Burke, as they were walking to their residence in Dublin's Phoenix Park.

The use of terrorist tactics was not popular among many Fenians. James Stephens, the IRB's founder, called it 'the wildest, the lowest and the most wicked conception of the national movement'.[70] Similarly, when Seán O'Casey was talking Ernest Blythe into joining the Brotherhood in 1905, Blythe 'having read something about the Invincibles … told him that [he] did not favour assassination and would have nothing to do with an organisation which countenanced it. Seán said that the Fenians were completely against assassination, and that their policy was to prepare to make open war on England'.[71]

The reality was, however, that both Fenian traditions of political violence – open insurrection, preferably having first built up a popular Republican base among the people, and clandestine assassination and sabotage – would play a role in the Irish Revolution. And there was a third tradition of violent direct action that would also be used in the years ahead: communal boycott and intimidation. These were tactics honed over at least a century of agrarian conflict in rural Ireland and most recently used in the Land War. Nationalist activist Mary Flannery, for instance, remembered that in County Sligo during the 1880s, when the tenant farmers were on rent strike, 'if people paid rent, organisations such as the "Molly Maguires" and the "Moonlighters" used to punish them by "carding them", that means undressing them and drawing a thorny bush over their bodies. I also remember a man who had a bit of his ear cut off for paying his rent ... The idea was to terrorise them'.[72] The land question remained a key part of the IRB's appeal in rural areas, where they were understood to be the most militant opponents of landlords, 'ranchers', agents and the police. In 1914, *Irish Freedom* argued for 'radical reform of the land system ... the landlords are the descendants of the robber horde sent over by Elizabeth, James Cromwell and William of Orange ...[they] should be given a last chance to sell to their tenants, the absentees first', before more radical action was taken.[73]

Of 1910, when he joined the IRB, Paul Galligan later recalled that he mostly attended lectures on Irish history: 'there was no drills or instructions in military subjects... There were no arms at this time'.[74] But this was shortly to change.

Since 1909, two IRB leaders in particular, Tom Clarke and Seán MacDermott, had been pressing for some kind of armed uprising in the years ahead.[75] Clarke was an old

Fenian bomber, who had participated in the dynamite campaign of the 1880s in England, for which he had subsequently served sixteen years at Her Majesty's pleasure in Portland Prison, many of them in solitary confinement. In 1907 he returned to Ireland from the United States, where he had gone after his release, and opened a tobacco shop on Parnell Street in Dublin. Unlike other nationalists of the period, he was neither much of a writer nor a speech-maker, but he quickly established himself on the Supreme Council of the IRB, where his militant past and determination to pursue armed action gave him a certain credibility.[76]

MacDermott, like many young IRB activists, was by origin from a poor rural area (Leitrim) and a Land War, nationalist background, but was recruited into the Organisation when he moved to the cities. In his case, the city was Belfast and his original mentor Bulmer Hobson. MacDermott lost his job on the trams in Belfast for, characteristically, defying regulations about smoking on duty, and moved to Dublin where under Clarke's influence he became commercial manager for the newspaper *Irish Freedom* and the leading IRB organiser in the country. An attack of polio in 1912 left him lame and, according to some observers, stirred in him either a wish to die or a rage that only the pursuit of insurrection could sate. Together, Clarke and MacDermott, more than anyone else, would make sure that the IRB would embark on armed revolt sooner or later.

However, the existence of the IRB alone, with its uncomplicated doctrine of complete Irish independence by any means necessary, cannot explain how the physical force of Irish Republicanism grew from a small minority into a mass movement. The Fenians operated within a wider pool of radical Irish nationalism.

Cultural nationalism

By the 1900s most recruits to militant separatism came from the milieu of cultural nationalism, and specifically from two organisations: the Gaelic League and the Gaelic Athletic Association (GAA). But what was cultural nationalism? The Gaelic League was founded by academics Douglas Hyde and Eoin MacNeill in 1893 for 'the preservation of Irish as the national language of Ireland and the extension of its use as a spoken tongue', as well as to 'cultivate a modern literature in Irish'. In the short term the League hoped to make Irish 'as in Wales, the medium of instruction in National Schools where it is the home language of the people'.[77]

The GAA predated the Gaelic League by nine years, having been founded in Thurles in 1884 to 'foster and promote native Irish pastimes', in practice to promote indigenous Irish games – hurling and Gaelic football – over 'English' (or 'foreign') ones such as soccer, rugby and cricket. Within three years it claimed to have a membership of over fifty thousand. While most were there simply for the sport, the explicit rejection of British sporting culture it represented was nonetheless significant. And while in the GAA, members were often exposed to Gaelic League and sometimes IRB and Sinn Féin ideas too.

Cultural nationalism necessarily had political implications. People who met in Gaelic League Irish classes inevitably began to discuss (usually in English) nationalist political questions. If Ireland was a culture completely separate from Britain and if, in fact, its culture was actually being killed off by the imperial power, the next logical step was that, to save Irish national identity, Ireland itself would have to separate completely from England. That many in the Gaelic League and the GAA reached this conclusion was no doubt in part due to the fact that the IRB from the start infiltrated both organisations to recruit and to proselytise.[78]

The IRB's role in the GAA was one of the areas where it clashed with the Catholic Church. In the 1890s the Church temporarily withdrew its approval from the sporting body as a result of the influence of the secret revolutionary organisation within its ranks.[79]

Cultural nationalism was a popular movement rather than a conspiracy, however. In large part, it was an attempt by a new generation of upwardly mobile Irish people to recover a truly Irish culture that they felt they had lost. European ideas of nationhood since the early nineteenth century had dictated that 'a nation' must have its own language and national customs – typically to be found among the simple but uncorrupted rural folk. Irish cultural nationalism, or the 'Gaelic revival', in looking for this pure identity, was in this respect no different from its German, or Czech, or Basque, or Ukrainian equivalents. Educated urban men and women would study the 'national language' and travel to the remote countryside to learn the language and ways of the 'real Ireland'.

In the summer of 1912, for instance, Gaelic Leaguers travelled to Achill Island, off the western coast, to attend the *Scoil Acla* summer school. In addition to classes in the Irish language, the programme offered figure dancing, music instruction, sporting activities and 'unrivalled scenery'. Those attending were encouraged to bring a 'Gaelic dress, or kilt, and any musical instrument you can. If a piper, do not forget the pipes. Also bring your bicycle'.[80]

But more than simply being a diversion for intellectuals following continental fashions, cultural nationalism also fulfilled an important psychological need for many Irish people. In the same way that the separatists' vehemence over Irish independence was fuelled by a rejection of ideas of Irish inferiority, so cultural nationalism was a mental challenge to the idea that Irish culture was necessarily backward, poor and primitive.

Frank O'Connor, for instance, who grew up beside a British Army barracks in Cork, son of an ex-soldier, at first looked to the antics of English public schoolboys as presented in popular 'Boy's Own' comics for models of behaviour, until he was introduced to Irish by a teacher, Daniel Corkery, himself a Gaelic League scholar. Returning home after memorising a simple poem in Irish, he was surprised to discover that his grandmother, whom he had always thought of as dirty and ignorant, could not only translate it but knew many better poems that he could not yet understand: 'I had at last discovered some use for that extraordinary and irritating old woman, because it turned out that Irish not English was her native language as it was of several old people in the neighbourhood'.[81]

Cultural nationalism therefore represented a kind of internal journey of discovery during a time of intense social change in Ireland. Irish society changed rapidly in the second half of the nineteenth century, after the terrible famine of the 1840s. Marriages took place much later in life, so that land did not have to be sub-divided and holdings could be better preserved in viable sizes. Literacy shot up in the following generations, as did social mobility. The extensive construction of railways and the beginnings of mass consumer culture also opened Irish Catholic life up to a much broader, though primarily British, frame of reference. While some of these reactions to the cataclysm of the 1840s would appear positive, a section of Irish people viewed their result, an English speaking, British-influenced mass culture, as the slow murder of Irish identity.

Patrick Pearse, at this date a lawyer, educationalist and Gaelic League activist, thought that if the language were allowed to die by his generation, 'they would go down to their graves with the knowledge that their children and their children's children cursed their memory'.[82] In the 1851 census, 23 per cent of the Irish population claimed Irish as their first language. By 1901 it was only 14 per cent.[83] The fear of the permanent loss of what made Ireland unique led to the formation of the Gaelic League and GAA, but also informed a wider cultural and literary movement.

The Gaelic revival, however, was as much a reinvention as a resurrection of Irish culture. The Gaelic League was founded in Dublin, where the English language had been predominant since at least the fourteenth century.[84] Many of its early adherents – notably Douglas Hyde and Lady Augusta Gregory – were 'Anglo-Irish' (of the Protestant upper class), whose ancestors had most likely never spoken the language in the first place. Patrick Pearse, the principal Gaelic League ideologue of the Easter Rising, had an English father. All of them learned Irish as adults. Ernest Blythe learned the language by going to live in an Irish-speaking district of Kerry, working as a farmhand and refusing to speak English.[85]

There was also an element of fantasy, or at least wishful thinking, about the 'revival'. It was one thing for nationalist activists in the cities to attend Irish classes and change their names from things like Charles Burgess to Cathal Brugha, or John Whelan to Seán Ó Faoláin, in symbolic defiance of British cultural hegemony. It was quite another to revive Irish as a working language. In the remaining Irish-speaking areas or *Gaeltachtaí*, poverty, poor land and poor prospects forced thousands of people to emigrate every year. Those who remained needed English to gain the education and prospects that most cultural nationalists already had. The language as a result continued to decline in spite of the League's efforts.

Nevertheless, the idea of a 'Gaelic revival' provided the mental basis to imagine a new Ireland formed on the basis of its 'true' nature prior to English conquest. Into this bottle could be poured almost anything nationalist revolutionaries could wish for. For the socialist James Connolly, the Gaelic past had been a form of 'Celtic communism'. To others it meant a conservative Catholic land, of small farms and industry. Regardless, the idea of a Gaelic Ireland was to be extremely important in early twentieth-century Irish nationalism. Patrick Pearse in a 1915 speech declared: 'Ireland must not only be free but Gaelic as well'.

Cultural nationalism also had an aspect of distaste for British popular culture, with its bawdy, 'immoral' sexual references. Imprisoned in Britain in 1917, for instance, IRB man Paul Galligan wrote to his brother:

> I never thought that British journalism had fallen so low until I got some of the magazines here. Even the best of them from a literary point of view are far below our Irish magazines, and morally – well the least said about this the better, but one and all attack the Catholic church ... It was disgusting to see in those magazines full page photographs of actresses, some almost naked and in such positions as to bring the outline of the figure fully before your gaze and one magazine labelled such filth as this with the title 'Artistic Poses of a Well Known Actress'. Those magazines are supposed to be the 'cream' of British literature and nearly all boast of being read in every house in England.[86]

A common trope in separatist literature was to lament the immoral and 'degrading' influence of the British garrison on public morality in Ireland – especially that in Dublin, which according to nationalists supported unaided the Monto, the city's infamous red-light district.[87]

Women

One other attraction of the Gaelic League was that it was one of the few nationalist organisations where men and women mixed freely, without parental or priestly supervision. Seán Ó Faoláin wrote of idyllic bicycle trips to the countryside around Cork where he and his first girlfriend, also a fervent Gael, would take romantic walks and correct each other's Irish.

The main women-only nationalist organisation was Inghinidhe na hÉireann (Daughters of Ireland), formed by Maude Gonne (a well-heeled English woman by origin, but nevertheless a veteran of the Land War, the Amnesty Campaign for Fenian prisoners and other such actions), on the occasion of a royal visit to Ireland in 1903. According to Helena Molony, it came into being as a 'counterblast to the orgy of flunkeyism which was displayed on that occasion, including the exploitation of the school children – to provide demonstrations of "loyalty" on behalf of the Irish natives'. The Inghinidhe (satirically nicknamed the 'ninnies' by its detractors, with a roughly correct phonetic rendering of the name) organised a 'Patriotic Children's Treat' as a rival to official parties held under the Union Jack for the royal visit and claimed to have attracted thirty thousand young patriots to it.[88]

They were, Molony recalled, 'Irishwomen pledged to fight for the complete separation of Ireland from England, and the re-establishment of her ancient culture'. To do this they taught evening classes on Irish history and culture, principally to children 'from the poorer quarters of the city [Dublin], where, at that time, the British Army got its most valuable recruits'. They also ran a campaign at one point to stop Irish girls from having sex with British soldiers. According to Molony:

> ...many thousands of innocent young country girls, up in Dublin, at domestic service mostly, were dazzled by these handsome and brilliant uniforms, with polite young men with English accents inside them – and dazzled often with disastrous results to themselves, but that is another side of the matter, and we were only concerned with the National political side. Of course the publication and distribution of these bills [leaflets] was illegal, in fact any statement derogatory to the forces of the Crown was regarded seriously by the authorities.

Constance Markievicz, like Maud Gonne of aristocratic Anglo-Irish background, also founded Na Fianna Éireann in 1909, as a nationalist rival to the 'imperialist' Boy Scout movement.

Women's suffrage was one of the principal radical battlegrounds in British politics in the years leading up to the First World War. The so-called 'suffragette' activists used sometimes violent direct action, such as throwing a hatchet at Prime Minister Herbert Asquith on a visit to Dublin in 1912 (it in fact hit and injured IPP leader John Redmond) to highlight their cause. *Irish Freedom* applauded the action as consistent with their 'fight for freedom', but although some Republicans were feminists, such as James Connolly, most Irish nationalists were not. The IPP's leadership were generally opposed to women's suffrage, with one leading member, John Dillon, stating that 'Women's suffrage will, I believe, be the ruin of our western civilisation. It will destroy the home, challenging the headship of man, laid down by God'.[89] In Ireland there were two women's suffrage leagues: one nationalist, led by Hanna Sheehy Skeffington, and the other Unionist.[90]

One might therefore assume that politicised, radical Irish nationalist women would also be ardent feminists, and indeed some were, such as Helena Molony, Maud Gonne and Constance Markievicz. In general, however, most women in nationalist movements, although in theory committed to universal suffrage, subordinated it to the 'national cause'.

Instead, nationalist women tended to assert their equality with the men by equal or superior zeal in pursuit of Irish independence. Helena Molony, for instance, expressed the view that the Sinn Féin political party, being 'definitely and explicitly against physical force', was too moderate. Moreover:

> ... the social ideals of Sinn Féin did not appeal to us. They wished to see Irish society (as their official organ once expressed it) 'a progressive and enlight-ened aristocracy, a prosperous middle-class, and a happy and contented working-class'. It all sounded dull, and a little bit vulgar to us, and certainly a big come-down from the Gaelic Ireland of Maedhbh, Cuchullain, and the Red Branch Knights, which was the sort of society we wished to revive.[91]

Sinn Féin

If the Gaelic League and cultural nationalism generally formed the social and cultural background of separatist nationalism, its foremost political expression was the party Molony thought dull: Sinn Féin ('Ourselves'), which was founded in Dublin by Arthur Griffith in 1905. Griffith was born in central Dublin and had worked as a printer, coming under the influence of the journalist and poet William Rooney, with whom he became active in the Gaelic League. Griffith was a member of the IRB until 1910, after which time he generally eschewed the use of physical force for political ends.

Griffith argued, in a book entitled *The Resurrection of Hungary*, that Irish nationalists should model their search for independence on that of Hungary. There, elected representatives had seceded from the Austrian Habsburg Parliament and set up their own parliament under the sovereignty of the Habsburg monarch. They had thus been recognised as equal parts of the Austro-Hungarian 'dual-monarchy'. In the same way, Irish MPs should withdraw from Westminster and declare an Irish Parliament to be in existence. If necessary, after a campaign of passive (though not armed) resistance, Ireland could be an equal but separate part of a 'dual-monarchy'.

Sinn Féin's economic policy was based on making Ireland self-sufficient and on the promotion of Irish industry. To this end, Griffith's newspaper *Sinn Féin* proposed such measures as Irish control over Irish banking and tariffs, the creation of an Irish merchant marine, reforestation (Ireland having been stripped of trees since the seventeenth century), a return to tillage farming instead of 'ranching' and other policies designed to increase employment and make Ireland economically independent. Insofar as separatism had a worked-out economic policy, this was it. The Sinn Féin agenda was also promoted in such bastions of Republican insurrectionism as *Irish Freedom*.

If Griffith's embrace of monarchy over Republicanism was to have little future in Irish nationalist circles, his advocacy of using elected representatives as a means of unilaterally declaring independence was largely to become reality in 1918–19. In 1913, however, all this lay in the future. At the time, Sinn Féin had no Members of Parliament and a handful of county councillors, mostly in Dublin city, where it had only four (down from a high of twelve in 1910) out of 80 seats, and had a working relationship with Labour councillors in order to stave off total domination of the city's government by the IPP.[92] A young councillor named William T. Cosgrave made a name for himself campaigning for slum clearance.

The IRB initially funded the Sinn Féin newspaper with money from Clan na Gael in America, and for a time their activists campaigned for Sinn Féin in elections. From about 1910, though, coinciding with the growing influence of Tom Clarke and Seán MacDermott, the Organisation became increasingly disillusioned with the murky compromises inevitable in electoral politics and instead concentrated on preparing for future armed revolt.

Sinn Féin had no explicit links with the IRB by 1913, though there was some crossover in membership. Nevertheless, because of the party's public profile, all separatists of the era were popularly referred to as 'Sinn Féiners'.[93]

Socialism

There was one final strand of the militant separatist movement – the very recent phenomenon of Irish socialist Republicanism. This ideology had its intellectual roots in populist traditions of Irish Republicanism for which, as *Irish Freedom* put it, 'the cause of Irish liberty is more the cause of the people than the plutocrats'.[94] Urban Ireland was a more unequal society than most even in contemporary Europe, with Dublin in particular having poorer housing, lower wages and higher rates of malnutrition among the unskilled working classes than virtually any other comparable European city. Irish revolutionary socialism had its concrete roots in the formation of all-encompassing trade unions for the unskilled in Ireland from 1907 onwards, which fought against these conditions. James Larkin, a Liverpool-born socialist and union organiser, had broken away from the British-based National Union of Dock Labourers in that year, and founded the Irish Transport and General Workers' Union (ITGWU) in 1909.

In theory, this was a revolutionary syndicalist union dedicated to the conquest of political power by the Irish working class. What it represented in practice was a formidable organisation of Irish workers across the barriers of trade and occupation – which in the short term mounted a major challenge to employers paying low wages, but also in time could be used as a powerful tool of political agitation. It was also, from the start, distinctively 'Irish'. Some of its leading organisers, such as P. T. Daly, were former Fenians.

In 1898 James Connolly, an Irish socialist of Scottish birth, had founded the Dublin-based Irish Socialist Republican Party, but with restricted franchise and faced with the entrenched dominance of the IPP in the city, it made little headway. By 1912, in anticipation of the granting of an Irish Home Rule parliament, the labour movement formed a political party, the Irish Labour Party.

By 1913 it also had its own Army of sorts. The Irish Citizen Army, roughly two hundred strong, was formed in November 1913, emerging originally from the ITGWU as a trade union militia designed to protect striking workers from police aggression. It was born during the protracted and bitter industrial dispute known as the Lockout in 1913–14, in which twenty thousand workers took on the Dublin business establishment over the right to be represented in the union of their choice. The dispute was extremely violent. Strikers physically attacked William Martin Murphy's trams and his 'scabs', beating to death at least two in the course of the dispute. The police baton-charged union rallies, and even made sorties into the slum buildings to beat up strikers there – accounting for at least two more deaths. The employers handed over revolvers to strike-breakers for self-protection, resulting in several fatal shootings of strikers.

The Citizen Army therefore was at first simply a self-defence organisation, as well as a way of keeping those out of work during the strike busy – drilling in the ITGWU's sports grounds with bats and hurling sticks. That it became a revolutionary armed cadre was essentially down to the influence of one man: its leader James Connolly. Connolly, who took over leadership both of the ITGWU and the Citizen Army when Larkin left for America after the Lockout's defeat. Connolly, who had worked variously as a soldier in the British Army, a carter and finally as trade union organiser – principally in Dublin and Belfast – was self-educated and a convinced Marxist. His ideology was a mixture of traditional Irish Republicanism and socialism, which he had elaborated in a short book entitled *Labour in Irish History*. The two sat awkwardly with each other at times. In the Lockout, for example, his 'class enemy', William Martin Murphy, the *bête noire* of the unions, was a Catholic and a former Nationalist MP, whereas the strikers depended heavily on financial support from sympathetic unions in Britain. For Connolly, nevertheless, 'only the Irish working class remains as the incorruptible inheritors of the fight for Irish freedom'.[95] His argument was that bourgeois Irish nationalists were too tied into the British imperial capitalist economy to be truly separatist. At the same time, the British Empire would never allow social revolution to take place in

Ireland, hence: 'The cause of Labour is the cause of Ireland, the cause of Ireland is the cause of Labour'.[96]

The mainstream nationalist press – notably the *Freeman's Journal* and the *Irish Independent* – was owned by the same William Martin Murphy with whom the unions fought in 1913 and as result it excoriated the 'atheist' socialism of Murphy's enemies. The IPP itself was more circumspect. Many of its MPs, who represented rural constituencies and had cut their political teeth on the land question, simply had nothing to say about the new phenomenon of militant labour. In Belfast, IPP MP Joe Devlin, who represented a largely working-class Catholic electorate, liked to frame himself as the true working man's representative.

The radical nationalists, by contrast, saw some potential in radical labour. They argued that class conflict in Ireland was so bitter because Britain had wrecked Irish trade. Some strikes, it argued, were the fault of employers, and some of workers, 'but the vast majority are the direct result of the British connection'. 'Class War', it argued, was 'incidental to commercial decadence ... independent Ireland would of course have disputes between capital and labour, but they would be fights to re-adjust a balance, not a fight to the death'.[97]

In the labour conflicts before the First World War, the IRB placed itself on the workers' side. They defended the ideas of socialists from their enemies in the press ('vast amounts of unmitigated rubbish is written on the horrors of socialism'), argued for a compulsory system of grievance resolution for workers and argued that the edge could only be taken off class conflict by better workers' rights.[98]

Arthur Griffith, writing in *Sinn Féin,* condemned 'Larkinism' for wrecking Irish businesses. Seán MacDermott too had his fears over the effects that strikes would have on Irish industry, writing that 'socialism and the sympathetic strike are dangerous and ruinous weapons in Ireland at the present time'. On workers' leader Jim Larkin, MacDermott wrote: 'Larkin is not a nationalist' [not entirely true, in fact], but also noted that 'he did good work with a difficult crowd and against terrible opposition in getting them better conditions'.[99]

The young Ernest Blythe, writing in 1913, thought that 'political freedom will not feed the poor or lift up the downtrodden'. Indeed, maintaining the status quo would 'leave the workers without honour and without security'. Writing under his Gaelicised name Earnán de Blaghd, he continued that he was also against reformist socialism (or, as he put it, 'the slave state') just then being introduced in embryonic form by the Liberal Government with the National Insurance Acts, as it would 'leave the people well housed, well fed and well educated, but in a slavish way. The squalor and misery of the present is preferable because it raises no such barrier against better things'. No, Blythe thought, the only answer was the revolutionary demand for the 'democratisation of industry' into a 'cooperative commonwealth'.[100] This was startlingly radical language, reminiscent of the most revolutionary of contemporary socialists.

But social questions were principally important to the IRB because they brought ordinary Irish people into conflict with the state forces. 'We dislike internecine strife in the face of the common enemy', they wrote of the 1913 Dublin Lockout, but 'the separatists of Ireland must realise that a great spiritual revolt has begun'.[101] 'We have the utmost confidence in the mass of workingmen, their ... love of Ireland will send them ... to Ireland's fighting Army when the time comes'. They advised workers to 'punish the police brutes' and to 'arm yourselves with bullets'. Of police violence during the lockout, *Irish Freedom* wrote that it was 'an example of the methods the

English Government is prepared to use to keep Ireland in submission'.[102]

In short, while the separatists were alive to the possibilities of social conflict to mobilise people against the British state, it was really a means to an end – that of an independent Ireland.

The nationalist revolutionaries in Ireland just before the onset of the Home Rule crisis were therefore a mixed bunch: a secret insurrectionary society; a political party dedicated to economic nationalism; a wider cultural and linguistic movement, with the recent addition of a union-based revolutionary socialism. There existed in Irish society the potential for the emergence of a more radical alternative to the Irish Parliamentary Party; one which would exploit that party's weakness among sectors of Irish society – workers, women, the landless – hitherto excluded from political life. But in 1912 the committed separatists were a minority and they knew it. However, two crises that swept over the British state in Ireland in 1912–14 would give them their chance to break the political monopoly of the IPP and, in time, the connection with Britain itself.

Chapter 3:

The Home Rule Crisis and the Birth of the Volunteers

States are never more vulnerable than when they try to reform themselves. The process of reform is, in itself, an admission that the existing system is imperfect and encourages further questioning of the *status quo*. Much more dangerously, though, when a state reforms itself – particularly when it gives power or rights to a group long denied them – it risks provoking violent opposition from those who benefited from the *ancien régime* and fear the new dispensation.

Throughout the century of the union between Great Britain and Ireland, this had been a problem for those in Britain who wanted to remove the legality of 'Protestant Ascendancy' (largely accomplished by 1900) and to institute some form of Irish self-government in line with the wishes of the majority. How much reform of British rule was possible in Ireland without provoking the resistance of those who identified with Crown and Empire and who still exercised a considerable degree of social, political and even military power?

Between 1912 and 1914, when the third Home Rule Bill came before, and was eventually passed by, the

British Parliament at Westminster, this question appeared to have found a disturbing answer. Unionists in Ulster first mobilised *en masse* to block the bill and then armed themselves to prevent its enactment. One of the two main political parties in Britain made noises supporting the Unionists, and elements of the British Army indicated they would not act against them.

All of this gave rise very rapidly to a situation which, in the long term, discredited Home Rule altogether, but even in the short term compromised the legitimacy of British rule in Ireland in the eyes of many nationalists. It also helped to create the conditions for the formation of a mass nationalist militia – the Irish Volunteers – through which those separatists who planned armed insurrection could organise.

The Third Home Rule Bill

Home Rule, defeated in the House of Commons in 1886 and in the House of Lords in 1893, came back onto the agenda following two developments in British politics. Firstly, in 1909 the Liberal Government faced down the House of Lords over the so-called 'People's Budget' (which introduced more taxes on the wealthy and brought in social welfare legislation), removing its right to veto legislation passed in the Commons. Secondly, in the subsequent elections of 1910, the Liberals won again, but narrowly, meaning that the Liberal Prime Minister Asquith needed the support in Parliament of the Irish Parliamentary Party. This meant that John Redmond could at last call in the long-standing Liberal promise to Irish nationalists of delivering Home Rule, and that this time it could not be blocked in the British upper house.

The Third Home Rule Bill had already taken two years in the drafting before it came before Parliament in

April 1912. It was a very carefully worked-out document – the main architect was Liberal MP Herbert Samuel – with much thought given to how much power could be devolved to an Irish Parliament and what safeguards there should be for the Protestant minority.[103]

The Bill stated clearly that: 'The executive power in Ireland shall continue vested in His Majesty the King, and nothing in this Act shall affect the exercise of that power... The Lord Lieutenant or other chief executive officer or officers for the time being appointed in his place, on behalf of His Majesty, shall exercise any prerogative or other executive power of His Majesty the exercise of which may be delegated to him by His Majesty'.

If that was not clear enough, the second clause made plain that Home Rule was devolution, not independence. 'Notwithstanding the establishment of the Irish Parliament or anything contained in this Act, the supreme power and authority of the Parliament of the United Kingdom shall remain unaffected and undiminished over all persons, matters, and things within His Majesty's dominions', it read. Moreover, the Imperial Parliament had the right to veto or reverse any legislation passed in the Irish Parliament.[104] The Prime Minister Asquith, in introducing the Bill, emphasised 'the over-riding force of the Imperial Legislation, which can at any time nullify, amend or alter any act of the Irish Parliament'.[105]

The number of Irish MPs at Westminster would be cut from 103 to 43; as Winston Churchill (at this point a Liberal minister) said, 'We think the Irish have too much power in this country and not enough in their own'.[106] The new Irish Parliament would consist of a House of Commons with 164 elected members and a Senate with 40 members nominated by the Imperial Parliament, which was intended to ensure representation for the Protestant minority. The Senate had the right to hold up legislation and appeal it to the Imperial Parliament but not, ultimately, the right to block it. The Irish Parliament would have the power to make laws, 'for the good government of Ireland', but not the power to legislate on a long list of items. The restrictions included powers generally reserved for a central parliament in a federal arrangement – the power to alter the position of the Crown and the Lord Lieutenant, the Army and Navy, the making of war and peace, foreign and colonial relations, foreign trade, coinage, were all withheld under Home Rule from an Irish Parliament.

But the Home Rule Bill also withheld many of the powers one would expect a local parliament to have. The acts relating to land purchase in Ireland, the old age pension and social welfare legislation, the raising of public loans, and even the postal service were all to be beyond the powers of the Home Rule Parliament. The Irish Parliament would also have to continue to collect the land loans – which farmers had taken out under the Land Acts – and would have to make up any shortfall if they were not collected. No radical agrarian or social change would be possible under Home Rule.

More crucially though, the new parliament would have no control over the collection of taxes, which would be collected by a central authority and sent to the Imperial Parliament, which would then give its Irish equivalent a budget of £6 million per year along with a £500,000 grant to make up any shortfall in revenue. The Royal Irish Constabulary and the 'management and control of that force' were also beyond the powers of the Home Rule Parliament.

There was scope in legislation for some of these powers to be devolved further. If the Home Rule Parliament returned budget surpluses for three years in a row, it could apply for further devolution of fiscal powers. After a minimum of seven years it could apply for more control over the police.[107] Still, there was no denying that Home Rule was a very cautious and very limited step towards Irish self-government. The proposed Irish Parliament would have none of the crucial powers of statehood. It could not collect its own revenue or set its own budget. It had no control over foreign relations or the military. While it could make laws, the body that would enforce them, the Royal Irish Constabulary, was beyond its control.

Despite all these limitations, IPP leader John Redmond welcomed the bill. 'The principle of devolution is the bond of Union,' he said. 'It has at its back the sanction of the Empire. Why, it is the foundation of the Empire today, and it is the bond, and the only bond, of union. I think it is true to say that no community of white men within the Empire has ever asked for this right and up to this has been refused the exercise of it'.[108]

It was initially difficult to work up much enthusiasm among the Party's grassroots supporters. In County Sligo on the west coast, IPP MPs urged the United Irish League – their local party organisation – to encourage continued fundraising, 'to show there was no apathy' on the Home Rule question.[109] But even the separatists expressed, if not satisfaction with Home Rule, at least the conviction that it would lead to better things. Though in public *Irish Freedom* called Home Rule 'a grotesque abortion', stating that 'we stand for full independence',[110] in private Seán MacDermott wrote to Joe McGarrity of Clan na Gael in 1913 of the Home Rule Bill: 'Even in its rottenest form I hope it will get through… whatever its fate may be we are in a better position to do work than we have been for many years'.[111]

However, Home Rule set off a storm of Unionist resistance.

Ulster says no

Some Irish Protestants were nationalists. Some, as we have seen, were even separatists. Most, however, were Unionists and were dismayed at the idea of Home Rule. *The Irish Times*, the Dublin-based Unionist newspaper of record, opined that Home Rule amounted to 'a conspiracy to interrupt and destroy the peace and prosperity of Ireland'. Irish Unionists desired, it said, 'to live in peace and harmony with their Nationalist fellow countrymen. But they will not shirk the challenge... They will go into the fight with the grim resolution of quiet men who have been wantonly assailed'.[112] Dublin's roughly 92,000-strong Protestant community, though, were a distinct minority (albeit a relatively well-off and influential one) among nearly 400,000 Catholic and mostly nationalist-voting fellow citizens.[113] Elsewhere in southern Ireland, Protestants were an even smaller minority. With the House of Lords' veto gone, they could not hope to block Home Rule on their own.

The only part of Ireland where Protestant Unionists dominated numerically was in north-east Ulster, and it was here that militant Unionist resistance to Home Rule was mobilised. As early as 1910, elements of Ulster Unionists began drilling and talking of mounting armed resistance, if necessary, to the break-up (as they saw it) of the Union. They were led by two charismatic figures: Edward Carson and James Craig. Carson was a Dublin barrister and MP and hoped to use the weight of Ulster Protestantism to block Home Rule for all of Ireland. Craig, by contrast, was a Belfast businessman and Ulster Presbyterian and from the start was principally concerned with keeping the north-east specifically out of the jurisdiction of the proposed Irish Parliament.

At first, neither nationalists nor the British Government took the Ulster Unionists' threats seriously. There was much talk of 'clowns' and 'playing soldiers'; *Irish Freedom* confidently predicted that 'Ulster won't fight.[114] But they were all wrong.

When Winston Churchill came to Belfast in February 1912 (before the Bill was presented) to promote Home Rule, he was badly jostled by Unionist crowds outside Celtic Park football stadium. Catholics in Belfast also felt Unionists' ire. In July of that year, as was typical of Belfast in moments of high political tension, rioting broke out where Catholic neighbourhoods adjoined Protestant ones during and after Orange Order parades. Catholic workers at the city's huge shipyards – which not long before had completed an ill-fated ship named the *Titanic* – were forced out of their jobs. The nationalist MP Joe Devlin claimed that two thousand Catholic workers and five hundred Protestants of Labour sympathies (Labour and socialist activists tended to favour Home Rule) were now 'walking the streets' – 'with the exception of those who are lying beaten and bruised and some of them dying in the city hospitals'.[115]

In September 1912, the Unionists staged a massive show of strength in Belfast. Some half a million men and women[116] signed a pledge known as the Ulster Solemn League and Covenant (based on the seventeenth-century Scottish Covenants which had pledged to resist kingly impositions in religion) to resist Home Rule. It was widely reported that many Ulstermen signed in their own blood, such was their earnestness, though a recent investigation found just one such name on the document.[117]

Regardless, the sheer weight of numbers behind the Covenant could not be ignored. The document itself read:

Being convinced in our consciences that Home
Rule would be disastrous to the material

well-being of Ulster as well as of the whole of
Ireland, subversive of our civil and religious
freedom, destructive of our citizenship, and
perilous to the unity of the Empire, we, whose
names are underwritten, men of Ulster, loyal
subjects of His Gracious Majesty King George
V., humbly relying on the God whom our fathers
in days of stress and trial confidently trusted, do
hereby pledge ourselves in solemn Covenant,
throughout this our time of threatened calamity,
to stand by one another in defending, for ourselves
and our children, our cherished position of equal
citizenship in the United Kingdom, and in using
all means which may be found necessary to defeat
the present conspiracy to set up a Home Rule
Parliament in Ireland. And in the event of such
a Parliament being forced upon us, we further
solemnly and mutually pledge ourselves to refuse
to recognize its authority. In sure confidence that
God will defend the right, we hereto subscribe
our names. And further, we individually declare
that we have not already signed this Covenant.

Not all Ulster Protestants were behind Carson and Craig. As
many as twelve thousand signed an 'Alternative Covenant'
endorsing Home Rule in October 1913, led by Roger
Casement and a Presbyterian minister named R. J. Armour,
but the demographic strength of militant unionism was
made clear by the Covenant.

To hammer home the point that Ulster Unionists were
deadly serious, in January 1913 they formed their own
militia: the Ulster Volunteer Force or UVF. In April 1914,
they took the final step when Major Frederic Crawford
(in several arms deals in Germany, Austria and elsewhere)

imported some 37,000 rifles of various makes and around 3 million rounds of ammunition. Of the rifles, 25,000 were landed at Larne on April 25, in a spectacular defiance of the law and of Home Rule, but one which the authorities made no effort to stop. A 'Provisional Government' of Ulster was set up, and plans were made to seize key positions in the province, should Home Rule be enacted.[118]

Their stance did command sympathy in influential places. Andrew Bonar Law, the leader of the British Conservative Party, visited Ulster at one stage and declared that he would support the Unionists, using 'all means in their power including force', to block Home Rule[119], an astonishingly militant posture for a constitutional politician. And it may not have been all talk. Senior Convervatives, maybe even Bonar Law himself, were involved in financing gunrunning into Ulster in 1914.[120] In May 1914, when the British garrison in the Curragh, central Ireland, was ordered to take up positions in Ulster – at this stage merely as a precaution against the possibility of civil unrest – over sixty officers, led by one brigadier general, refused, saying they would prefer to resign their commissions.

The Ulster Unionist resistance to Home Rule therefore fatally compromised the idea that the British organs of state could be impartial reformers in Ireland, as well as dangerously militarising Irish politics. Before plunging into the crisis caused by the emergence of rival paramilitary groups, though, it is necessary to pause to reflect on what motivated such hostility to Home Rule among Ulster Unionists.

'Home Rule is Rome Rule'

At one level, Unionist opposition to Home Rule was part of the tradition that dated back to the seventeenth century but had really solidified at the end of the eighteenth, uniting Ulster Protestants of all classes against the 'Popish' enemy. In the 1790s, Protestant 'Ultras' and the newly formed Orange Order (1796) had resisted granting rights to Catholics and ultimately participated in the suppression of Republican insurrection. At its crudest, the Orange tradition maintained that Protestants were simply the rightful masters in Ireland – God had granted their ancestors victory over the Catholics in the wars of the seventeenth century and they meant to maintain the position they had gained therein. If they did otherwise, the treacherous Catholics would turn on them.

For instance, an 'Address to the Protestants of Ireland' in 1843 stated: 'We scorn the idea of there existing a physical force superior to our own... the deliverance we Irish Protestants have recorded in the annals of our nation [at the battles of] Aughrim, the Boyne and Derry [show] we are the masters of this land... we hold it for Him [God].[121] And identical language was still being used in the twentieth century. For instance, William Moore MP told his listeners at the Orange commemorations on 12 July 1911 in Belfast that 'We are dealing with an enemy in whose ideas of justice, tolerance or fair play towards the Protestant minority we have not an ounce of confidence... the lessons of the last three hundred years have not been wasted on Irish Protestants, and the moral from them is as true today as it was in [the rebellions of] 1641 or 1798'.[122]

As the nineteenth century went on, even the most hardline Ultra-Protestants began to drop the hope they had had up to then of simply converting the Catholics to Protestantism and instead began to focus on maintaining the British connection to support their position in Irish society.

But such loyalty to the British Empire had always been highly conditional on its maintaining Protestant supremacy in Ireland. Should the British Parliament renege on its side of the bargain, warned an evangelical Dublin preacher named Tresham Gregg in 1843, 'we will rally around the standard of our native land and raise the cry "Erin go Bragh". What signifies "British supremacy" if it is not identical with the Ascendancy of Protestantism? Who cares one fig for the integrity of the British Empire if it be not the empire of immortal truth?'[123] In 1913, this attitude reached its high point in Ulster with the preparation for armed defiance of the British Government.

However, Unionist opposition to Home Rule as articulated in the Covenant was not simply based on sectarian grounds. Unionists had three basic objections to Home Rule as it was proposed in 1912. The first, as was noted in the Covenant, was that Home Rule would be 'disastrous to the material well-being of Ulster as well as of the whole of Ireland'. What this meant was that Ulster's industries would be heavily taxed to subsidise the underdeveloped rest of Ireland, that the Dublin Parliament would run up a disastrous public debt and that it might even cut off free trade to Britain and the rest of the Empire in order to foster domestic industry in the south. The last of these fears had little basis. Belfast's export industries needed free access to the British market, but so too, vitally, did the agricultural exporters – especially the cattle trade – of the south. The first and second fears – that the Irish Parliament would be high-taxing and free-spending and would bankrupt the country – would simply not have been within its power under the 1912 Bill, though the Unionists looked nervously at the clauses allowing for further devolution if Home Rule went smoothly.

The second Unionist objection to Home Rule, as expressed in 1912, was that it would be 'subversive of our civil and religious freedom'. Economic interest explains much hard-headed Unionist sentiment in Ulster, but it was probably the question of religious freedom that made men prepared to take up arms to resist it. Home Rule, as the slogan went, would be Rome Rule.

The fear that the Catholic Church would be enormously powerful in a self-governed Ireland that would be about 75 per cent Catholic was not an unreasonable one. Might the Catholic Church in effect be established as the Protestant Church of Ireland had been up to 1869? The Catholic Church actively sought to absorb as Catholics the children of 'mixed marriages' through the *Ne Temere* decree. It also sought to control areas such as education and health care. However, the Home Rule Bill specifically stated that the 'Irish Parliament shall not make a law so as either directly or indirectly to establish or endow any religion, or prohibit the free exercise thereof, or give a preference, privilege, or advantage, or impose any disability or disadvantage, on account of religious belief or religious or ecclesiastical status, or make any religious belief or religious ceremony a condition of the validity of any marriage'.[124]

John Redmond in Parliament sought to assuage Unionist fears by telling them that 'We in Ireland regard no insult as so grievous as the insult that we, as a nation, are intolerant in matters of religion.[125] And on the outer fringes of Irish nationalism, the *Irish Freedom* organ of the IRB wrote: 'Sectarianism is the decay of the genuine nationalist ideal... All sects must stand together'.[126] Nationalists did not plan religious discrimination in a self-governed Ireland. Moreover, Redmond had reluctantly agreed to a nominated senate precisely in order to offset the Catholic advantage in numerical representation.

But the third Unionist fear, that Home Rule would be 'destructive of our citizenship and perilous to the unity of the Empire', probably had a grain of truth in it. Home Rule itself would not of course have meant Irish independence; far from it. John Redmond assured Unionists that 'we are not separatists'. The question remained, however, once nationalists had their devolved parliament, would they be happy with what the elite of the IPP called a 'union of equals', or would they have pushed for more independence? In the 1880s, Parnell, the original Home Rule leader, had famously said that 'no man has the right to fix the boundaries of a nation'. The separatist movement would without doubt have remained in place and probably grown stronger under Home Rule. In time, either the Irish Parliament would have pushed for greater autonomy or been itself outflanked by more radical voices.

What Edward Carson wanted was to 'save' southern Unionists – and, indeed, all of Ireland as he saw it – from Home Rule by means of Ulster's militancy. However, the secondary objective, and the one favoured by Craig, was to exclude north-east Ulster from the Home Rule Bill, at least initially. Even in 1912, Redmond made noises in Parliament indicating that he would accept a compromise along such lines. The delicate question was how much of Ulster would be excluded and for how long. Three counties, Cavan, Monaghan and Donegal, had large nationalist and Catholic majorities and, despite having substantial Unionist minorities, had to be let go. Two more counties, Fermanagh and Tyrone, had slight nationalist majorities. Whether they would be included in a partitioned Ulster statelet would spill much ink and not a little blood in the years ahead. If they were included then north-eastern Ulster might just be a viable entity; without them, it would be too small to be viable.

Partition was, however, exceptionally unpopular in most of Ireland and was the first in a series of concessions to Unionists that eventually discredited the IPP in the eyes of Irish nationalists. The IRB newspaper *Irish Freedom* (for once, echoing what most nationalists thought) declared that 'Ulster is as much a part of Ireland as Dublin, Kerry or Clare', and judged the broaching of partition to be 'another surrender by the IPP'.

Ernest Blythe recalled that when 'the Partition issue became very much alive', Seán MacDermott sent him to Belfast to work on an anti-partition campaign. Catholic and nationalist west Belfast, centred on the Falls Road, was understandably one of the districts most concerned by partition. But it was also the personal fiefdom of Irish Parliamentary Party MP Joe Devlin, and normally Republicans could expect, at the least, a sharp-tongued reception there. The prospect of partition, however, changed all this.

Blythe remembered that on the Falls Road, 'A very big crowd came to listen to us. We attacked Partition strongly without saying anything against Joe Devlin, and got a very good reception. We held a number of similar meetings and had no trouble anywhere'. However, it was clear to Blythe after a couple of months that 'we could not alter the general complexion of political affairs in Belfast'.[127] It was in the south that nationalists would have their rejoinder to the Ulster Volunteers.

The Irish Volunteers and the Howth Gunrunning

Many erstwhile moderate nationalists were outraged by how the Unionists had been allowed to arm and to block a law that had the clear assent of the majority. Kevin O'Shiel, a law student in Dublin, who had previously regarded the 'Sinn Féiners' as 'either idealistic idiots or designing mischief makers', found that 'our pristine childlike faith in Liberal promises began to dissolve... it was but the old, old game all over again... the effect of the Curragh mutiny was terrific but it was mild compared with that of the Larne gun-running... it violently shook our faith in constitutionalism'.[128] For those who sought full independence, the Ulster crisis was therefore a massive opportunity.

In November 1913, in response to the formation of the UVF, nationalists formed their own paramilitary force: the Irish Volunteers. In fact, IRB elements led by Bulmer Hobson took the lead even if the formal leadership tended to be public figures and cultural nationalists. Their initial intention was not to fight the Ulster Volunteers, but to pressurise the Liberal Government in order to guarantee the passage of Home Rule. Eoin MacNeill, the founder of the Volunteers, was a Gaelic League scholar and academic. He wrote that the Volunteers would 'show the Tories that the alternative to Home Rule was a policy of repression and coercion beyond any they had experience of', and would 'show the Ulster minority that nationalist Ireland could not be treated with contempt'.[129] Seán MacDermott wrote, 'we are not out against Carson's Volunteers but to insist on our own right of citizenship'.[130]

Whether or not the average Irish nationalist saw things in such a broad-minded light, the Irish Volunteers were popular, attracting ten thousand members by the end of 1913.[131] According to *Irish Freedom*, 'The young men who stand together... for Gaelic League and Sinn Féin and Republican principles, who are crowding into the Volunteers, can save Ireland and will'.[132] Just like the Gaelic League and the GAA, but much more so, given that this was to be an armed paramilitary group, the Volunteers was the perfect mass front for the IRB to infiltrate and control.

In north Dublin, Paul Galligan, the young Cavan man who had joined the IRB three years earlier, recalled that 'on the formation of the Irish Volunteers in November 1913', he and his comrades in the IRB 'were instructed to immediately join and take control... Our [IRB] class was distributed over the different units in the city area. I joined at Blackhall Place... Our instructors were ex-British Army men and they were doing the drilling and organisation, but our men of the IRB were really in charge'.[133]

By June 1914, when the Volunteers took part in the annual rally at the grave of the United Irishmen leader Theobald Wolfe Tone in Bodenstown, County Kildare, Galligan recalled that 'it was noticeable that the IRB were well in control of the Volunteers now'. His IRB centre, Tom Hunter, was also the commander of the Volunteers' Second Battalion. Ernest Blythe, by this time back in Kerry, similarly got himself elected as captain of the local Volunteer Company, displacing an ex-soldier.[134]

A women's auxiliary, Cumman na mBan (roughly 1,500 strong) was formed to assist the Volunteers, absorbing many of the militants of Inghinidhe na hÉireann, though some of the most radical of the latter, such as Helen Molony and Constance Markievicz, elected to join the socialist Citizen Army instead, where they were given equal standing with the men.[135]

Fearing that he would be undermined by the radical nationalists, John Redmond quickly tried to bring the Volunteers under his party's control, and in June 1914, after repeated meetings with Eoin MacNeill and Bulmer Hobson, managed to get himself and his appointees co-opted into the governing council of the Volunteers. For Tom Clarke and Seán MacDermott, the most militant advocates of insurrection among the IRB and the most contemptuous of the Irish Parliamentary Party, this was a despicable betrayal by MacNeill and Hobson, and for this they never truly forgave them. In future plans for insurrection, the formal leaders of both the Volunteers and IRB would be left in the dark.

The general public knew nothing of this, of course, and in the short term, the endorsement of the Volunteers by the Redmondites merely made the group more popular: its membership soared to 180,000 by the late summer of 1914.[136] This was a time when military values and the idealised vision of the 'manly soldier' were at their height in Europe. In the United Kingdom the forming of 'Volunteer' militias was legal as long as their purpose was to defend the security of the Empire, which both Volunteer formations in Ireland could, ostensibly, claim they were trying to do. Martial values were also a key part of the Irish separatist identity; the armed citizen could no longer be treated as an inferior by the British. The increasingly bellicose Gaelic Leaguer and Volunteer Patrick Pearse wrote in November 1913, 'We must accustom ourselves to the thought of arms, to the sight of arms, to the use of arms'.[137] Without arms, the Irish Volunteers (just like their Ulster equivalents) could be dismissed as a stage Army. *Irish Freedom* editorialised, 'A dozen rifles are more effective than a thousand resolutions in Parliament'.[138] But as yet, the Volunteers had no rifles at all. This all changed in the most dramatic fashion on 26 July 1914.

IRB man (and now Volunteer) Paul Galligan's battalion was mobilised on that day for a route march to the fishing village of Howth, north of Dublin. 'Through my IRB contacts, I knew there was something serious on, but did not know exactly what it was'.[139] In fact, they were to march to Howth harbour, to unload from the yacht the *Asgard* a cargo of nine hundred rifles and thirty thousand rounds of ammunition that Bulmer Hobson, the IRB leader, had secretly purchased in Germany. The rifles were obsolete single-shot Mausers from 1871 – most

ill-matched against the rapid-firing Lee Enfield rifles and
machine guns (not to mention artillery) with which the
British Army was equipped, and three generations behind
what German troops carried in 1914. But no matter. It
was the symbolism of Irish nationalists with weapons that
was important.

Along the way to Howth, a march of about 15
kilometres or 10 miles from Dublin city centre, Paul
Galligan watched as the Fianna (the nationalist boy scouts
now acting as the youth wing of the Volunteers) brought
up handcarts full of oak batons 'which were handed out to
selected men'. At the quay in Howth, Galligan 'saw a yacht
coming into the harbour. She hove-to at a point in the pier
and made fast and the crew started handing out rifles to the
Volunteers'.[140] A Cumann na mBan activist remembered
that, at the sight of the arms being taken off the *Asgard,* 'we
cheered and cheered and cheered and waved anything that
we had and cheered again'.[141]

Galligan saw the coastguard fire off rockets to warn the
authorities, but by that time all the rifles had already been
handed out and the battalion was ready to march back to
the city. The commissioner of the Dublin Metropolitan
Police, upon hearing of the arms landing, ordered
the police, backed by British troops, to intercept the
Volunteers, declaring: 'a body of more than one thousand
men armed with rifles marching on Dublin constitutes
an unlawful assembly of a most audacious character',
and ordering the police to seize the weapons.[142] To the
rank and file of the DMP, however, most of whom were
Catholics and probably nationalists of a sort, this seemed
like a blatant double standard. The Unionists had been
allowed to arm but the nationalists were not. Whether
because of this, or because they, unarmed, did not want
to face down a thousand armed men, many policemen

failed to obey the orders to intercept the return march from Howth.[143]

As a result of the police's unwillingness to act, a battalion of troops – the King's Own Scottish Borderers – were called out. Along the Howth Road, on the way back into the city, Galligan's Volunteer battalion saw that 'British soldiers were drawn up across the road with bayonets fixed'. The soldiers had been ordered to seize the Volunteers' arms. The two groups of armed men came to a nervous halt close to each other and a Volunteer captain, Judge, went to talk to the British troops. A melee broke out. One Volunteer named Burke who went to Judge's aid was stabbed with a bayonet in the knee. In the confusion, Paul Galligan and the other Volunteers were ordered to disperse and take their rifles with them. They slipped away across country and through the north Dublin suburbs. Galligan and his club-mates from Kickham's Gaelic football club made their way to their clubhouse and left the rifles there.[144] Though other companies lost a small number of rifles in similar scuffles, most made their way to various company headquarters.

The day, which became known as the Howth gun-running, was a triumph for the Volunteers and a humiliation for the authorities. The British had not opposed the landing of Unionist arms at Larne but had now forcibly attempted to halt nationalists doing the same thing. Worse, from the British point of view, they had not succeeded in preventing the importation of the Mauser rifles. Another batch was brought ashore secretly the following month at Kilcoole, County Wicklow. And even worse was to come for the British. The Scottish Borderers, who had failed in their mission to disarm the Volunteers, returned to the city to be jeered at: 'Go back your own country,' they were told, and stoned by a hostile nationalist crowd as they were marching back to the Royal Barracks along the Dublin quays. The troops opened fire on the taunting crowd on Bachelor's Walk, killing three bystanders and injuring thirty-seven.[145]

Irish Freedom exulted, 'The Volunteer Movement has been formally baptised in blood. Proudly and in broad daylight the armed nation has been upheld. The young men are ready to fight for Ireland. Ultimate victory is very close now'.[146] They were particularly impressed by the reaction of the policemen of the DMP, a body they had previously excoriated for their role in baton-charging both radical nationalists and striking workers. 'While innumerable acts of brutality can be credited to the DMP, cowardice, individual or collective cannot be alleged'. By their 'manly attitude' in refusing to disarm the Volunteers, the police, 'usually instruments of foul anti-Irish work... may have lit the flame that will paralyse English government in Ireland'.[147]

The crisis over Home Rule really did appear to be growing out of the control of either the British authorities or John Redmond. Two rival militias now existed in the country, both armed, and the forces of the state – both in the Army and the police – had, in different ways, appeared to show that they could not be relied upon to put them down should the need arise.

The brink of civil war?

The Home Rule Bill was passed into law on 18 September 1914. Did Ireland really stand on the verge of civil war?

Enforcing Home Rule would have meant antagonising the Unionists. However, the exclusion of Ulster to some degree had already been accepted, even by Redmond, by mid-1914. An Amending Bill was passed in July 1914 by which six counties in north-east Ulster were 'temporarily excluded' from Home Rule. The suppression of the Ulster

Volunteers by British forces was therefore no longer an imminent possibility. Had they been ordered to do so, the same officers who threatened to resign at the Curragh in May 1914 insisted that they would have carried out their duty.[148] Putting down the nationalist Irish Volunteers would have presented an even more tricky task, should it have been deemed necessary. Repression followed by further radicalisation of the nationalist public was of course precisely what the separatists wanted. In private correspondence, Seán MacDermott wrote of the Bachelor's Walk shootings: 'It will do good and all is well. That ought to open the eyes of the fools as to what Liberal government is'.[149] Conversely, it was precisely the opposite of what Redmond was hoping to achieve. Fortunately for him, the Chief Secretary for Ireland, Augustine Birrell, despite the incidents at Howth and Bachelor's Walk, voiced the opinion that to clamp down on the Volunteers would be counterproductive.

Would the rival Volunteers have fought each other? It is easy to read history backwards and assume so, but in the world of 1914 it was not as unusual to have large bodies of men drilling and even training with weapons as it would be today. Both sides, in public anyway, stated that they merely wished to uphold the law: for the Unionists, the Union; for the nationalists, to ensure the passage of Home Rule. On the ground, even in Ulster and its borderlands, both sides seemed to be able to live together, though tension was high. In any case, outside of Dublin and one or two other localities, the nationalist Volunteers were still essentially unarmed. So civil war was probably not as imminent in 1914 as it might first appear.

Nevertheless, actually implementing Home Rule to the satisfaction of all the parties, especially now that both were armed and mobilised, was a daunting task for the

Liberal Government. Dramatic events at the other end of Europe suddenly took a hand, however. In Sarajevo on 28 June, a Serbian nationalist by the name of Gavrilo Princip assassinated the Archduke Franz Ferdinand of Austria – setting in motion what we know as the First World War. Germany invaded Belgium on 4 August 1914 and Britain declared war on Germany on the same day.

Home Rule was suspended for the duration of the European War. The Great War seemed to have averted the Home Rule Crisis's coming to a head. But the demands of war on the Irish population and the opportunities it afforded those who dreamed of an end to British rule altogether meant that, by 1918, the Home Rule project was dead.

Chapter 4:

From Great War to Easter Rising

On 20 September 1914 at Woodenbridge, County Wicklow, some two weeks after Britain had declared war on Germany, the leader of the Irish Parliamentary Party John Redmond addressed supporters of his party. He told them that Britain's fight was Ireland's – that the war was for 'small nations' and the Catholic religion, both of them attacked by the Germans when they invaded Belgium. 'The interests of Ireland – of the whole of Ireland – are at stake in this war. This war is undertaken in the defence of the highest principles of religion and morality and right'.

The parliamentary leader then did something no nationalist leader had ever done publicly before: he told his followers to join the British armed forces. 'It would be a disgrace forever to our country and a reproach to her manhood and a denial of the lessons of her history if young Ireland confined their efforts to remaining at home to defend the shores of Ireland from an unlikely invasion... I say to you, therefore, your duty is twofold. I am glad to see such magnificent material for soldiers around me, and I say to you: Go... wherever the fighting line extends, in defence of right, of freedom, and religion in this war'.[150]

In the north, the Ulster Volunteers – who had been preparing, perhaps, to defy His Majesty's Government by force of arms – also flocked to the colours to prove their loyalty to the Empire. Just under 200,000 Irishmen would go on to serve in the First World War and almost 30,000 would die in it by November 1918.[151]

The war provided an acid test for political identities in Ireland; it forced people to choose sides on a range of divisive questions. Were they ultimately loyal to the British Empire? Would they die for it? Was such a loyalty compatible with Irish nationality?

Initially it seemed as if Redmond had managed to square some of these circles. His message was that Britain's cause was Ireland's, and indeed the Irish Volunteers', cause. New Irish divisions raised for the war would be the nucleus of a post-Home Rule Irish Army. Their service would help to ensure that Irish self-government would indeed come to pass. And initially he seemed to win the argument. The Home Rule crisis was temporarily defused. Some people who had been wary of the Volunteers were much more comfortable with the idea of a loyal militia after August 1914.

The split in the Volunteers

Redmond's support for Britain in the war split the Volunteer movement wide open. Those in the IRB, and also other 'advanced nationalists' like Eoin MacNeill, who had founded the Volunteers, furiously rejected the idea that the Volunteers might join the British Army for the duration of the war. Redmond and his appointees, who had only recently joined the Volunteers, were purged by the disgusted separatists. Most of the rank and file, though, followed Redmond.[152]

The split was acrimonious but, unlike many others in Irish nationalist history, bloodless. The two sides abused each other in the press, but they parted ways and even divided weapons by mutual agreement. On one side were the original Irish Volunteers, around 13,500 strong, infiltrated by the IRB and nominally led by MacNeill, who refused to support the British war effort and resolved to keep their organisation intact and in Ireland until Home Rule was passed. On the other side were the over 140,000 'Irish National Volunteers' who followed Redmond, many of whom went on to join the British Army.[153]

In Paul Galligan's Dublin Brigade at the time of the split:

> ... all companies... were ordered to parade and a notice was read which asked all Volunteers who were prepared to stand by the executive of the Volunteers [MacNeill's wing] to take a pace forward. Most of the men took a pace forward. Many of those who did not [take a step forward] did not take any further part in Volunteer activities after this. The Redmond or National Volunteers were now formed as a distinct organisation... We lost a large amount of rifles and equipment owing to these defections.[154]

The initial support of mainstream Irish nationalists for the British war effort in Europe was a sickening blow to the radicals in the IRB. Seán MacDermott told a crowd in Tipperary in 1914: 'The Volunteers were not brought into existence to fight for England. To hell with England! Let her fight her own battles. The Volunteers are only intended to fight for Ireland!'[155] *Irish Freedom* asked if Redmond was a 'madman or traitor?' for 'conspiring with those whose aim is to remove Ireland from the roll of nations'. It concluded that his pro-war policy was 'either incredible stupidity or damnable treachery'. For separatists it pledged: 'Hatred to the Empire and remember Bachelor's Walk!'[156]

But initially it was Redmond's vision of an Irish patriotism that was compatible with the Empire that seemed to win the argument. Some 130,000 Irishmen volunteered for the duration of the war, along with nearly 60,000 serving and reserve Irish servicemen, and 24,000 of these originated from the Redmondite National Volunteers. Another 26,000 came from the loyalist Ulster Volunteers.[157]

Both recruitment and anti-recruitment rallies were held across Ireland in the autumn of 1914. Ernie O'Malley, the future IRA leader and writer, whose family were moderate nationalists, remembered getting into a fistfight with separatists in Dublin who tried to seize his Union Jack coloured hooter, which he had bought as a souvenir in 1914.[158] His older brother Frank went on to serve and to die as an officer in the East African campaign.

Such was the initial enthusiasm for the war that in late 1914 Redmondite MP Stephen Gwynn exulted that the radical nationalists were 'snowed under and I think were almost dumbfounded by what they found around them. They held no meetings and had no press'.[159] He might have added, though, that one reason why the 'Sinn Féiners' had no press was that titles such as *Irish Freedom* of the IRB and James Connolly's *Irish Worker* were shortly afterwards closed down under the Defence of the Realm Act, and their presses seized for anti-war agitation.

Ireland and the World War

If the separatists were appalled by the Irish reaction to the outbreak of the war, the Great War and the demands it forced the British state to make of its citizens nevertheless put the United Kingdom in a most dangerous position in Ireland. Mathew Nathan, the Undersecretary for Ireland, thought that Redmond had not carried his constituency with him.

Despite Redmond's initial triumph in 1914, the mood in nationalist Ireland was nowhere near as pro-British as it was in the top echelons of the Irish Party. In Sligo, for instance, after the passing of the Home Rule Bill in September 1914, the Redmondite MP Thomas Scanlan arrived in the town by torchlit procession and declared that 'Ireland is now and shall for all times be a nation once again... but this same Statute binds Ireland indissolubly to the British Empire'. A group of labour activists from the Transport Union heckled him with calls of 'To hell with the Empire', and the meeting broke up with what the local paper called 'a spirited bout of fisticuffs'.[160]

There is, however, no doubt that many nationalist recruits did believe in Redmond's pro-war policy, and that they were serving Ireland by joining up. Senior Irish Party stalwarts such as Thomas Kettle and Redmond's own brother Willie served and died in the war. But although recruitment for the war was reasonable in Ireland, it was only about two-thirds of the rate of recruitment in Britain itself. Moreover, as the war went on and casualties mounted, recruiting fell sharply. Some 44,000 Irishmen enlisted in 1914 and 45,000 followed in 1915, but this dropped to 19,000 in 1916 and 14,000 in 1917.[161] Even from very early on in the war, moreover, the idea of conscription was deeply unpopular in Ireland. A former Lord Mayor of Dublin, Alderman J. J. Farrell said in 1915: 'In Dublin young men have been advised to go to war by the effective means of depriving them of work. In England there are millions of men fit to fight if only they are willing. The Government do not want anything from Dublin or the south [of Ireland] but blood and money. If the two Volunteer forces in Ireland made up their minds that there would be no conscription, there would be none'.[162]

A considerable proportion of recruitment in Ireland was motivated not by ideology but by economic considerations. Around 50,000 of the Irish wartime recruits were dedicated Unionists or Redmondite nationalists, judging by the proportion who came from the Ulster and National Volunteers. Out of the remaining 80,000 who had no experience in either of the paramilitary formations, most were urban and poor. In Dublin city, a survey of 169 recruits from Corporation workers shows just nine 'salaried professional' workers joining up and 113 unskilled labourers, for whom the Army signified a pay rise and a chance to learn a trade.[163]

Similarly, for the poorest of the working class the 'Separation Allowance' paid to wives and families of serving soldiers could mean a marked increase in standard of living. Farmers' sons were under-represented across the country, even in Protestant Ulster, as they could not be spared from farm work. In County Galway, police reported that recruiting was 'slow and entirely confined to the towns'.[164] Economic motivations therefore played a significant part in military recruitment, as they did in Britain itself, where voluntary recruiting slowed when the war economy began to offer more jobs. Other Irish recruits simply liked the idea of being part of something big and important. Future IRA leader Tom Barry later wrote, 'I went to the war for no other reason than that I wanted to see what war was like, to get a gun, to see new countries and to feel a grown man'.[165]

The Irish appetite for total war, such as it was, was given a stunning blow when Irish units first suffered mass casualties. At Gallipoli in August 1915, for example, the 10th Irish Division (whose ranks, especially the Dublin Fusiliers, included 'Pal's Battalions'* of Redmondite Volunteers)

---

*   'Pals' battalions' were wartime recruits of the New British Army raised after 1914 who raised their own units from among their friends and colleagues.

suffered devastating casualties while trying to land on Turkish beaches, with up to two-thirds of the regiment being killed or wounded. When news of the losses reached Ireland, along with reports that Ian Hamilton, the Officer Commanding, had criticised the Irish troops, it shook even 'Castle Catholic' (Catholic Unionist) Katherine Tynan. She wrote to a friend, 'For the first time came bitterness, for we felt that their lives had been thrown away and their heroism had gone unrecognized... Dublin was full of mourning'.[166]

As the war went on the demands it placed on the citizenry grew. Poverty and unemployment could deliver some recruits for the British forces, but they could also work against the popularity of British rule in Ireland in wartime. Wartime food prices rocketed, creating a boom for big Irish export farmers, but hard times for their labourers and for urban workers. On the land, always a volatile issue in Ireland, rents accordingly went up and at the same time, due to wartime pressures on public finances, the land reform of the Congested Districts Board slowed almost to a halt.[167]

Taxes, both direct and indirect, were also by necessity raised to pay for the war effort. It was not only the working class that was outraged by wartime demands. Dublin employers, still recovering from the general strike in that city in 1913, complained to the government and to John Redmond that they were being beggared by the 'excessive profits tax' introduced to stop war profiteering'.[168]

By 1915, Irish public opinion was wavering on the war. In November of that year, seven hundred Irishmen trying to emigrate to the US were blocked at Liverpool on the basis that they should be in the Army. Redmond remarked that it was 'very cowardly of them to emigrate' rather than enlist – provoking a hostile public response from a Catholic bishop of Limerick, Edmund O'Dwyer, who stated, 'Their crime is that they are not ready to fight for England. Why should they? What have they or their forbears ever got from England that they should die for her?'[169]

One contemporary thought that 'behind it all was the vague feeling that to fight for the British Empire was disloyal to Ireland'.[170] As early as November 1915, with no end to the war in sight and with Home Rule still not enacted, British sources were reporting signs of disaffection. Also in 1915, the Catholic Church turned against the war and recruitment. Worst of all for the Home Rule Party, it was already plain by then that the version of 'fighting for Ireland' promoted by Redmond was no longer credible. The 'Irish Divisions' (the 10th and 16th), very far from being a proto-Irish Army, were led by British officers and filled at a fairly early stage with recruits from elsewhere.[171] By contrast, the 36th Ulster Division, recruited in large part from the UVF, kept its own officers and political identity – a clear sign that Irish nationalism was still distrusted by the British Government.

A short, victorious war for Britain might have brought Redmond political triumph, and his loyalty to the Empire might have undermined the Ulster Unionists' position in British politics. But as the Great War dragged on, Irish enthusiasm for it faltered as casualties mounted. Wartime meant hardship induced by food shortages, price increases and rationing, and for activists, extra repression under the Defence of the Realm Act (DORA). All of these factors undercut Redmond's pro-British, pro-war stance. Worst of all, Home Rule continued to be postponed.

This convergence of circumstances, the frustration of constitutional nationalist demands by Unionist defiance, the formation of armed paramilitary groupings, and the opportunity offered by Britain's entry into a major

European war, was a combustible cocktail. Taken together, they would give to the most radical elements of Irish nationalism the opportunity for armed rebellion in 1916.

The roots of insurrection

The war gave those who wanted rebellion access to German arms and aid. It also distracted British attention from Ireland. 'England's difficulty', the old Fenian saying went, 'is Ireland's opportunity'.

There were, however, within the Volunteer leadership two distinct schools of thought on the use of armed force. One, the position held by Eoin MacNeill and Bulmer Hobson, was that the Volunteers should not fight unless the British tried to ban their organisation, take their weapons and arrest their activists. If this happened, the Volunteers would fight in self-defence. Hobson, head of the IRB, argued that the organisation's constitution of 1879, which said that the IRB would not launch another rebellion until it had the support of the majority of the Irish people, supported this case.[172] But both Hobson and MacNeill were isolated within the separatist camp by their co-operation with the Irish Parliamentary Party in 1914.

The other camp, led initially by Tom Clarke and Seán MacDermott, favoured launching a rising regardless of what the British did. This faction made a decision in principle to launch a rising immediately after the outbreak of war in Europe, and in May 1915, Clarke and MacDermott (as well as like-minded Volunteer officers such as Patrick Pearse, Thomas MacDonagh, Eamon Ceannt and Joseph Mary Plunkett) formed a secret 'Military Council' to plan an uprising. Clarke and MacDermott represented the veteran Fenians; the others were drawn first into the Volunteers via the Gaelic League and sworn into the IRB only in the previous two years. In Pearse's case he had joined 'the Organisation' in 1913, and in the case of the others, after the outbreak of war.[173]

Pearse in particular came to be the spokesman for the Rising, and indeed was to be named as 'President' of the 'Republic' the rebels proclaimed at Easter 1916 – facts that have probably inflated his role in the separatist movement. In some ways he was most unlike the veteran IRB men Clarke and MacDermott. Unlike them, he had a high public profile as a Gaelic League scholar, poet, editor of the League's journal *An Claidheamh Soluis* ('The Shining Sword'), and headmaster of an Irish-speaking school, St Enda's, in south County Dublin. He had no previous background in the IRB and no connection to either the world of political violence (as did Clarke) in the 1880s, or to militant land struggles (as did MacDermott). As late as 1912 he had stood on a platform with John Redmond in support of the Home Rule Bill – though in a typical rhetorical flourish, he had warned there would be 'red war throughout Ireland [if] we are betrayed again'.

The Ulster crisis and the suspension of Home Rule apparently signified that Irish self-government was indeed 'betrayed', and thereafter Pearse moved closer to the separatists, contributing sometimes to *Irish Freedom* before being sworn into the IRB and finally being co-opted onto the Military Council. Pearse, and to some extent also Volunteers such as MacDonagh, Plunkett and Ceannt, despite their lack of a separatist background, were to the forefront in pushing for military action.

The tension between those who acknowledged the need for popular support before taking up arms and those who felt that armed struggle would push the people in the right direction was a theme that would run through the coming years. Neither MacNeill nor IRB General Secretary Hobson nor IRB President Dennis McCullough were informed of the plans of the Military Council for an uprising.

What kind of revolution would it be, this secret conspiracy; one that not alone did not try to first build a mass base among the population before launching an insurrection, nor brief those who would be the fighters on the ground, but did not even tell all of its own leadership? Not one that could hope to overthrow British rule by mass insurrection, nor even by a *coup d'état*. The rebellion that would eventually come off in 1916 was basically an armed demonstration to show that separatists were really serious about fighting, and if necessary dying, for an independent Ireland.

That they would conceive of it in this way can only be explained by the bitter disillusionment they felt with Irish participation in the Great War on the British side. *Irish Freedom* might declare in bold headlines that 'Germany is Not Ireland's Enemy', but apparently the mass of people did not agree with them in 1914. One Volunteer, Joseph O'Connor, recalled acidly that that the populace who had been moved to fury against the British Army by the Bachelor's Walk shootings were, weeks afterwards, joining up to that same Army. 'In a couple of days after these happenings [the Howth gunrunning and Bachelor's Walk shootings], war broke out between Germany and England. The effect in Ireland was immediate. People who were what one would have thought rebels on Sunday were completely pro-British the following Sunday... One of the sickening things in all this pre-'16 period was the inconstancy of the ordinary people'.[174]

The coming insurrection would therefore be in some ways a mark of desperation. The separatists wanted an independent Ireland – not Home Rule – and complained that 'even this paltry measure of freedom is not granted until some unknown future date'.[175] In late 1914 their dream looked further away than ever. Something radical would have to be done.

Speaking in Tralee in 1914, Seán MacDermott told his listeners, 'Nationalism as known to Tone and Emmet is almost dead in the country and a spurious substitute as taught by the IPP exists... The Irish patriotic sprit will die forever unless a blood sacrifice is made in the next few years. It will be necessary for some of us to offer ourselves as martyrs if nothing better can be done to preserve the national Irish spirit'.[176]

Desmond Fitzgerald, another IRB man, Gaelic Leaguer and 1916 rebel, said that if a rising was not launched before the end of the First World War, 'Irish nationality would flicker out'. 'The reaction of the Irish people after the declaration of war filled me with the conviction that we had reached a point where the Irish people had accepted completely their absorption by the British'. If that happened 'it would be futile to talk of ourselves other than as inhabitants of that part of England that used to be called Ireland. In that state of mind I had decided that extreme action must be taken'.[177] Similarly, lower down the organisation's ranks, Paul Galligan wrote to his brother after the Rising, 'we were surrendering the last shred of Irish nationality and we knew that we had to fight to keep Ireland from becoming a British province'.[178]

It was, in the separatists' view, better to fight and, if needs be, die 'honourably' than to accept subjugation, political defeat and cultural annihilation. The idea of 'saving' Irish nationhood from oblivion was a powerful one, going to the heart of the separatists' identity as unbowed, defiant fighters against the subjugation of Ireland. It was repeated too often and by too many rank-and-file activists to simply put it down to the thinking of romantic intellectuals such as Pearse.

The Marxist materialist James Connolly (who should in theory have rejected such 'subjective' ideas) wrote in the *Workers' Republic,* scorning a recruiter who had claimed that the trenches were no more dangerous than the Dublin slums: 'You can die honourably in a Dublin slum. If you die of fever, or even of want, because you preferred to face fever and want, rather than sell your soul to the enemies of your class and country, such death is an honourable death, a thousand times more honourable than if you won a V.C. committing murder at the bidding of your country's enemies. These are war times. In times of war the value of the individual life is but little, but the estimate set upon honour is even higher than in times of peace'.[179]

The sight of thousands of Irishmen serving in the British Army in the European War to many separatists sounded the death knell for what they understood 'Ireland' to mean. Armed conflict with the British Empire, 'striking a blow for freedom', was therefore not only a political tactic –although it was that too – but also a way of 'redeeming' Irish nationality by defining it in armed struggle against the British state.

Planning the Rising

In 1914, the IRB had apparently had in its clutches a militia over 150,000 strong, perhaps ready to fight for Home Rule. In 1915 the Irish Volunteers had no more than 10,000 men. On the face of it, this was a catastrophe for the separatists. The split with the National Volunteers was not, as it turned out, such a disaster for those inside the Irish Volunteers who favoured insurrection.

Certainly the split had cost them a lot of manpower, but it had also streamlined the Volunteers into a much more homogenous and politically committed force than it had been in mid-1914.

The National Volunteers, by contrast, without such a coherent and ideologically driven core grouping, fell away quite quickly. Though only about 20 per cent of their number joined the British Army as Redmond had urged, the remainder tended to fall into inactivity. In County Sligo the RIC reported that only 280 of the original Volunteers were 'Sinn Féiners', while the National Volunteers took some 4,000 men with them. But by 1915, the National Volunteers were reported to be completely inactive in Sligo; apparently they believed they would be sent to the front if they kept drilling.[180]

The RIC concluded of Redmond's National Volunteers that 'it is a strong force on paper, but without officers and untrained, it is little better than a large mob'. The National Volunteers staged a rally, some 20,000 strong, on Easter Sunday 1915 in Dublin's Phoenix Park, but their Inspector General Maurice Moore saw no military future for the organisation: 'They cannot be trained, disciplined or armed, moreover, the enthusiasm has gone and they cannot be kept going... it will be of no practical use against any Army, Orange or German'.[181]

The Irish Volunteers, by contrast, increased slightly in numbers as the war went on and went about procuring more weapons wherever they could. The 'Howth Mausers' were supplemented by modern British Lee Enfield rifles surreptitiously bought or stolen from soldiers and Martini carbines similarly extracted from the police.

There was also the complicating factor of the Irish Citizen Army. In 1914, with the departure of James Larkin, the founder and leader of the ITGWU, to America, James

Connolly found himself at the head of the union and of its militia. With the aid of another former soldier, Michael Mallin, he had armed, uniformed and trained the small force. Connolly seems to have prioritised this work over maintaining the Transport Union, which was down to a mere ten branches and 5,000 members by early 1916. By 1915 the Citizen Army too was preparing for insurrection against British rule. Connolly, who since the war had started was writing belligerent articles about armed rebellion in his newspaper, *The Workers' Republic*, was co-opted onto the Volunteers' Military Council in early 1916 to avoid the risk of him either pre-empting British repression or even starting a rebellion on his own.

It was this group, the Military Council, a conspiracy within a conspiracy, that was to plan the Rising. The military plan, apparently composed by Joseph Plunkett, was kept so secret that no record of it has survived, but so far as historians have been able to reconstruct it, it was this. The main body of Volunteers were to seize central Dublin and also its main port at Kingstown (now Dun Laoghaire). There they were to hold out for as long as possible and await reinforcements from the surrounding counties. In the west, the plan issued to Volunteers in Galway, Clare and Limerick was to hold 'the line of the Shannon' (River) and keep the British garrisons there pinned west of it.

The thinking was that, if retaking Ireland could be made too costly for the British, they might prefer to negotiate rather than divert major resources from the Great War's Western Front. The plan was supposedly based on Robert Emmet's blueprint of 1803. One Volunteer saw Thomas MacDonagh poring over a copy of Emmet's original plan shortly before the Rising.[182] Apparently Plunkett, who visited Germany in 1915, hoped for a German military landing in Ireland, but even with German aid, this all sounds hopelessly unrealistic for a poorly armed militia of 10,000 or so men. Admittedly, the Germans had promised arms to the insurgents, via Roger Casement (an Ulster Protestant and former British diplomat turned radical separatist), but small arms alone in the hands of amateur soldiers could not hope to defeat the British military, and given the Royal Navy's dominance at sea, a German seaborne invasion of Ireland was never likely to happen.

However, there was a secondary objective. Connolly wrote, 'If the British use artillery in Dublin they are doomed'.[183] While he was quite wrong in thinking that the British would not use heavy weapons in putting down the rebellion, he may have had a point. If British rule could be reduced to the use of blunt physical force to put down a nationalist rebellion, it would be fatally compromised in the eyes of Catholic and nationalist Ireland. Irish people would have to choose between British repression and Irish insurgents. In such a scenario, the willingness to compromise that underpinned the politics of Home Rule and the Irish Parliamentary Party would be swept away.

Although the plans for the Rising were the work of a small, closed group, they do not seem to have misled the rank and file, who by and large were eager to fight. According to Citizen Army member Helena Molony, the ordinary Volunteers wondered why launching the rebellion took so long: 'There was a good deal of silent anger among the Volunteers at this "go slow" atmosphere. Their discipline, loyalty and trust in their leaders kept them silent, but these young men knew what they had enrolled for, and one hundred per cent of them were resolved to "strike a blow" and live up to their maxim – "England's difficulty is Ireland's opportunity"'.[184] In the lead-up to the Rising, Volunteer companies were put to work making improvised hand grenades, so it seems most unlikely that they did not know that action of some kind was imminent. Nevertheless, the price to pay for the extraordinary secrecy exercised by the Military Council was great confusion among the rank and file.

Even those with senior IRB connections knew only that something was going to happen in the coming months. Seamus Doyle, a Volunteer and IRB officer from Enniscorthy, for instance, recalled that in late 1915, 'I was aware through IRB circles at this time that a Rising was planned, but I had no idea when it would take place'. In March of 1916, he met Pearse at the Robert Emmet commemoration in Wexford, and Pearse told him that 'the insurrection was near at hand'.[185] Richard Mulcahy, a prominent Dublin Volunteer and IRB member whom, unbeknownst to him, Seán MacDermott and Tom Clarke had pencilled in to command a unit which would blow up the telegraph system in Dublin, was only told of the Rising and his expected role in it days before it broke out.[186]

'Defiance to England'

Against this background, the Volunteers, Citizen Army and also a small group called the Hibernian Rifles (a separatist offshoot of the Ancient Order of Hibernians) trained and paraded intensively. In August 1915 the Volunteers, along with the Citizen Army and representatives from Sinn Féin, the GAA and even elements of the National Volunteers, staged a show of strength in Dublin at the funeral of Jeremiah O'Donovan Rossa – a veteran Fenian bomber of the 1880s – an occasion that would strike many as a symbol of the open rejection of not only the war but also the legitimacy of the British state.

On the day of the funeral, Paul Galligan (by this time adjutant to Military Council member and Volunteer head of training Thomas MacDonagh) had orders to keep a clear passage and right of way for the Volunteers marching from the city centre to Glasnevin cemetery, from Grattan Bridge over the River Liffey to City Hall. A company of Volunteers were put at his disposal to keep the street clear. 'A superintendant of the DMP approached me in a furious temper', Galligan recalled. 'He wanted to know under what authority I had stopped the thoroughfare. I informed him I was acting on the orders of my commanding officer'. The superintendent accompanied Galligan to see MacDonagh and, after an argument, MacDonagh ordered Galligan to put the policeman under arrest. The Volunteers were armed and the Dublin Metropolitan Police were not, so there was little the superintendant could do about it. The humiliated policeman was detained until after the funeral. The superintendant was still in Galligan's custody when the main body of Volunteers marched past in their dark green uniforms, wearing their distinctive Boer-style wide-brimmed hats and carrying rifles and bandoliers of ammunition. When the funeral procession passed, Galligan's Volunteers formed part of the rearguard and the column proceeded to Glasnevin.[187]

At the graveside Patrick Pearse gave the oration, which concluded: 'The Defenders of the Realm have worked well in secrecy and in the open. They think that they have pacified half of us and intimidated the other half... but the fools, the fools, the fools! They have left us our Fenian dead and while Ireland holds these graves, Ireland unfree shall never be at peace'.

In those times, before megaphones, not many people actually heard Pearse on the day itself, but the oration later became a classic summation of the Republicans' defiant attitude to British rule. More impressive still, to many onlookers, was the volley of rifle shots that crashed out over the grave when Pearse had finished speaking. A watching priest, Father Curran, thought that 'it was more than a farewell to an old Fenian. It was a defiance to England by a new generation in Ireland'.[188]

While such occasions were thrilling and radicalising for some, to others they seemed merely ridiculous posturing. Initially, the Irish Volunteers (nicknamed inaccurately the 'Sinn Féin Volunteers' after the split) were unpopular with the general public for their anti-war 'pro-German' stance, while so many Irishmen were serving in the British forces.

In Cork, teenaged policeman's son Seán O'Faoláin went along with the view that the Volunteers were 'nothing but vulgar corner boys with no common sense'. Watching forty or fifty of these 'rudely accoutred fellows with no uniform other than a best around ordinary working clothes, only a very few bearing rifles', he thought, 'they were disgracing our country while real glorious war was flashing and booming in Flanders and France'.[189]

Most rank-and-file Volunteers were of the 'respectable working class' – that is, those who could afford to pay dues for arms and uniforms – and one of the social groupings they came into conflict with was the poorest of the urban population. This was particularly pronounced when they came into contact with the despised 'Separation Women' who were taking the British Government allowance while their menfolk were at war – and invariably, according to separatist prejudice, drinking the money away.

In Limerick city in 1915, where a thousand Volunteers paraded armed through the streets, Ernest Blythe recalled that 'the rabble of the city, particularly the "separation women" got into the mood to make trouble'. At the train station, where the Volunteers from Dublin returned after the parade, stones were thrown, punches exchanged and some Volunteers had their rifles taken. 'One Volunteer officer who lost his head ordered his men to load their rifles. Fortunately his instructions were countermanded, otherwise in the heat of the turmoil, irreparable damage might have been done'.[190]

Republicans tended to blame British war propaganda, which insisted they were dupes of the Germans, for such outbursts of public hostility; but it seems clear that at this point, open insurrectionary nationalism, as opposed to a vague anti-war feeling, was quite unpopular.

This was true among the richest as well as the poorest classes. William Martin Murphy's *Irish Independent*, for instance, was openly hostile to the separatists. After the Rising, Murphy himself said 'that the authorities allowed a body of lawless and riotous men to be drilled and armed and to provide themselves with an arsenal of weapons and explosives was one of the most amazing things that could happen in any civilised country outside of Mexico', and no doubt many well-off Home Rulers felt the same.[191]

The Volunteers were indeed a regular sight on the streets of Dublin in 1915–16, uniformed in dark green and armed with rifles. On St Patrick's Day 1916 they staged a mock insurrection in central Dublin, including an 'attack' on Dublin Castle, without any intervention by the police or military.

Elsewhere, the Volunteers were similarly aggressive. In Galway, Gilbert Morrissey recalled that his company of Volunteers openly defied the police, parading their newly acquired 'Howth Mausers' in the town of Athenry. When the police, 'a District Inspector, Head Constable, two sergeants and 27 men', surrounded them and attempted to seize the weapons, 'our O/C [Officer Commanding] ordered the twelve rifle-men to fire three rounds each'. The RIC District Inspector backed down and had a talk with the Volunteers' officer, Larry Lardner, 'who told him that Carson's Volunteers were carrying rifles in the north without hindrance and that we would do so in the south, and he got away with it. From that onwards we carried rifles and shotguns in the open'.[192]

The view from Dublin Castle

With hindsight it seems almost astonishing that the British allowed an armed and openly hostile nationalist group to parade and manoeuvre in full view on the streets of the Irish capital and elsewhere. Even more so given that the British knew from intercepted telegraphs from America to Berlin that the Volunteers, via John Devoy and Clan na Gael in the US, were in contact with and had been offered help by the Germans.[193]

In fact there was fierce debate on whether to move against the Volunteers within the British administration in Ireland. Augustine Birrell, the Chief Secretary, and Mathew Nathan, the Undersecretary, were both of the opinion that clamping down on the radical nationalist groups would be more politically costly than it was worth and would alienate the broad nationalist community. On the other hand, the Lord Lieutenant, Viscount Wimborne and British military intelligence argued insistently that 'seditious' groups must be disarmed.

However, despite having extensive emergency powers under the wartime Defence of the Realm Act, the British state in Ireland was only intermittently repressive. Seán MacDermott was given four months' hard labour for a 'seditious' speech in Tuam, County Galway in early 1915, but this put only a short halt to his preparations for insurrection. *Irish Freedom* was closed down in December 1914 for its agitation against recruitment of Irishmen for the British forces.[194] Connolly's *Irish Worker* was closed down for 'seditious language', but only weeks later was replaced with the almost identical *Workers' Republic*. A number of IRB activists, notably Ernest Blythe, were arrested and deported to England for anti-recruitment agitation. On the whole, though, the Volunteers were largely left alone in the months before the Rising.

Birrell's policy was naturally fiercely criticised after the rebellion, but was it really as misguided as it seems? Birrell was a highly experienced and not unsympathetic observer of Irish nationalist politics. He knew that Irish self-rule was coming in some form, and in the meantime, keeping a semi-loyal population in line under a broadly democratic system needed a soft touch. Repression would be counterproductive by alienating a much broader constituency than the separatists themselves. Piaras Béaslaí, in 1916 an IRB man and Volunteer, thought Birrell was in fact one of the biggest problems they faced: 'As one who was working tooth and nail to bring about an insurrection, I can testify that one of the biggest obstacles was the cleverness of Mr. Birrell's policy'.[195]

There is even a suggestion that elements of the British state allowed the Rising to happen so they could get around Birrell's liberalism and put down the Volunteers. Just before the Rising, British military intelligence intercepted a telegram to Berlin giving the date and location of the rebellion. Whether Birrell and the Dublin Castle administration were informed we do not know.[196] What we can be sure of, though, is that despite ample warning of what was about to happen, the Rising caught the British totally unprepared.

The brink

Two dramatic events immediately preceded the insurrection. One was the attempted landing of the

German arms for the Volunteers, along with Roger Casement. The other was the last-minute revelation of the imminent rebellion to the leaders of the Volunteers and the IRB.

The Germans had placed only a low priority on the aid to rebels in Ireland. What they sent was very much second-rate weaponry, captured from the Russians in 1914. Nevertheless, it was substantial. Aboard a ship named the *Aud* were 20,000 rifles, 10 machine guns and hundreds of thousands of rounds of ammunition. To put this into perspective, the Volunteers had at most 5,000 or so weapons in their possession in the whole country, and many of these were of obsolete patterns.[197]

The *Aud* narrowly avoided several British patrol ships and convinced others that it was a Norwegian trawler. It anchored off Fenit in County Kerry for hours, waiting for the local Volunteers to respond to their signals. In the meantime, it attracted the attention of British vessels in the area, which pursued it into Cork harbour. Realising the game was up, the ship's captain scuttled the vessel and its weaponry. A party of five Volunteers, sent by car from Dublin to try and contact the ship, drove in pitch darkness over the edge of Ballykissane Pier (Castlemaine Harbour in Dingle Bay) near Killorglin, drowning three of them. They were the first casualties of the Rising. The following day a U-Boat landed Roger Casement nearby at Banna Strand near Fenit. Casement, who had tried in vain both to raise a Volunteer unit from Irish prisoners of war held by the Germans (he got only 55 recruits) and to persuade the Germans themselves to send an expedition to Ireland, intended to try and stop the Rising, which he was convinced would be a bloody failure. Before he could do anything, however, he was arrested by a suspicious policeman.[198] He would be hanged in August for treason.

The loss of the German arms shipment was a major blow to the prospects of the rebellion, especially outside of Dublin. Even with the arms, the prospect of a nationwide rebellion was a long shot. Without them it would be all but impossible.

On 21 April 1916, Volunteer companies around the country were informed that they would parade with full kit on Easter Sunday, 23 April. Only the Military Council and the very restricted number of people they had told knew that this was actually the signal for rebellion. At the last minute, the leadership of the Volunteers and IRB were also informed. Some Volunteers seemed to believe that the British were about to suppress their organisation and arrest their leaders. Paul Galligan wrote to his brother, 'it was decided to fight for this reason, that [Easter] Monday would see all the Volunteer officers arrested and a general lifting of arms take place... From Easter Sunday it was a race between us and the Government but we got there first, even if it was only with a small force'.[199]

This was the argument used by the Military Council to Eoin MacNeill, when the plans for the rebellion were revealed to him the day before the planned uprising. It was based on a Dublin Castle document, leaked by a sympathetic civil servant to Dublin Corporation Alderman Tom Kelly the week before the rebellion, which revealed a plan by the British military to arrest the leaders of Sinn Féin, the Irish Volunteers, the National Volunteers and the Gaelic League. Citizens of Dublin were to be confined to their houses and the city streets patrolled by troops. Patrick Pearse's school at St Enda's was to be surrounded, as was MacNeill's house and that of the Catholic Archbishop of Dublin.

The British administration denied utterly the authenticity of the document and the British Army later asserted that it was merely a contingency plan to be used if conscription was imposed on Ireland. It also seems a little too convenient for the insurrectionists to have discovered this document just before they planned their uprising. On the other hand, many separatists did seem to believe it. Seán MacDermott, just before his execution, swore to the priest who gave him absolution that the document was genuine.[200]

MacNeill, however, was not convinced; nor was Bulmer Hobson. MacNeill was summoned to a house in suburban Dublin and told bluntly that the Rising was to go ahead the following day, with or without his consent. Pearse told him petulantly, 'We don't need you any more'. MacNeill, though, after at first appearing to go along with the idea, very nearly stopped the event in its tracks. He took out an advertisement in the *Sunday Independent* newspaper which advised the Volunteers that 'All manoeuvres for today are cancelled'.[201]

Michael O'Rahilly (known as 'The O'Rahilly' in separatist circles) drove around the country, in a frenetic two-day period, trying to enforce the countermanding order. In the event, MacNeill and O'Rahilly's efforts only postponed the Rising for a day. The Military Council managed to get word to reliable units that the 'manoeuvres' would be going ahead on Monday instead. O'Rahilly himself quixotically joined the Rising himself and would die in it.

Seán MacDermott woke up on Easter Sunday, 23 April 1916, expecting to be launching an insurrection in Dublin city. When he found out that it had been frustrated by Bulmer Hobson and Eoin MacNeill, he was enraged and crestfallen. 'It was the first and only time', one Volunteer remembered, 'that I saw Seán really upset'.[202] Of Hobson, who had originally recruited him into the IRB in Belfast and mentored his political development, he said that he would 'damn soon deal with that fellow', and had him kidnapped and held at gunpoint until the Rising could be put back on track. Some IRB men even wanted to shoot him, but were dissuaded. Dennis McCullough, President of the Organisation, based in Belfast, was more pliable and reluctantly agreed to go along with the rebellion.[203]

In the meantime, MacNeill's last-minute order to call off the Rising caused almost indescribable chaos amongVolunteer units around the country. Seán MacEntee, commander of the Volunteers in County Louth, sent a contingent south to seize the RIC barracks in the village of Ardee, only to get word on the Sunday that the Rising had been cancelled. He had to send three messengers after them on bicycles before he managed to halt the column. Finally having caught up with his men on Monday, he got further information that the rebellion was actually going ahead. MacEntee ended up cycling to Dublin from Drogheda, all through the night through sheets of pouring rain, to get confirmation. Having eventually met his superiors, he got back to Louth in time to discover that most of his men had dispersed. He finished the week back in Dublin, where he fought in the rebel headquarters at the General Post Office.[204]

MacNeill's 'countermanding order' has often been blamed for the Rising being confined to Dublin, and there is some truth in this. In Cork, for example, around one thousandVolunteers came out on Easter Sunday – as many as in Dublin – but they went home after receiving a string of contradictory orders from the capital.[205] On the other hand, as events would show, in the absence of sufficient arms and coherent planning there was little enough the rebels in the provinces could have done anyway.

It is therefore more than likely that the serious fighting of Easter week would have happened in Dublin – the centre of Volunteer organisation and weaponry – regardless of MacNeill's order. In Dublin itself, the countermand cost the Rising some manpower, but perhaps not as much as is sometimes claimed. On St Patrick's Day that year, 1,400 Volunteers mobilised for exercises in Dublin – where they occupied the city centre for an hour. In the actual rebellion, about a month later, only slightly fewer men – 1,200 or so – fought in the Rising.[206] Those who did not turn out on the first day of the Rising generally joined their units once it was clear that the long-awaited fight was indeed underway. For the most part, the delay simply meant a day of nerve-jangling waiting and a sleepless night for Dublin Volunteers.

Early on Monday, 24 April 1916, the Volunteers and Citizen Army assembled at various points in Dublin, marched out and took over pre-selected strongpoints in the city centre. The Rising – the armed insurrection against British rule long dreamt of by separatists but barely conceived of by anyone else – had begun.

Chapter 5:

The Easter Rising

On Easter Monday, James Stephens, a writer, nationalist and registrar of the National Gallery in Dublin, started hearing strange rumours. There had been rifle firing in the city all day. Returning from lunch to his office, he encountered a crowd of onlookers at St Stephen's Green:

> 'Has there been an accident?' said I. 'What's all this for?' A sleepy rough looking man answered, 'Don't you know? The Sinn Féiners have seized the city this morning'. 'Oh', said I... 'They seized the city at eleven o'clock this morning. The Green there is full of them. They have captured the Castle, they have taken the Post Office'. 'My God', said I staring at him, and turned and went running towards the Green... I saw the gates were closed and men were standing inside with guns on their shoulders.[207]

Ernie O'Malley, a medical student, was strolling through Dublin that morning; it was a bank holiday and he had the day off. On O'Connell Street (or Sackville Street, as it then was) he saw:

> Large groups of people gathered together. From the flagstaff on top of the General Post Office, the

GPO, floated a new flag, a tricoloured one of green, white and orange... 'What's it all about?' I asked a man who stood near me, a scowl on his face. 'Those boyhoes, the Volunteers have seized the Post Office, they want nothing less than a Republic', he laughed scornfully... On the base of [Nelson's] Pillar there was a white poster. Gathered around it were groups of men and women. Some looked at it with serious faces, some laughed and sniggered. I began to read it with a smile but my smile ceased as I read 'POBLACHT NA H-EIREANN, THE PROVISIONAL GOVERNMENT OF THE IRISH REPUBLIC'.[208]

There were some dead horses lying on the street, testament to a skirmish between the Volunteers and a troop of British cavalry. 'Those fellows,' O'Malley was told, 'are not going to be frightened by a troop of lancers. They mean business'.[209]

Dubliners woke up on Easter Monday morning and found the city centre occupied by armed men (and some women) in a mixture of dark green uniforms and civilian clothes. James Connolly had mobilised the main body at Liberty Hall, the Transport Union's headquarters. He was in command of the men O'Malley saw who took over the GPO and most of Sackville Street. Also north of the Liffey, Volunteers under Ned Daly took over the Four Courts, the centre of the Irish legal system, and the clump of little streets behind it. The men Stephens encountered on Stephen's Green were mostly Citizen Army fighters, commanded by Michael Mallin. Most unwisely, they dug in on the Green, which was overlooked by high buildings on every side.

Several hundred metres away, another body of Volunteers under Thomas MacDonagh had occupied Jacob's Biscuit Factory on Aungier Street. Further to the west, there were two main Volunteer strongpoints: one in the South Dublin Union, a vast complex of workhouses and hospitals on the site of present day St James' Hospital, under the command of Eamon Ceannt; the other in Jameson's Distillery at Marrowbone lane, overlooking the Grand Canal. Finally, at the other end of the canal to the south-east was a garrison led by Éamon de Valera, ensconced in Boland's Mill. A detachment of this force guarded the canal crossing at Mount Street Bridge and another covered the military barracks at Beggar's Bush.

Dublin's old centre can be imagined as an elongated oval, like a misshapen rugby ball, bisected by the River Liffey, which runs from one end of the oval to the other. Its perimeters are bounded by two canals, the Royal on the north side and the Grand to the south. Running roughly parallel to the canals are two 'Circular Roads', again named North and South. This was the area the insurgents wanted to hold. However, in 1916 this district was abutted by no fewer than six British Army barracks: three around the southern rim of the oval along the Grand Canal; another at Kilmainham, at the oval's western point; one more in the Phoenix Park; and another, the Royal Barracks, just beyond the Four Courts on the River Liffey. Broadly speaking, with the exception of the headquarters at the GPO, the Volunteer's positions had been chosen as defensive sites against a counterattack from these barracks.

However, strategically speaking, there were some major flaws in their dispositions. The rebels had left two imposing and highly symbolic buildings in British hands, right in the centre both of the city and of their positions: Dublin Castle, the centre of British rule, and Trinity College. The Castle was attacked by a small party of Citizen Army fighters, but after shooting a policeman they retired to the rooftop of the adjacent City Hall, from where they exchanged shots with rapidly arriving British reinforcements. No attempt was made to take Trinity, the Protestant and largely Unionist university, which stood right in the path between the rebel garrisons north and south of the Liffey. A scratch force of armed students was put together to defend it and, as the week went on, further British forces were funnelled in.

Just as seriously, the Volunteers failed to take or put out of action either of Dublin's two main train stations at Amiens Street (now Connolly) and Kingsbridge (now Heuston), which the British would use to bring in reinforcements from their garrisons in the Curragh and Belfast. Finally, while some of the bridges over the Grand Canal (those at Marrowbone lane and Mount Street particularly) were strongly held, others were not manned at all. The result was that instead of a compact city centre stronghold, the insurgents ultimately found themselves in isolated positions which had to withstand British counterattacks more or less alone. By the end of the week, communications between the rebel posts were only kept open by the odd Cumann na mBan (female) messenger who braved the hostile areas in between.

For most of Dublin's citizens, the Rising was a bolt out of the blue, and from the civilians the Volunteers at first experienced utter incomprehension and not a little hostility. Ernie O'Malley recalled the reaction of people in his middle-class neighbourhood: 'The loyalists spoke with an air of contempt, "The troops will settle the matter in an hour or two, these pro-Germans will run away"... The Redmondites were more bitter, "I hope they'll all be hanged... Shooting's too good for them. Trying to stir up trouble for us all"'.[210] In the working-class areas around Sackville Street, Jacob's biscuit factory and the South Dublin Union, many people had dependents serving in the British Army in the Great War. Wives of soldiers were paid 'separation money', and these women were bitterly hostile to the insurrection. O'Malley heard women abusing the Volunteers outside the GPO: 'You dirty bowsies, wait till the Tommies bate yer bloody heads off... if only my Johnny was back from the front you'd be running with your bloody well tail between your legs'.[211] Elsewhere the Volunteers had occupied places of work and welfare (such as it was) of poor working-class people.

In several cases the rebels had to use force against the locals to occupy their positions. At the Jacob's factory, a Volunteer named Seán Murphy recalled: 'Some civilians had... attacked one of the Volunteers and in order to save his life they had to shoot one of the civilians'.[212] At the South Dublin Union, the Volunteers found themselves involved in a riot with locals and had to 'lay out' two with rifle butts before they got into the complex.[213] At Stephen's Green, where the Citizen Army had seized passing cars and carts at gunpoint to serve as barricades, James Stephens saw a carter try to remove his livelihood from the barricades, only to be shot dead by the insurgents. 'At that moment the Volunteers were hated'.[214]

If the initial civilian reaction was largely one of bewilderment, the British military were almost equally astonished. Many of their officers had been at the races in Fairyhouse for the Bank Holiday Monday and there were only around 400 troops left in the city.[215] Lord Wimborne, the Lord Lieutenant, his worst fears having come to pass, declared martial law and handed over power to General W. J. Lowe.[216] If nothing else, the rebellion had at least freed him to clamp down on 'sedition', as he had been recommending for months.

On the first day of the Rising there were, by and large, only skirmishes between the Volunteers and the British military. Two troops of British cavalry, sent out to investigate the strange happenings, were badly shot up on O'Connell Street and on the quays in front of the Four Courts. A bomb was detonated at the British Army's arms dump in Phoenix Park, which failed to destroy the arsenal, but the Volunteers did shoot dead an unfortunate teenager who tried to alert the local police.[217] On Mount Street, a group of reserve volunteer soldiers, nicknamed the 'Gorgeous Wrecks' in Dublin (because of their advanced age and their tunics' inscriptions 'Georgius Rex'), on their way back from a route march in the Dublin Mountains, unwittingly stumbled upon the rebel position and four were killed before they scrambled into safety at Beggars Bush barracks.[218]

In fact, had the rebels known of the weakness of the British garrison, they could have taken such important points as Dublin Castle (garrisoned by only seven soldiers),[219] Trinity College (no garrison) and Beggars Bush (held initially by the Army catering staff and 17 rifles)[220] with relative ease. Only at the South Dublin Union, which was attacked by troops from the adjacent Richmond Barracks, was there serious fighting on the first day, and there the British command ordered a halt until they had come to terms with what they were dealing with.

Three of the unarmed Dublin Metropolitan Police were shot on the first day of the Rising, and their Commissioner pulled them off the streets. The decision, though understandable, unleashed an orgy of looting, especially around Sackville Street, as slum dwellers from the surrounding area took the once-in-a-lifetime opportunity to ransack the city's shops and boutiques.[221] Ernie O'Malley recorded that for the slum dwellers, 'this was a holiday. Some of the women... walked around in evening dress. Young girls wore long silk dresses. A saucy girl flipped a fan with a hand wristletted by a thick gold chain… She strutted in larkish delight, calling to others less splendid, "How do yez like me now?"[222]

The holiday for some was a nightmarish breakdown of social order for others. According to another onlooker, 'a horrible procession poured into the streets, mainly women and girls… they started with sticks and stones, a breach would be made [in a shop], the door would be forced in', and if the shopkeeper resisted 'they would beat him and down him without mercy'.[223] Labour leader William O'Brien:

> … saw a good many of the shops in O'Connell Street being looted. I saw a young fellow standing on the ledge of McDowell's Jeweller's shop at the Pillar, breaking the window, taking out fistfuls of watches and chains and throwing them to the crowd. Later, a number of fires started; one, particularly, in Laurence's shop in the block between Earl Street and Cathedral Street. Amongst the crowd I heard talk of fires in other directions.[224]

A total of 425 people were arrested after the Rising for looting.[225]

The Volunteers, who wanted to convey an image of themselves as a disciplined Irish Army, tried but largely failed to keep order and were reduced to shooting over the heads of looters to try and disperse them. So, sitting in mostly disconnected positions, with a civilian population at best ambivalent, at worst downright hostile, the Volunteers awaited the British counterattack.

Most Dubliners expected the Rising to be crushed within hours and were very surprised when it was not. In fact, it took several days for the British military machine to rumble clumsily into action. Reinforcements arrived from the military depot at the Curragh, clambered off the train at Amiens Street from Belfast and landed at the port in Kingstown (now Dun Laoghaire). General Lowe had only 1,600 troops under his command on Tuesday, but had 16,000 men in the city by Friday, backed up by field artillery rushed from Athlone and a gunboat, the *Helga*, which sailed down the River Liffey.[226] Effectively, the British would suffocate the Rising with overwhelming force. Nevertheless, the task proved far from straightforward. Lowe's first move was to open a line of communication along the River Liffey and to throw a cordon of troops around the Volunteers' strongholds.

Where the rebels sat in fixed positions, as at the GPO, they were steadily isolated and bombarded into surrender. When James Stephens returned to Stephen's Green on the Tuesday, he found it littered with dead and wounded Volunteers, caught by fire from the surrounding buildings. The insurgents there retreated to the College of Surgeons, where they remained for the rest of the week.[227] The neighbouring Jacob's factory saw little fighting, as did Boland's Mill and the Four Courts.

The Volunteers' headquarters at the GPO took the brunt of the British artillery bombardment. Most of Lower O'Connell Street was reduced to rubble and flames, and the Post Office itself became an inferno. James Stephens, observing the blaze from his window, wrote: 'I saw a red flare that crept to the sky and stole over it and remained there glaring; the smoke reached from the ground to the clouds, and I could see great red sparks go soaring to enormous heights; while always in the calm air there was the buzzing thudding and rattling of guns'.[228]

Inside the building were the Rising's principal figureheads, James Connolly and Patrick Pearse, along with the IRB veterans Clarke and MacDermott. Connolly, a former soldier, was a whirlwind of activity, building barricades, issuing orders and scouting the surrounding positions. On Thursday he was badly wounded in the leg by a ricochet on Abbey Street. He was treated by a captured British medic and then carried on a stretcher back to the firing line, where he kept himself occupied by reading a detective novel.[229]

Pearse, the writer and educationalist, in the words of one participant, 'sat out there in the front on one of the high stools, people would come up and talk to him'.[230] By Friday, the grand buildings of Dublin, having burned fiercely for two days, were crashing down around them. A sortie led by O'Rahilly tried to break out of the GPO and to occupy a fallback position on Moore Street, but was shot up badly by fire from the ever-closer British barricades. O'Rahilly himself was killed and lay sprawled, face up, on Henry Street in full view of his comrades.[231]

Despite the dangers involved in breaking cover, it was clear by that evening that an evacuation of the GPO could not be put off any longer. The survivors, nominally led by Pearse and Plunkett, though in fact commanded by a 21-year-old Volunteer named Seán McLoughlin, made a chaotic dash out of the blazing Post Office and into Moore Street. McLoughlin went first to see if the way was clear, but looked back to see 'the whole garrison coming towards me at the run. There was terrible confusion, almost panic. No one seemed to have any idea what to do... Another party entered from the opposite door and they opened fire on each other – one man was killed and several wounded. I was incensed with rage, calling, "Have you all gone mad – what the hell is wrong!" and I drove them towards the wall threatening them'.[232]

McLoughlin had them break into the houses in Moore Street and they proceeded to tunnel through the walls of adjacent buildings. He recalled, 'Seán MacDermott, who was the most active man there, said, "What shall we do in the meantime?" I said, "The most sensible thing you can all do is to have a few hours sleep"'.[233]

Elsewhere, the thick walls of the rebels' positions usually protected them from British shells and bullets, but the psychological strain of waiting, inactive, for the British counterattack proved excruciating. In Boland's Mill, Éamon de Valera refused to sleep for six nights, pacing furiously up and down the post. He ordered nearby Westland Row railway station to be burned, only to change his mind and have his men then put out the blaze under fire from British snipers. One Volunteer in the mill cracked under the pressure and shot one of his comrades before being clubbed down. Nevertheless, the garrison there was spared coming under direct shell fire due to a brainwave of de Valera's. He had a tricolour flown on a neighbouring empty building, which the British obligingly pounded with artillery.[234]

Where the British assaulted the Volunteers' positions dominating the routes into the city, fighting was much bloodier. There they were drawn into street fighting, with its invisible snipers and sudden close-range crossfire, which negated their superiority in men and firepower. This happened mainly at three locations: Mount Street Bridge, South Dublin Union/Marrowbone Lane and North King Street.

At Mount Street, on the approach to the city centre from the port at Kingstown, a Volunteer outpost manned by only 17 men, armed with rifles and handguns, inflicted 240 casualties on attacking British troops.[235] The rebels occupied the stately Clanwilliam House, commanding the crossing over the Grand Canal, and two houses on Northumberland Road, a leafy, upper-class, red-bricked neighbourhood. They were faced by a British regiment, the Sherwood Foresters, just off the boat from a training depot in England, and so inexperienced that they had to be shown on the pier at Kingstown how to fire and reload their weapons.[236] On top of that, they had left behind their grenades, and their Lewis machine guns had somehow been misplaced in the crossing.[237] Marching up through the suburbs, they were warmly applauded by the crowds still enjoying the Spring Show at the Royal Dublin Society, until they stumbled into the crossfire at Northumberland Road. Ten were hit in the first attack.[238]

Although there was an alternative crossing of the canal available just a street away at Baggot Street, which would have flanked the Volunteers' position, General Lowe ordered that the bridge at Mount Street be taken 'at all costs'.[239] For the rest of the day, at the sound of whistles every twenty minutes, waves of hapless troops led by officers with drawn swords charged up the road, only to be shot down. By the evening, the road was carpeted with dead and wounded British troops, many moaning in pain and trying feebly to drink from their water bottles.

The survivors crawled into the gutters and doorways at either side of the road for some cover, while others huddled under a low wall at the canal. For the Volunteers, despite the hopeless odds, it was exhilarating. Inside Clanwilliam House, one Patrick Boyle shouted to Tom Walsh over the noise of battle, 'Isn't this a great day for Ireland?' 'Isn't it that?' 'Did I ever think I'd see a fight like this? Shouldn't we all be grateful to the good God that he has allowed us to take part in a fight like this?' No sooner were the words out of Boyle's mouth when he was hit in the head and killed.[240]

De Valera, with over a hundred fighters, was only two streets away in Boland's Mill, but his command never reinforced the Volunteers at Mount Street. Eventually, on the Thursday, the position was stormed when the British brought up machine guns and explosives. Four Volunteers were killed and another captured. The rest slipped away.[241] The Sherwood Foresters suffered 4 officers and 24 other ranks killed, along with over 220 wounded, some of whom died later.[242] After the fighting, the area presented a grisly sight, carpeted with British casualties. Dead and wounded soldiers '... lay all over Northumberland Road, on the house steps, in the channels along the canal banks and in Warrington Place', witnesses recalled. 'The place was literally swimming with blood'. Four civilians had also been killed in the crossfire. The locals, 'all of good class', emerged from their homes to congratulate the British troops.[243]

The British never took the Volunteer positions at South Dublin Union and Marrowbone Lane, which blocked the route into the city from the south-west. They attacked it on Thursday and ferocious close-quarter fighting took place in the hospitals and workhouses. The British troops had to fight for every building, in wards where patients still lay as bullets and grenades flew around them.

The Volunteers, too few to hold the whole complex, made their stronghold in the nurses' building. A determined charge of British troops broke into it, only to find the inside of the building barricaded. Volleys of rifle fire and grenades were exchanged at point-blank range. Volunteer officer Cathal Brugha at one point held the barricade alone, badly wounded by a grenade blast, until the other Volunteers in the building heard him singing and came back to help him. The British soldiers, who were no less raw than the inexperienced Sherwood Foresters who had been massacred on Mount Street the day before, were the first to break off the nightmarish, claustrophobic combat, retreating to the Union bakery. From there, they and the Volunteers eyed each other until Sunday.[244]

In the distillery on Marrowbone Lane, near the Union complex, the British made several unsuccessful frontal assaults from over the canal. Volunteer Robert Holland was put in a top-floor room with a Cumann na mBan woman, who loaded his two rifles while he fired. By Thursday evening he 'could see quite a lot of [British soldiers'] bodies all around outside the wall and as far as Dolphins Barn Bridge. I could just see a pit and Red Cross men working at it putting bodies into it'.[245]

The rebel position around North King Street, behind the Four Courts, straddled the route towards the GPO – only about ten minutes' walk away – along the north side of the River Liffey, in a mesh of little streets and tenements. Ned Daly's Volunteers had barricaded each of the streets, and it was here that the most vicious street fighting of the week occurred. Even with the aid of an armoured car, the British troops made slow progress in taking the street.

At close range, death was waiting around every corner, from behind every chimney and behind every barricade. Starting on Thursday, the British tried to smother the enclave. Mostly they avoided direct fire by tunnelling through the walls of the slum houses, but one Major Sheppard, in much the same spirit as Lowe at Mount Street, decided on a frontal assault. The platoon that made the bayonet charge on one of the barricades was blasted by heavy Mauser bullets, losing fifteen men, including Sheppard himself, who fell wounded. The Volunteers afterwards scrambled over the barricade to take arms and ammunition from the dead and wounded. One, Frank Shouldice, recalled how 'one by one we knocked them all over. It was a terrible slaughter and to this day I can't understand why they tried to rush things'. Another thought that 'some officer... lost his head and sent those lads out to their deaths'.[246]

By the end of the week, the area was still not cleared. It was also here that the worst atrocity of the Rising took

place. The South Staffordshire regiment under a Colonel
Taylor advanced, in two days, 150 yards down North King
Street, resulting in 11 dead and 28 wounded. The troops,
no doubt infuriated at their losses and in any case under
orders to take no rebel prisoners, broke into the homes of
the locals and shot or bayoneted 15 civilian men whom
they accused of being rebels.[247] Ellen Walsh, a resident
of North King Street, recalled soldiers pounding on her
door until she opened, and demanding, 'Are there any
men in this house?' Thirty soldiers ransacked the house
'like wild animals or things possessed'. They took the two
men in the house aside, one of them Walsh's husband, and
killed them.[248]

A woman at Number 177 North King Street told an
inquest of the death of one of the civilians, one Paddy Bealin:

> They brought Paddy down into the cellar again
> and when they brought him into the cellar they
> were told to shoot him. [She asked the soldier]
> 'Why couldn't you let him off?', and he said, 'No
> because the officers have seen him'. The soldier
> said that the man said his prayers and though he
> was not of his creed the soldier helped him say his
> prayers, because he pitied him and then they said
> they could not shoot him fair faced. They told him
> to go down to the foot of the stairs and they let
> bang at him.[249]

The surrender

On Friday, 28 April, Pearse issued orders to surrender. The
remnants of his command from the GPO were cornered in
and around Moore Street. O'Rahilly was dead, Connolly
was badly wounded – his leg wound had turned gangrenous.

There was talk of trying to break through to Daly's men around the Four Courts, but it proved to be no more than that. Seán McLoughlin, the young Volunteer who had assumed a kind of military authority, was tasked with assembling a bayonet squad to try to cut their way out, but it looked a hopeless task. The Volunteers and Citizen Army fighters were tightly ringed by British rifles, machine guns and artillery on all sides. Civilians who tried to escape from Moore Street towards the British barricades were swept away by storms of bullets from the barricade in front of the insurgents' eyes. Some Volunteers remembered seeing three elderly men with white flags shot down;[250] others recalled the deaths of a husband and wife and their young daughter, who were shot as they tried to flee their house; others the deaths of another family who had tried to use a woman's apron as a flag of truce.[251] It was these shootings, apparently, that moved Pearse to surrender; he told his comrades, 'We must surrender to save the lives of the citizens'.[252]

Seán McLoughlin had been preparing to lead his 20 bayonet men in a charge towards Denmark Street when Pearse told him to stand down. 'Pearse said to me: "I am sending a message to the British to end this fight". I said: "Does it mean surrender?". He said: "I don't know until we have heard from the British."' A disconsolate McLoughlin went and sat down with Tom Clarke and said, 'somewhat bitterly', '"That's a curious way to act". He patted me on the back and said: "Don't take it like that, Seán; there are bigger things involved, you did your best."'[253]

Pearse sent a tersely written note via a Cumann na mBan nurse named Elizabeth O'Farrell, stating that he wished to surrender to 'prevent the further slaughter of the civilian population and in the hope of saving our followers, now hopelessly surrounded and outnumbered'.[254] Pearse's surrender came late on Friday afternoon. The survivors of the GPO garrison emerged blinking from their Moore Street enclave and assembled at Nelson's Pillar, where they piled their arms – Seán McLoughlin defiantly tossed his sword (which he carried as a Volunteer officer) at General Lowe's feet – and were marched to captivity in Richmond Barracks.

Word still had to be got to the other rebel strongholds, however, none of which had yet been taken by the British. Elizabeth O'Farrell, accompanied by a priest, volunteered to bring the news to the Volunteers around the city. At first, many of them didn't believe her. De Valera sent her away and had to be persuaded by officers who knew her that she was genuine. Thomas MacDonagh in the Jacob's factory thought the British had forged the note or forced Pearse to sign it. In Marrowbone Lane, full with over 100 Volunteers and Cumann na mBan women, the rebels were convinced they were winning and had organised a victory *ceilidhe* (Irish dancing) for that night.[255] James Stephens was clear that despite the surrender at Moore Street, the insurrection was still not over on Saturday: 'There is much rifle fire, but no sound from the machine guns, 18 pounders or trench mortars'.[256]

It was Sunday 30 April before the last rebel garrisons, at South Dublin Union and Marrowbone Lane, reluctantly surrendered.[257] Frank Robbins, a Citizen Army man, left an evocative account of the surrender in the College of Surgeons: 'The act of surrender was a greater calamity than death itself. Men and women were crying openly with arms around each other's shoulders'. It was only when British troops arrived that they recovered their composure: 'we had nothing to be ashamed of'. They might have failed, but 'others had failed before and they had not been ashamed or afraid of the consequences, why should we be?'[258]

Joe McGrath, a rebel commander at Marrowbone Lane, told his men to escape, and did so himself with a 'Toor a loo boys, I'm off'.[259] Michael Mallin, the Citizen Army commander, also told anyone who thought they could escape to do so, as did John McBride in the Jacob's factory, adding that if they ever got the chance to fight again, 'don't get inside four walls'.[260] De Valera, on the other hand, insisted that his men had to follow the surrender order to the letter, and they marched in formation into captivity.

Ernie O'Malley wandered into O'Connell Street – a scene of devastation – after the fighting had ended. 'The GPO was a shell from which the tricolour still floated. The stout walls were blackened, but they still held... The lower portion of O'Connell Street was in ruins. What houses still stood were being hauled down by wire ropes attached to traction engines. Houses were smouldering on Moore Street, Earl Street, Abbey Street and the Quays... Everywhere glass had been shattered or neatly drilled by bullets'.[261] The material damage caused by the five days of fighting in central Dublin came to over £2.5 million.[262]

Bodies littered the streets, and the authorities handed out bills calling on citizens to inform them immediately for fear of an epidemic.[263] The chaotic fighting across the city had seen people die randomly, often by stray gunfire, and left casualties strewn in unpredictable places. Paddy O'Connor, a teenage Fianna member from a strongly Republican family of railway workers, had stolen into the city with his brother while the fighting was still going on. Across from the South Dublin Union, where the insurgent garrison told them to go home, the two boys came upon 'the bodies of three dead Volunteers, lying in the fields. I did not recognise any of them'. On the Sunday, after they had been taken into custody in Beggars Bush barracks, the brothers watched a British soldier who was repairing a flagstaff suddenly topple over, dead, shot by an unseen sniper.[264]

Part of the popular memory of the Rising is that the Volunteers were pelted with abuse and missiles by hostile Dubliners as they marched under escort to prison. And there is no doubt that this did happen to many rebels. There had long been hostility between the Volunteers and some of the poorest class who depended on government aid, or as one separatist called them, 'the rabble of the city'. According to Frank Robbins, the Citizen Army man taken prisoner at the College of Surgeons, 'as they marched us into Richmond Barracks', crowds, 'waving hats and Union Jacks' stood at the kerbsides to hoot and jeer them. '"Shoot the traitors!", they cried. "Bayonet the bastards!"'[265] In one of the slum districts, the women pelted them with rotten vegetables, and some even emptied the contents of their chamber pots over them.[266]

Similarly, Robert Holland, a Volunteer captured at the surrender of the South Dublin Union, remembered that as he was likewise being marched to Richmond Barracks, 'men, women and children used filthy expressions at us'. Worst of all for Holland, a member of the Volunteer Company from the working-class Inchicore area, was that he knew many of his assailants. The prisoners 'heard all of their names being called out at intervals by the bystanders. My name was called out by some boys and girls I had gone to school with... This was the first time I ever appreciated British troops, as they undoubtedly saved us from being manhandled that evening.[267]

This may not, however, be the full story. For one thing, all of the areas around barracks where the prisoners were taken would have had a disproportionate number of soldiers' families in them, who were naturally antagonistic to the insurgents. James Stephens thought that the wider mood in the city, although 'definitely anti-Volunteer', was more ambivalent. First of all, the people he talked to respected that the Volunteers were 'putting up a decent fight'. 'For being beaten does not greatly matter in Ireland, but not fighting does matter'. 'Had they been beaten on the first or second day, the city would have been humiliated to its soul'.[268] So in some sense, despite being opposed to the Volunteers' actions, many people seemed to instinctively identify with them as fellow Irish nationalists.

Stephens believed that while the fighting was still going on, people had not yet taken sides: 'None of these people were prepared for insurrection. The thing had been sprung on them so suddenly they were unable to take sides'.[269] A Dublin Unionist, A. M. Bonaparte-Wyse, thought that 'the sympathies of the ordinary Irish are with Sinn Féin'.[270] Likewise, a Canadian journalist, F.A. McKenzie, found that 'in the poorer districts… there was a vast amount of sympathy with the rebels, particularly after the rebels were defeated'.[271] The experience of Ernie O'Malley, the medical student who came upon the GPO takeover on Easter Monday, was extreme. He actually joined in the fighting on the rebel side, sniping at British troops with a borrowed rifle and then helping fugitive Volunteers to get away after the surrender.[272]

The Rising outside of Dublin

Elsewhere in the country, there were risings of significance in only three places: Ashbourne in County Meath; rural County Galway; and Enniscorthy in County Wexford.

The fighting in Ashbourne was really an adjunct of the Dublin insurrection, as the North County Dublin Volunteers under Thomas Ashe and Richard Mulcahy, unable to get into the city, took an RIC barracks and ambushed a police force that came to retake it, killing 11.

In Cork, which outside of Dublin had the largest concentration of Volunteers and the most rifles, the

Volunteers briefly mobilised on Easter Sunday before eventually dispersing when faced with a stream of contradictory orders from Dublin. They were persuaded even to surrender their arms by local Catholic clergy and the Lord Mayor – a humiliation that their leaders, Tomás MacCurtain and Terence MacSwiney, would later go to great lengths to wipe out. The only shots fired in the 'rebel county' in 1916 were those of the Kent brothers, who resisted when the RIC came to arrest them, killing a head constable. Two of the brothers were shot in the ensuing gun battle and another later executed.[273]

In County Wexford the Volunteer movement had largely followed Redmond in 1914, with the exception of the town of Enniscorthy, where it was heavily infiltrated with IRB members. In the months leading up to the Rising, their leaders knew that something was going on, but the last order they received from Pearse in Dublin was to mobilise on Easter Sunday and 'obey your orders'. Since, especially with Eoin MacNeill's countermanding order, it was not at all clear what they were in fact expected to do, most Volunteers in Wexford, like their counterparts in Cork and elsewhere, simply did nothing. Sinnott, the Brigade commander in Wexford town, told his subordinates, 'in consequence of the conflicting orders he would not have anything to do with the matter'.[274]

The commandant in Enniscorthy was Cavan man Paul Galligan, who was not only a trusted IRB man, but also assistant to Military Council member Thomas MacDonagh – sent to Wexford to train the Volunteers there. When the Rising broke out he travelled to Dublin to try to find out what was happening and what was expected of him.

Connolly said to me that they had enough men in Dublin and that it would be better to join my unit in Wexford. After a talk with Pearse and Plunkett in which I could hear the word 'mountains' being used, Connolly instructed me to go back to Wexford as quickly as I could to mobilise the Enniscorthy Battalion and to hold the railway line to prevent troops coming through from Wexford as he expected they would be landed there. He said to reserve our ammunition and not to waste it attacking barracks or such like.[275]

When Galligan got back to Enniscorthy on the Thursday, after a 200-kilometre cycle, the local Volunteers occupied the town, surrounded and isolated the RIC barracks, hoisted the Republican flag over the town hall, and set about fortifying their positions against a counterattack. A party led by Galligan also took over the nearby town of Ferns. The diary of Seán Etchingham, a local Republican from Gorey, conveys the exhilaration of the Enniscorthy rebels: 'We had at least one day of blissful freedom. We have had Enniscorthy under the laws of the Irish Republic for at least one day and it pleases me to learn that the citizens are appreciably surprised... a more orderly town could not be imagined. The people of the town are great. The manhood of Enniscorthy is worthy of its manhood'.[276]

By Sunday morning, there had still not been any sight in Enniscorthy or Ferns of hostile British forces. Later that afternoon, an RIC district inspector and sergeant had arrived at Ferns under a flag of truce with a copy of Pearse's surrender order. At first, Seamus Doyle, the Volunteer commandant, and his officers in Enniscorthy refused to believe the document. He and Seán Etchingham applied to the British commander, French, for permission to travel to Dublin and see Pearse in person. French put them in a military car and had them driven them to Arbour Hill prison in Dublin where Pearse was being kept.

Doyle recalled that Pearse looked 'physically exhausted but spiritually exulted. He told us that the Dublin Brigade had done splendidly – five days and nights of continuous fighting... Etchingham said to him, "Why did you surrender?" Pearse answered, "Because they were shooting women and children in the streets. I saw them myself"'.[277]

Pearse had not been aware of the Rising in Enniscorthy, but agreed to sign a written order to the Wexford Volunteers confirming the surrender that Doyle and Etchingham brought back to Enniscorthy.[278] Reluctantly, the Volunteers there surrendered and 270 men were arrested, of whom ten, including Paul Galligan and Seamus Doyle, were sentenced to imprisonment and penal servitude.[279]

In the eastern part of County Galway, the Volunteers and IRB were synonymous with a local secret society led by a blacksmith named Tom Kenny, who had been fighting landlords, bailiffs and the police on and off for several years. Here at least, the Rising had an important class aspect. The middle class, the shopkeepers and the landowners were either Unionists or moderate nationalists, while the insurgents were, according to the RIC, 'persons of no importance... the agricultural class of young men and shop boys'.[280] Central IRB leadership was provided by Liam Mellows, an activist originally from Wexford but sent to Galway to oversee training.

Like Galligan in Wexford, Mellows managed to get word from IRB leaders Clarke and MacDermott in Dublin on the Tuesday that, despite the countermanding order, the rising was back on. He brought out a large number of poorly armed men – up to 600, according to some reports. According to Gilbert Morrissey, 'Each man had some sort of weapon, such as a shotgun, pike or bayonet'.[281] They made an ineffective attack on a police barracks at Athenry and killed two RIC men in skirmishes before commandeering some local landlords' houses and waiting for word from Dublin.

By the Friday, 350 Volunteers (many had already gone home by this point) under Mellows were ensconced at Myode Castle and Lime Park. Even had they wanted to make an Alamo of their positions, they were not equipped to do so, with only 50 rifles between them. When they heard the news of the arrival of a British warship in Galway Bay, which landed 200 Royal Marines and began shelling the area, they dispersed. Liam Mellows wanted to 'fight it out until the end', but a sympathetic priest, Father Fahy, persuaded them that they had, 'made their gesture and must preserve their lives for the next fight'.[282]

Mellows and Kenny escaped, eventually to America, but many others did not. Gilbert Morrissey and his brothers evaded arrest for a few days, but he was 'captured in the general round up by police and British forces that had landed at Galway. Myself and three other brothers were taken to Galway jail, also all the company and several others who were in sympathy with us. After a week I was sent to Richmond Barracks, Dublin; from there with 200 others marched to the North Wall and put on a cattle boat for Glasgow'.[283]

Unlike Dublin (and leaving aside the engagement at Ashbourne), the Rising was largely bloodless in the provinces – only two wounded in Enniscorthy and two killed (both RIC) in Galway. This was largely because of the lack of arms outside the capital. Moreover, in contrast to popular sentiment in Dublin, the occupation of Enniscorthy by the Volunteers appears to have been quite popular among the townspeople. According to Seamus Doyle, 'Feeling in the town was generally friendly towards us, excepting the families of some British Army soldiers'.[284]

But another feature of the Rising in the provinces was that the National Volunteers – the force aligned to the Irish Party – actually mobilised to aid the British forces. In Galway, the Craughwell company of the National Volunteers offered their services to the RIC and hid out in the barracks there while the town was occupied by the rebels.[285]

In Enniscorthy after the Rising, two hundred of the Volunteers' various political opponents, who had lain low during the rebellion ('National Volunteers, Hibernians, and Unionists', according to one Republican), helped the RIC to patrol the town. As one separatist, Máire Fitzgerald, bitterly recalled, 'the rats all came out of their holes to welcome the British soldiers'.[286] Volunteer John O'Reilly was shocked to see the British Army entering Enniscorthy, 'accompanied by some of the Wexford (so called) National Volunteers or Redmondites'.[287]

Had the nationwide Rising been better organised, more prolonged and better armed, it could conceivably have developed into fighting between rival Irish nationalists. Evidence from elsewhere indicates that the reaction of the National Volunteers in Wexford and Galway was not exceptional. In Sligo, the magistrates were preparing to enrol 'local volunteers', both Unionist and Redmondite, should the Rising break out in that county.[288]

The aftermath

By Sunday 30 April the Rising was over. General John Maxwell had arrived in Dublin on Friday, just in time to take Pearse's surrender. He arrived in a burning city, with its main street in ruins. The fighting, according to British figures, had cost the lives of 447 people and wounded 2,585. Of these, 116 were British soldiers, another 368 of whom were wounded. Sixteen policemen (13 RIC and three DMP) were killed. The British counted rebel and civilian casualties together, giving a total of 318 killed, 2,217 wounded. It was later ascertained that 62 of these were combatants – 50 Volunteers and 12 Citizen Army men.[289] The true death toll may actually be higher, however; a recent study puts the fatal casualties at 482.[290]

Asquith, the British prime minister, said of the insurgents, 'they conducted themselves with great humanity... they were misled I believe into this terrible business...[and] fought very bravely and without outrage'.[291] The Volunteer prisoners equally had little animosity towards the ordinary British soldiers.[292] However, if the combatants had 'fought fair' and by and large treated each other decently when they became prisoners, the civilians had suffered from both sides. More than once on Easter Monday the Volunteers had shot civilians who got in their way. A great many of the civilian casualties were no doubt caught in the crossfire, and both the Volunteers and the British tried to move civilians out of danger in combat zones.

However, in at least three separate incidents, British troops deliberately killed non-combatants. The worst example was in North King Street, where the soldiers had broken into houses and killed 15 men they found there. An inquiry was held, but it took no action against Colonel Taylor.[293] General Maxwell's conclusion was that such incidents 'are absolutely unavoidable in such a business as this' and 'responsibility for their deaths rests with those resisting His Majesty's troops in the execution of their duty'.[294]

In Portobello Barracks, an officer named J. C. Bowen-Colthurst had murdered six civilians, including two journalists and the well-known pacifist and unorthodox nationalist Francis Sheehy Skeffington, who had been trying to organise 'citizen police' to stop the looting. When asked by British pickets if he was in sympathy with 'the Sinn Féiners', he most imprudently answered, 'yes, but I am not in favour of militarism'. He was taken to a cellar and shot.[295] Bowen-Colthurst, described as 'off his head' by his fellow officers, was finally brought under control when a Major Vane arrived at the barracks, to find it surrounded by crowds shouting 'murderer'.[296] A court martial was held but it found Bowen-Colthurst insane and not liable for his actions.[297] A third case was that of a British sniper on a roof in Lower Mount Street who 'went off his head and began to indiscriminately slaughter passers-by'.[298]

In the burning GPO, Pearse wondered if they had done the right thing after all. 'After a few years', he consoled himself, 'people will see the meaning of what we tried to do'.[299] What was amazing about the aftermath of the Rising is that the sea change in public opinion took only a few months. In the immediate aftermath, the Rising was condemned across the board in Ireland. Irish Party leader John Redmond said the rebels were his 'irreconcilable enemies', who had 'tried to torpedo Home Rule'[300]. Within two years, Redmond and the Parliamentary Party would have sunk below a tide of sympathy for radical nationalism.

For this, the British response was largely to blame. Birrell and Nathan, the Chief Secretary and Undersecretary, who had consistently refused to disarm the Volunteer movement on the grounds that it would antagonise the broader nationalist community, resigned. Their lenience was subsequently blamed for the Rising. General Maxwell, in the wake of the surrenders, declared martial law across all of Ireland. In a process of dubious legality, the leaders of the Rising were tried in secret, and fifteen shot in small batches in the period May 3–12. The British Government had told Maxwell not to execute the insurgents under martial law, but rather to wait for civilian law to be retored, under which they could be tried for treason. Maxwell, nevertheless, had them tried by court-martial and then shot within a day of the verdict of treason being returned. The results were often quite arbitrary; Willie Pearse, for instance, seems to have been executed for no more reason than being the brother of Patrick, the Rising's main spokesman. Éamon de Valera, conversely, who had been a rebel commandant, was left alive.[301]

Pearse, Clarke and MacDonagh were the first to be shot, only four days after their surrender. A Unionist journalist, Warren B. Wells, described in a letter to Maxwell the Irish public mood as 'something of the feeling of helpless rage with which one would watch a stream of blood dripping from under a closed door'.[302] Joseph Plunkett famously married his fiancée just before being executed. James Connolly, who was badly wounded, had to be tied to a chair in order to face the firing squad. Pearse wrote a sentimental poem to his mother before his death. Fearing the emotions that Maxwell was letting loose, the British Government intervened to commute the death sentences of another ninety rebels, including Eoin MacNeill and Éamon de Valera, before they could be shot.

The executions of the Rising's leaders created some of the event's most enduring mystique. 'They died like lions', the medical witness at the executions reported.[303] The peculiar power of the martyr is that their death seems to almost prove the validity of their cause. What more proof could there now be that Irish freedom was a serious cause, for which people would lay down their lives? How, a new generation of young men and women would ask, could one talk of Home Rule and compromise after their deaths?

The insurgent leaders, in a manner quite unsettling to twenty-first century sensibilities, seem to have been quite well aware and even happy about the propaganda value of their executions. Seán MacDermott, perhaps the man most responsible for bringing about the insurrection, met one of his comrades, Seán Murphy, a Volunteer and long-time IRB member, as they were being marched into captivity:

> 'Well that's all Seán,' Murphy said, 'I wonder what's next'. MacDermott replied, 'Seán, the cause is lost if some of us are not shot'. Murphy was taken aback. 'Surely to God you don't mean that Seán, aren't things bad enough?' 'They are', he said, 'so bad that if what I say does not come true they will be very much worse'.[304]

In a letter written while awaiting execution, MacDermott wrote that 'I feel happiness the like of which I have never experienced. I die that the Irish nation might live! [...] I know now what I have always felt, that the Irish nation can never die. Let our present day place hunters condemn our action as they will, posterity will judge us aright from the effects of our actions'.[305] Similarly, James Connolly told Seán McLoughlin just after the surrender, '"There is no hope for me; all those who signed the Proclamation will be shot". I said: "Are you sure of that?". He said "Certain the British can do no worse and we do not expect any mercy... We have tried our best; it was better than we hoped and it has not ended as it might have done, in disaster"'.[306]

General Maxwell also sent mobile columns of cavalry, infantry and armoured cars throughout the country to disarm the Volunteers and arrest nationalist suspects. A total of 3,430 men and 70 women were rounded up.[307] The repression after the Rising was spread much further than the actual fighting. It was this that did much to inflame nationalist opinion against the British military. In Roscommon town (population: 1,800), for example, 700 troops arrived on 7 May. They occupied the centre of town, sealed off the routes out and conducted a house-to-house search. Some 27 men were arrested and taken away. And this in a town where nothing had happened during the Rising, with the exception of the raising of a tricolour flag over some local buildings.[308]

The same thing was repeated throughout the country. County Cavan was, according to a local Republican, scoured by patrols of the Enniskillen Fusiliers of the 36th Ulster Division (largely recruited from the Ulster Volunteers), who carried out ten arrests.[309] If the authorities had set out to antagonise nationalists in Cavan, they could hardly have devised a better plan than this – to employ predominantly Protestant, Unionist units to carry out wholesale searches and arrests in an area where no Rising had occurred.

Of the prisoners, 1,400 were released within a week and the remainder were deported to British prisons or to an internment camp at Frongoch in Wales.

'You took care that no plea of mercy would interpose': the public reaction

Taken together with the executions and the rumours emerging of the killing of civilians by British troops in Dublin, the repression of the Rising rapidly alienated nationalist public opinion. In Galway city, where crowds had pelted the Volunteers with mud and stones after their arrest, the police reported shortly afterwards that 'the alleged excesses committed by the military in Dublin, and the executions of the leaders of the insurrection subsequently stirred up a considerable amount of sympathy for the rebels, even amongst persons who were hitherto regarded as loyal'.[310]

Tim Healy, a former Irish Party MP now affiliated with the All For Ireland League, who had been bitterly hostile to the 'Sinn Féiners', was even more antagonised by the military occupation of Dublin after the Rising. 'Among moderate Catholics who are intensely loyal, I find nothing but Sinn Féin sentiment... The looting of the soldiers, downright robbery and ruffianism against innocent people – the shocking ill-treatment of the prisoners, the insolence of the military in the streets, the foul language used to women and the incompetence shown, all have aroused the contempt and hatred for which there is no parallel in our days'.[311]

The Catholic Bishop of Limerick Edmund O'Dwyer wrote to General Maxwell in the aftermath of the executions, telling him, 'you took care that no plea of mercy would interpose on behalf of the young fellows who surrendered to you in Dublin', while another Bishop Fogarty thought that the people did not want armed rebellion but that 'the brutal shootings and deportation of young insurgents after the surrender have filled the country with such anti-English feeling as I never saw before'.[312]

In Parliament, John Dillon, the deputy leader of the Irish Party, railed against the executions and wholesale arrests. 'You are doing everything possible to conceivably madden the Irish people... you are letting loose a river of blood... it is the first rebellion in Ireland where you ever had the majority on your side, it is the fruit of our life work... and now you are washing out our life work in a sea of blood'.[313]

Nationalist opinion on the Rising, as expressed in the editorials of provincial newspapers, swung rapidly from viewing it as a 'mad plot', or 'German conspiracy', to being a 'fight for Irish freedom'. The cause of the Rising was put down to the provocations of the Ulster Unionists and the indefinite delay of Home Rule. The rebels were, after all, 'our own flesh and blood'.[314] The County Wexford RIC reported that 'Although the majority of people did not approve of the rebellion and were anxious that law and order should be maintained, they were unwilling to see any of the rebels punished and their punishment excited considerable sympathy'.[315]

But was the British repression so savage? By comparison with suppression of the Paris Commune of 1870, also an insurrection in a capital during wartime, where the French had summarily executed up to 20,000 rebels and sent thousands more to penal colonies, the reaction to the Easter Rising was rather mild. Similarly, only eleven years before, after putting down the first Bolshevik insurrection in Moscow in 1905, the Tsarist regime had sentenced 5,000 political activists to death and exiled another 38,000, while summary reprisals against the concurrent peasant uprising in rural Russia saw 15,000 executed and 45,000 exiled.[316] So why was there so much outrage in Ireland over a mere 16 executed and 1,500 imprisoned?

The problem of the British in Ireland was twofold. First, although not especially bloody when compared to international precedents, the response to the Easter Rising was much harsher than the punishment meted out to previous generations of Irish rebels in 1867 and 1848. It was also far more severe, as many in Ireland commented at the time, than the treatment of the Afrikaner revolt in South Africa in 1914 (an effort to restore the Boer Republics lost in 1902), for which only one insurgent was executed and those imprisoned were given relatively light sentences. So by the standards which Irish people knew best, the repression of the Rising seemed unusually severe.

Secondly and more vital, was that the Rising took place in the context of the stalling of Home Rule. Much of nationalist Ireland did not entirely accept the legitimacy of British rule in the first place – a sentiment that became especially virulent after the Ulster crisis of 1912–14. By 1916, the fragile unity that Redmond had engineered around Irish support for the war in exchange for self-government looked increasingly creaky. The post-Rising repression, no matter how justified from a British point of view, could only explode the very fragile Irish nationalist consent for the existing state in Ireland. The Rising, though completely defeated militarily, was in hindsight the start of nationalist revolution and the end of British rule in most of Ireland.

Chapter 6:

The Tipping Point, 1916–18

It was not until 5 June 1916, roughly a month after the Rising's end, that Dublin Corporation met again at City Hall, itself pockmarked by bullets from the fighting, in a city centre still partially in ruins from the shelling and the great blaze that had engulfed its main street. The order of business was begun with motions of sympathy for the families of those members who had died – including the relatives of Volunteer officer and late Labour councillor Richard O'Carroll, gunned down in Portobello Barracks, and Thomas Esmonde MP, whose son was lost aboard *HMS Invincible* in the Battle of Jutland.

The Lord Mayor lamented the 'calamity of rebellion' – especially the material destruction of rate-paying properties – and called for the release of Alderman Tom Kelly of Sinn Féin, but otherwise passed no judgment on the Rising, for or against. The question was already too potentially divisive.[317] The Irish Catholic bishops similarly could not agree on a position and in the end issued no formal statement on the Rising.

In Sligo at a United Irish League rally in September 1916, the speaker began: 'There has been a rebellion (applause) and the men who fought in that rebellion fought as nobly as any men ever fought in any cause (loud and continued applause). They fought a good fight, but gentlemen, it was a foolish fight (several voices: "No!")'.[318]

A year on from the Rising, on 9 April 1917, Dublin commemorated the insurrection with a riot. A Republican tricolour was hoisted over the ruined GPO and another over Nelson's Pillar, the spiralling monument that overlooked it. 'That was the signal', *The Irish Times* reported, 'for an outburst of cheering and various other demonstrations of approval on a wide scale'. When the police, after some effort, sawed down the temporary flagpole, they were stoned by inner-city youths, who used as missiles the debris of the building work that was rebuilding O'Connell Street. The police temporarily had to retire from the north inner city as what *The Irish Times* sniffily called 'young toughs' looted shops, damaged a Methodist Church and overturned several trams.[319]

Once the smoke had cleared in 1916, the bodies had been buried, the leaders of the Rising thrown into quicklime graves and the others deported to imprisonment, the nationalist public very quickly began to look back on the Easter Rising much more favourably than most of them had during the six days in which it had raged. It is difficult to exaggerate what a powerful propaganda gesture the Rising had been in the context of the values of Ireland of that time. The insurgents had fought 'bravely and manfully'. They had acted with 'honour' and, apparently, respected civilians and their property. They had 'fought for Ireland' and 'Dublin Castle' had murdered them. The Irish Party might condemn them as 'foolish' but even they could not totally disavow what they had done.

The Rising as a symbol was hugely important, but the insurrection also had concrete results. Martial law was kept in force until November 1916, meaning that British repression, or as the separatists had it, 'English tyranny', was now something real that touched most parts of Ireland. In the context of the Great War dragging on, the looming threat of conscription being imposed on Ireland, the war's exacerbation of social and class conflict and the continued postponement of Home Rule, the argument that Ireland should separate altogether from the Empire began to look attractive to many more people. By the end of the war in 1918, the new Union of Equals once promoted by the Irish Parliamentary Party looked less plausible to many in Ireland than the Irish Republic of the 'Sinn Féiners'.

Hard time

None of this was apparent, however, to the Volunteer, Cumann na mBan and Citizen Army fighters taken prisoner after the rebellion. A great many of them were insulted and stoned by the Dublin public as they were led into captivity. There, in barracks and jails around the city, they spent several dismal days herded together in squalid conditions. Some activists were picked up and imprisoned on the slightest of grounds. One such was labour organiser William O'Brien, who, though sympathetic to the Rising and particularly to his friend and colleague James Connolly, took no part in the insurrection. He was inspecting the damage done to the union headquarters at Liberty Hall when a watching detective had a corporal stop him. 'This policeman approached and said "What is your name?" I replied, "O'Brien". He turned to the Corporal and said "He is an enemy". The Corporal said, "Left turn! Quick march!" and I walked into the [temporary prison at the] Custom House'.[320] Arthur Griffith, the leader of Sinn Féin, was similarly presumed to have had something to do with the rebellion – of which he in fact had known nothing, having been out of the IRB for almost two decades by 1916 – and was arrested.

Dozens of men, including Eoin MacNeill, the head of the Volunteers, Thomas Ashe and Éamon de Valera, the last surviving commandants of Easter Week, and Paul Galligan, the leader of the Rising in County Wexford, had been sentenced to death and spent a few agonising days awaiting execution before the British Government intervened to halt the firing squads. Galligan wrote that 'In fact I was sorry, for I was prepared for the death and it would have been a relief then as the whole week of the Rebellion I had not a single hour's sleep and when then on 21 May after sleeping for three weeks on cold floors and in your clothes without a change, death was preferable to another week of it'.[321]

Over 1,500 prisoners were shipped out on cattle boats across the Irish Sea and into British prisons. Most were, within a few weeks, concentrated into an internment camp recently vacated by German prisoners of war at Frongoch in north Wales. Conditions there were often grim, the food was bad and discipline strict, but they had the advantage of being all together and they could organise collectively. It is no coincidence that the future leaders of nationalist revolution in Ireland – military leaders like Michael Collins, Richard Mulcahy and others; political leaders such as Gearóid O'Sullivan; or the trade union leaders Cathal O'Shannon and William O'Brien – were all interned together at Frongoch. The camp was certainly not comfortable, but William O'Brien thought the conditions there were 'not bad', and above all the prisoners were free to discuss and to organise. Gilbert Morrissey from Galway recalled, 'I took part in the hunger strike inside the camp which lasted for two days and all other activities organised by our Camp staff for our rights as prisoners of war. We occasionally went on route marches and on these occasions were accompanied by an armed guard'.[322] This sort of relative freedom was unthinkable for some of the other rebel prisoners.

Those the authorities considered mid-ranking leaders of the rebellion were imprisoned at Reading. Among them were Ernest Blythe, who had missed the Rising due to having been deported to England but was nevertheless picked up afterwards, and a host of other prominent separatists such as leading Sinn Féin members Arthur Griffith and Herbert Moore Pim, P.T. Daly, a labour organiser who had been an old Fenian centre, and the Cork Volunteer leaders Tomás MacCurtain and Terence MacSwiney.[323]

The men deemed the most dangerous, however – those who had been identified as the surviving leaders of the 1916 insurrection – were imprisoned in much grimmer and more oppressive conditions. Some 120 men, including MacNeill, de Valera, Thomas Ashe (who had led the Volunteer action at Ashbourne), William Partridge, the most senior surviving Citizen Army officer, and the Wexford leaders Paul Galligan and Seamus Doyle, were given sentences of between five and ten years of penal servitude at Dartmoor and Portland Prisons.

The lot of the high-security Irish prisoners in Britain was extremely grim. Like high-risk British convicts, the Irish prisoners at Dartmoor and Portland were not allowed to speak or interact with other inmates, and were allowed to write and receive only one letter every four months. They could be flogged for infractions but more typically were put for three days in solitary confinement on nothing but bread and water. The psychological pressure that this regime exerted on the prisoners – particularly the isolation and inadequate food – was enormous and would drive more than one prisoner into mental and physical breakdown.[324]

William Partridge of the Citizen Army fell ill with Bright's disease and died not long after his release. Paul

Galligan wrote to his brother, 'I have often heard this war [the First World War] spoken as "hell with the lid off", but the originator of this expression never put a week in with us in Dartmoor jail'.[325] 'I always read with horror the sad incidents of suicide but I will never read of suicide in future without pity and compassion for I know the battles those souls had to fight and it is only our Irish Catholic faith that brought us unsullied through it all'.[326]

On arrival at Dartmoor Prison the Irish prisoners were stripped naked, lined up for inspection and searched. Éamon de Valera later told a friend that 'the shyness of the Irish lads gave the impression of their being cowed'.[327] The Volunteers at Dartmoor were housed in single cells with no heating, and bedding consisted of a thin mattress placed on the cell's floorboards. The cold was so severe that many of the prisoners developed acute lumbago or back pain. They exercised every morning before work, but again no communication was allowed with any of the other incarcerated Volunteers. Their work, making mail bags, also had to be done in silence.[328]

The story of the sixty-five men at Dartmoor is interesting not only for the harsh conditions they endured, but especially for the insight it gives into the personality of one Éamon de Valera, who would go on to dominate Irish politics for the next half-century. De Valera, a mathematics teacher in pre-Rising days, had been one of the many cultural nationalists and Gaelic Leaguers attracted to the Volunteers at the time of the Home Rule crisis and subsequently drawn into the conspiracy for insurrection after the outbreak of the Great War. Though he had been sworn into the IRB in 1915, his sympathies lay in the direction of open mass politics rather than clandestine secret societies, and he remained suspicious of the Brotherhood.

At Easter 1916, his military leadership at Boland's Mills had struck the men under his command as erratic. Apart from his failure to reinforce the outpost at Mount Street, or his changes of mind when setting fire to the train station at Westland Row, he had seemed panicked and even hysterical at times. According to one Volunteer, de Valera had celebrated British artillery missing their target by running up and down the Mill shouting, 'Hurrah, what a rotten shot'[329]. At this remove, the almost reverential loyalty that de Valera later inspired among his followers can seem difficult to understand, but Dartmoor gives us a clue.

The prison governor there referred to him as 'a real firebrand and fanatic... he is decidedly a "personality" and the others seem to look up to him as their leader'[330], while Paul Galligan recalled later that, 'His fight for his fellow prisoners, to my mind, marked him out as our future leader'.[331] From the very start, according to what de Valera told Frank Gallagher in 1928, 'after the indignity of the first personal search when convicts are publicly stripped naked, he decided that a fight was necessary'.[332]

When Eoin MacNeill arrived in the prison, de Valera had his first opportunity for a confrontation. The prisoners were lined up in two rows for the morning inspection when MacNeill came down the stairs. MacNeill's popularity was at a low ebb after the countermanding order but he was still nominal commander of the Volunteers. Seamus Doyle remembered, 'Commandant de Valera, who was standing at the end of one of the lines, stepped out on our front and gave the order: "Irish Volunteers, eyes left". We gave the salute. There was commotion among the warders and Commandant de Valera was taken away'.[333]

He was hauled before the governor. 'Why did you do that?' he was asked. 'To salute my commander in chief in the proper manner', de Valera replied. 'Do you not know that any such action is mutiny, the most serious crime a prisoner can commit and that flogging is the punishment?' De Valera replied, 'I know nothing about that, I only know we are soldiers and owe respect to our commanders'.[334]

What really stuck in Paul Galligan's memory, however, was another occasion when de Valera sacrificed himself for another prisoner. 'In the opposite cell to de Valera there was a huge big man called Phil McMahon... he was always hungry as the prison food was insufficient for him'.[335] Other accounts state that the prisoner was Jack McArdle and that he had been put on three days' ration of bread and water for some minor infraction.[336] Either way, 'De Valera somehow discovered that McMahon had insufficient food and... threw a small loaf of bread across to McMahon'.

His action was spotted by the warders and de Valera was again taken to see the governor where he argued that 'the bread was his and he did not require it and he had the right to give it to any man who required more food'. De Valera was put in the punishment block or 'cachot' on bread and water for three days. Shortly afterwards, he and Desmond Fitzgerald were transferred to Parkhurst Prison on the Isle of Wight.[337]

The prison experience, though extremely gruelling, was relatively short. It was the great weakness of British rule in Ireland that while it was not truly democratic, it could not bring itself to be a really efficient tyranny either. Instead, when faced with opposition in Ireland, bursts of repression were followed with hasty attempts at conciliation.

So it was in December 1916, when David Lloyd George replaced Asquith as British Prime Minister. Lloyd George released all of the internees at Frongoch, and transferred those at Dartmoor and Portland and other high security prisons to the lower security facility at Lewes in Sussex.

Lloyd George was anxious to assuage Irish-American as well as Irish opinion in an effort to get the United States into the First World War.

At Lewes, where they were allowed free association, the prisoners' experience took on a completely different aspect; all 120 of them, for instance, marched in military formation to Mass on 24 April, the first anniversary of the Rising. Thomas Ashe, who had taken over as President of the IRB (the old Supreme Council having either been wiped out or discredited by 1916), corresponded extensively in secret with his comrades in Ireland, who by this time were busy reorganising the movement. Éamon de Valera organised a strike, where the prisoners refused to do prison work and ended up rioting, smashing everything in their cells. Despite another brief dispersion into other prisons after this episode, the remaining prisoners were released on 18 June 1917 as part of a general amnesty, having served just over a year of their sentence.

Most prisoners, whether released in late 1916 or mid-1917, came home to ecstatic receptions. In County Clare the police reported, 'the release of so many interned rebels instead of exciting gratitude appears to stimulate resentment. These men generally appear unsubdued by internment, and their release is by ignorant country folk regarded as proof that they were interned without any just cause and that the police who arrested them in pursuance of orders acted vindictively'.[338]

A new generation

Back in Ireland, out of the ashes of the Rising emerged a new generation of Republican militants. Most of them were young; very few were over 30. The vast majority were Catholic. Many had no previous involvement in separatist politics, but were radicalised by the rebellion itself and its aftermath. Many of them later describe their conversion to physical force nationalism after the Rising as an almost religious experience.

Kevin O'Higgins, a law student from a family of impeccably constitutional nationalists, with two brothers in British uniform in France, had joined the Volunteers shortly before the Rising but had taken no part in it. However, he summed up the emotional power of the event in a poem written shortly afterwards in tribute to Pearse: 'Peace to Your Soul! For one short glorious week you cast defiance in the Saxon's teeth. Not all the bloody vengeance they can wreak can rob the patriot hero of his wreath'.[339] What the short verse may have lacked in subtlety it made up for in expression of the intensity of commitment felt by the post-1916 generation of activists.

Ernie O'Malley, the medical student who had stumbled across the Rising's headquarters at the GPO on Easter Monday 1916, joined a fund for rebel prisoners almost immediately after the rebellion and joined the Volunteers themselves not much later. His intelligence and above all ferocious dedication to military training soon saw him become one of the most trusted new officers in the movement. Liam Lynch, a former Hibernian, joined the local Volunteers in Midleton, County Cork when he saw local Republicans the Kent brothers being dragged away by the RIC. According to his grandmother, he was still a Redmondite in 1916, 'until the day the British attacked the Kents of Bawnyard and he saw Thomas Kent being brought in bleeding through the town of Fermoy, his poor mother dragging along after them'.[340] In Monaghan, in the south Ulster borderland, Eoin O'Duffy (previously secretary of the Gaelic Athletic Association and Gaelic League in County Monaghan) made the short jump from cultural to armed nationalism after the Rising.[341] They all entered an intensely activist world of public drilling, demonstrations and eventually, guerrilla warfare.

Everywhere it was noted that the post-Rising separatist generation was a movement of young men. For Mossie Hartnett in County Limerick, who had joined the local Volunteers in 1915, post-Rising militancy was a generational as well as a national liberation. By joining the Volunteers and then Sinn Féin and becoming a fulltime organiser, 'I was free of parental control. My parents did not take kindly to the new movement'.[342] Ernie O'Malley also acknowledged the personal fulfilment he attained through separatist struggle, later describing his career in the IRA as a transformation from being 'a sheltered individual, drawn from the secure seclusion of Irish life to the responsibility of action'.[343] Similarly, O'Duffy's new role as a nationalist activist was not a political rebellion against his tyrannical father, but it was a remarkable opportunity to be his own man and important in his own right.

Women also played an increased role in the separatist movement immediately after the Rising, with so many male activists dead or imprisoned. Kathleen Clarke, the widow of Tom, was the first to organise a fund for the families of prisoners. Once the Frongoch internees had been released, however, women tended to revert to their previous support role. Michael Collins, who had made his way to the top of the rival National Aid Fund, quickly overshadowed and then absorbed Clarke's organisation. As we will see, veterans of the Rising like Collins had an almost mythical aura to the new young generation of activists.

What the new generation of activists signed up to was not exactly a new ideology. Generally speaking, they tended to absorb the existing thinking of the separatist movement: Republicanism, cultural nationalism, militant (and if needs be, military) methods and sometimes a hint of social radicalism. In many cases their thinking was simple enough; pursuit, by all means necessary, of an Irish republic that would sever all ties with the British Empire. Rather than a set of ideas, what they signed up for was the struggle: the mental rejection of all things British and the unswerving dedication of the converted to the cause.

Sinn Féin and the new revolutionary movement

The Volunteers and the IRB remained central to this cause, but so too, from 1917 onwards, was the political party, Sinn Féin. Sinn Féin had never been a Republican party or a proponent of revolutionary violence. Nor had it had any part in the Easter Rising, though some members of the party such as William T. Cosgrave and Desmond Fitzgerald had indeed fought in it. For all that, the rebellion was popularly named the 'Sinn Féin Rising', and General Maxwell had interned its leaders, including Arthur Griffith, and closed their remaining press after the rebellion.

This proved to be a costly political mistake, not only in apparently confirming the iniquity of 'English tyranny', but also in reacquainting the actual Sinn Féiners with the more militant IRB and Volunteer activists in Frongoch, Reading and Lewes. Even before the last prisoners had been released from prison, a new Sinn Féin was taking shape in Ireland, but it was really galvanised with the release of the Rising veterans. In Cavan, for instance, when the last prisoners were released in June 1917, the RIC noted that Sinn Féin took off in the county, growing from 4 clubs with a mere 108 members to 53 clubs and 2,623 members by December of that year.[344]

The new Sinn Féin had some continuity with Arthur Griffith's original party in that its principle strategy was to win elections in Ireland, and having done that, to abstain from the Westminster Parliament, declare an Irish Parliament to be in session and to secede from the United Kingdom. What made the new party different were three factors. One was the new air of militancy and purpose provided by veterans of the Rising. The second was the changed times. The war, political repression and the ongoing failure to implement Home Rule was undermining acceptance of British rule. Thirdly, this Sinn Féin, after considerable internal debate, declared itself for an Irish Republic, the same as that which had been declared in 1916.

This last point had been surprisingly difficult to agree upon. Griffith declared himself agnostic on the subject of a Republic and was lukewarm about the militant legacy of Easter Week. Young Corkman and now leading IRB member Michael Collins, by contrast, had barged into a meeting declaring, 'If you don't fight the [Longford] election on the Republican ticket you will alienate all the young men'.[345] It was only in October 1917, and at the insistence of Collins, de Valera and other Rising veterans such as Cathal Brugha and Joseph McGuinness that Sinn Féin pledged itself to the pursuit of an Irish Republic.[346]

In 1917 the new, Republican Sinn Féin had its first electoral success, when Count George Plunkett, father of Joseph, one of the executed leaders of 1916, won a by-election in Roscommon. Sinn Féin followed this victory up with two more in Counties Clare and Longford. These elections were fought on the same old restricted franchise as the elections of 1910, so they did not signify the protest of an emerging social group. Rather, they were a judgement of the existing electorate on the failure of the IPP to deliver Home Rule, and an indictment of its increasingly unpopular pro-British and pro-War stance. The Clare by-election was particularly poignant in this regard. The seat had opened up because Willie Redmond, brother of Party leader John, had been killed at the front in France – serving, as his brother had urged, in the cause of Home Rule. The man who succeeded him as MP for the western county was the last surviving commandant of Easter Week, Éamon de Valera, elected only weeks after he had been released from prison.

In October 1917 the first Convention of the new Sinn Féin was held in Dublin. Over 1,700 delegates from 1,000 clubs, representing 250,000 members, took a unanimous decision to demand an Irish Republic at the peace conferences and, as Cavan delegate Paul Galligan put it, to 'demand nothing less as we want now to completely sever our connection with England'.[347]

At this point, it was not at all clear whether or not Sinn Féin and the Volunteers planned another round of insurrection. Nevertheless, in the post–Rising climate, political violence never went away. At a 3,000-strong rally in Dublin for the release of the remaining prisoners in June 1917, Cathal Brugha, who had been badly wounded in the rebellion, gave an inflammatory speech, for which he was placed under arrest by a watching RIC inspector. A vicious riot ensued, in which the unfortunate policeman was felled, mortally wounded with a blow from a hurling stick.[348] The inspector, John Mills, was one of the first mortalities of post–Rising political violence in Ireland.

The Republicans too soon had fresh martyrs. Thomas Ashe, President of the IRB and one of the most senior Volunteer leaders to have survived 1916, was rearrested only two months after his release from prison in August 1917 for a 'seditious speech' during the Longford election campaign.

Sentenced to two years' hard labour, he went on hunger strike in protest and died after attempted force-feeding by the prison authorities. Ashe, 36 years old at the time of his death, was a charismatic native of Kerry and the manner of his death was deeply shocking to nationalists. Paul Galligan wrote to his brother about Ashe, 'The poor fellow, I knew him well. We were in Dartmoor and Lewes together and he was a fine type of man in every sense of the word, but his death was a second 'Easter Week' in terms of the change of public opinion'.[349] Some 15,000 people filed into Dublin City Hall, past his body, to pay their respects.[350]

At Ashe's funeral in Glasnevin Cemetery in Dublin the uniformed Volunteers staged a show of strength – like the O'Donovan Rossa funeral where Pearse had given his famous oration just two years before. This, however, was a much more sombre and angry occasion. After Ashe's remains were lowered into his grave, three volleys of rifle shots crashed out from the Volunteer firing party into the air. Michael Collins, after Ashe's death the leading light in the IRB, stepped forward and told the mourners: 'Nothing additional remains to be said. The volley you have just heard is the only one which it is proper to make over the grave of a dead Fenian'.[351]

Collins, whose blunt oratory at Ashe's graveside was characteristic, was only 27 years old. Born in West Cork into a family of middle-sized farmers with a strong Fenian tradition, he had emigrated to London as a teenager, worked there as a bank clerk and also joined the Irish Republican Brotherhood. He had fought in the Easter Rising and had emerged from imprisonment in Frongoch in Wales to become a member of the IRB's Supreme Council. Possessed of a dynamic and powerful personality, he was known for his macho horseplay but also for his capacity to build strong personal relationships with his friends.

A sense of his personal charisma, particularly among young Republicans, can be glimpsed in his trip to Longford to persuade Seán MacEoin, at this date a blacksmith, to take over command of the local IRB and of the Volunteer Company. MacEoin was working in his forge when Collins arrived, and told Collins that the work would be impossible for him as his mother was a widow and he had promised his dead father he would look after the family. 'You must,' Collins told him. 'Well', MacEoin recalled saying, 'the man who says "must" to me must be a better man than I am... come out to the wood and we will see if you are a better man or not'. If urban nationalist leaders might be intellectuals, local Volunteer commanders were often tough men used to settling disputes with their fists. MacEoin and Collins wrestled in the wood beside the forge. MacEoin 'got him down without too much hardship', until he felt, 'to my Holy terror', Collins' teeth sink into his ear, whereupon the Corkman pinned him to the ground and said, 'Now aren't I a better man?' 'Now from that moment on', MacEoin concluded, 'the friendship between himself and myself remained until death'.[352]

As well a hard-man image, Collins also had a marked talent for networking, and by late 1917 had worked his way to the top, or near-top of the prisoners' National Aid Fund, Sinn Féin, the IRB and the Volunteers. All such positions, but especially those in the Volunteers and the IRB, would enable him to play a central role in the coming struggle. The Rising had torn a swathe through the previous generation of IRB leaders – most were either dead or, like Bulmer Hobson and Eoin MacNeill, had their reputation in ruins – leaving a free run for ambitious and dedicated young activists like Collins.

Collins had a far less mystical frame of mind than some of the 1916 leaders. He was unimpressed, during the fighting in 1916, upon seeing the insurgents in Moore Street down on their knees praying. 'Are you fucking praying too?' one participant recalled him remarking scornfully.[353] Nor was he as taken with the theatrical and propaganda-of-the-deed aspects of the Rising as were many members of his generation. 'It had the air of a Greek tragedy', he wrote to a friend. Violence in future, under Collins' management, would be deployed in a much more steely, pragmatic manner.

Not one of Collins' close circle of personal friends, but his key ally in the military movement, was the new Volunteer Chief of Staff, and also IRB Supreme Council member, Richard Mulcahy. In terms of personality the two men were very different. Mulcahy, a 31-year-old originally from Waterford, was so shy that in his pre-Volunteer days he had sometimes turned back from his frequent trips to Dublin's National Library because he feared that under the bright lights of the reading room he might meet someone he knew.[354] While Collins, as Ernie O'Malley recalled, was often found at hotel bars in Dublin, 'Mulcahy however never touched drink'.[355]

Nevertheless, the two shared some other characteristics. Both were self-educated and compulsive workers and demanded equally high standards of their comrades. 'Unsatisfactory' and 'appalling' were among the most common adjectives the two would fire off in communiqués to underperforming Volunteer officers. Both had worked in large bureaucratic institutions (Collins in the post office and then banks in London, and Mulcahy in the postal service in Dublin) and had a talent for organisation and record keeping. Both were basically bourgeois revolutionaries; in Collins' case not unsympathetic to organised labour, but essentially not very interested in social questions except as a means to rally support for national independence.

Finally, both had been involved in quite bloody fighting during the Rising, Collins in the GPO and Mulcahy at Ashbourne in County Meath, where eleven RIC men had been killed in a two-hour gun battle. Both seem to have been hardened by the experience and fully anticipated further armed conflict in the coming years.

Land and Labour

If the separatist movement had been revitalised by the fallout from the Rising and the war, its subsequent success nevertheless cannot be explained unless the wider Irish context of the period 1916–18 is taken into account. The social discontent that had been quietly festering since 1914 began to bubble over as 1916 turned into 1917 – exacerbated as the usual safety valve for social distress in Ireland, emigration, was cut off by the war.

On the land, as noted in the previous chapter, wartime conditions opened up a stark divide between export farmers on the one hand, who made a fortune exporting food to Britain, and labourers and smallholders on the other, who were hit with higher food prices and higher rents. In the winter of 1917–18 especially, poor farming families went hungry.

This was a particularly explosive schism where it coincided with boundaries of nationality and religion, as it did in the north midlands and west, where there was still a significant class of Anglo-Irish, Protestant landlords. Even when class division was not reinforced by such cleavages, though, it could still result in violence against 'ranchers' and 'land-grabbers', who, it was argued, occupied all the best land for cattle grazing, raised the cattle for export and contributed little to the local economy. From early 1917 onwards the RIC noted a resurgence in 'cattle-driving', where cattle were driven off the ranches, which were then occupied by smallholding families. By the middle of that year several hundred landowners required police protection against agrarian agitators. In County Clare, for instance, those who were landless and hungry began driving cattle off the ranches and allotting them to small farming families. Local Volunteer leader Michael Brennan recalled that 'we decided to cash in on this. Cattle drives became very popular and all over the County Volunteers took part in them as organised units.[356]

All of these demands – 'the land for the people' and 'division of the ranches' – had been the bread and butter of nationalist politics since the 1880s, but the Irish Party was now talking about 'conciliation' on the land at the same time that the only real avenue of reform, the Congested Districts Board, was being wound down due to scarcity of wartime funds. Concretely, what this meant was that, whereas in 1914 the Board was attempting to buy some 267,000 acres on 159 landed estates, by 1918 no such redress was possible for landless or uneconomic farmers.[357]

Maverick Home Ruler turned Sinn Féiner Laurence Ginnel, for one, toured the land-hungry regions advising evicted tenants to take, 'whatever measures are appropriate' to regain their holdings.[358] It was therefore no surprise that the new Sinn Féin Party grew most quickly in areas of agrarian agitation – a swathe of the west and north midlands from Sligo to Cavan and in the south and west from Clare to Kerry.[359]

Discontent at wartime hardships and food shortages also helped the growth of the Republicans in urban areas. On the Dublin docks, the local Volunteers gained much of their mass appeal in 1917–18 by seizing and slaughtering animals set to be exported and instead distributing the meat among the poor. A young Volunteer, Charlie Dalton, was given tea by grateful locals whom he had watched do the same for 'British Tommies' marching off to war in 1914. 'We were now', he recalled, 'the heroes of the people'.[360]

The labour movement and in particular the ITGWU also experienced a resurgence in these two years, growing from a post-Lockout low of some 5,000 members to over 60,000 by 1918. This was largely the work of William O'Brien, who, once released from Frongoch, set about reorganising the union devastated by defeat in the strike of 1913 and decapitated with Connolly's execution in 1916. However, the rush into the unions was, on the part of both urban and rural workers, essentially a defensive reaction, trying to bring wages up to the level of rising food prices and inflation. The subsequent strike-wave with 120 disputes in 1917 and 200 every year from 1918 to 1920 should be understood in these terms.[361] It was still, however, a contributing factor in the gathering radicalisation of Irish politics.

Labour did not fall into the Sinn Féin movement in quite the same way as the land agitators. Rather, it developed its own political voice – the Labour Party of Ireland – founded in 1912, but which only became a viable entity at national level in 1917–18. It was committed, at least rhetorically, to the legacy of James Connolly and the struggle for the 'Workers' Republic'. On top of that, several of its senior members, such as O'Brien and Cathal O'Shannon, had been interned with the Republicans and had a close relationship with them (though others such as Englishman and moderate socialist Tom Johnson remained more suspicious).

Burying the Parliamentary Party

By late 1917, Paul Galligan reported to his brother that 'Nothing but the full independence of Ireland will satisfy the Irish people. Redmond is a man of the past and his policy is only supported by a dwindling minority… Sinn Féin clubs, at least two and in some cases three, are already established in every parish, this in itself will give you an idea of what Sinn Féin has accomplished'.[362]

Despite the growing disenchantment with the British authorities and the Home Rule project, however, the IPP and their strong-arm organisation the Ancient Order of Hibernians still stood in the way of the Republicans gaining control of nationalist opinion. By 1917, the Irish Party had lost what the Republicans had in abundance: youthful vigour and enthusiasm. They found themselves in 1917 ceding cherished nationalist ground to the 'Sinn Féiners'. Nationalists had always proudly celebrated those who had fought for 'Irish freedom', but now it was the 'Sinn Féiners', the veterans of the Easter Rising, who could portray themselves as the rightful inheritors of what Patrick Pearse had called 'the Fenian dead'.

The Irish Party, by contrast, had condemned the rebellion and found itself, despite the protests of its leaders such as John Dillon, associated with the British execution of the Rising's leaders and the mass arrest of activists afterwards. Just as damaging, by 1917, was John Redmond's stance on the World War. Recruitment had slowed to a trickle, and there was deep apprehension in much of Irish society at the prospect of conscription being introduced.[363]

For all of these concessions of nationalist ground, the IPP had expected to get Home Rule in return. And this, despite being passed into law in 1914, had not happened. In 1917, the British Government tried again to implement it with an 'Irish Convention', attended by both nationalists and Unionists. Sinn Féin, fresh from their by-election victory in Clare, were invited, but refused to attend as Irish independence would not be on offer.

The Convention could conceivably have been a forum where the shortcomings of the 1912 Home Rule Bill could have been redressed. Giving a Home Rule Parliament fiscal autonomy was proposed by nationalists, as was the completion of land purchase from landlords. Both of these were vetoed by Carson and the Unionists, but naturally the greatest stumbling block was partition. Ulster Unionists insisted on it if Home Rule was going to be enacted, and despite some conciliatory noises, nationalists refused to countenance it. Southern Unionists led by Lord Middleton – by now more fearful of Sinn Féin and of their dominating a partitioned southern Ireland than of Home Rule – proposed an all-Ireland settlement within the Empire with religious and political safeguards for Protestant Ulster. This too was rejected by the Ulster delegation, and the Convention broke up in early 1918 without agreement.[364]

By this point the IPP was old and weary. It had surrendered much of its ideological inheritance in the search for compromise, and was identified too closely with the British establishment and the war. John Redmond himself died in March 1918, aged 61. He was succeeded as party leader by John Dillon.

Nevertheless, in late 1917 and early 1918 the IPP staged something of a comeback, winning by-elections in South Armagh, Waterford and East Tyrone. True, the old restricted franchise still applied. The Party also controlled much of the local press. Nor had it risen above the tried and trusted tactics of street fighting to beat its opponents off the streets at election time. In South Armagh, Cavan Volunteer James Cahill recalled that 'The Ancient Order of Hibernians were ferocious in their attacks on members of the Sinn Féin organisation. Occasionally they were assisted by the Orangemen... Frequently Hibernians or Orangemen would conceal themselves behind walls or hedges and attack us with stones as we cycled past'. The RIC, according to Cahill, did not intervene in such affrays unless it looked like the Volunteers were winning. 'We were', he recalled, 'very fortunate that none of our members got seriously hurt'.[365]

All of these things stood in the Irish Party's favour. No doubt also there was still much disquiet in some quarters about the Sinn Féiners and their radicalism, and it is possible that the IPP could have weathered the separatist storm had they not been overtaken by a final, mortal blow: the British attempt to impose conscription on Ireland.

Conscription

From the British perspective, drafting Irishmen into the war effort must not have seemed unreasonable. The Great War was consuming lives at an unprecedented rate, and conscription had been introduced into Britain itself in early 1916. If Ireland was a part of the United Kingdom and if, as the Irish Party had promised in 1914, Ireland was behind the war effort, it was the logical step. Instead, what it highlighted was how far away from the rest of Britain Irish loyalties now lay.

In the spring of 1918, the Germans launched their final offensive on the Western Front, initially routing British and French forces. Reinforcements were needed urgently, and in April the British Parliament approved the extension of conscription into Ireland.

Opposition to conscription united Irish opinion like no other issue. Every facet of nationalist political organisation came out against it – all the political parties, the trade unions and the Catholic Church – and not only condemned conscription but encouraged resistance to it. The IPP, who had always argued that it was by working inside the British system that Irish demands could be fulfilled, were suddenly made to look impotent. Even though the IPP withdrew from Westminster in protest, and its leader John Dillon shared platforms with Éamon de Valera, it was Sinn Féin, the party that advocated Irish independence and armed resistance if necessary, which became the voice of the anti-conscription campaign.

Even some Irish Party members who had followed John Redmond and joined up for the War were turned into separatists by the conscription crisis. Daniel Sheehan, an Irish Party MP and Captain in the British Army, told the House of Commons in so many words that everything he had signed up for in 1914 had been a fraud. 'You state that you are fighting for justice, freedom and liberty. It was in the belief this country was fighting for those principles that I and others offered our services in the earlier months of the War. I ask what freedom, what justice, or what liberty is the Irish conscript going to get?'

He raged that, contrary to the promises made to Redmond in 1914, there was no Irish legislature, and no Irish units led by Irish officers:

The officers were a horde of English Cockneys... A similar pledge was given in the case of Carson's Army, and it was observed; but it was not observed in the case of the Irish Brigade.... I tell you that you may take our men at the point of a bayonet – you will not get them in any other way, but you will not succeed in killing the spirit of Irish nationality, and at the end you will find you have lit a flame which is not likely to die out in our generation.

You have not trusted Irishmen. You have not dealt fairly with them since this war broke out. You have

heaped insults and humiliations upon them... I
remember reading with horror what I regarded as
a butchery of a Labour leader [James Connolly] in
Dublin in Easter Week. Although he was not able
to stand up to be shot, although he was wounded,
if he had been a soldier serving in any other part of
the world he would have received the honour due
to a soldier, but he was brutally butchered, maimed
and mangled.

You are teaching us once again that we cannot
trust you, and that if we are to exist as a nation
we must fight for our nationality... That is a right
which we Irishmen are asserting for our people,
and if need should arise, we will be ready to seal it
with our blood.[366]

The conscription crisis, in other words, brought separatist
rhetoric, of English tyranny and military occupation and
the obligation of national resistance – all of which had
seemed outlandish to moderate nationalists in 1910 – into
the mainstream. The Catholic Bishops issued a thunderous
statement: 'the attempt to force conscription upon Ireland
against the will of the Irish people and in defiance of the
protests of its leaders [is] an oppressive and inhuman law
which the Irish people have the right to resist by all the
means consonant with the law of God'.[367]

The Irish Trade Union Congress, led in particular by
William O'Brien and the ITGWU, called a general strike
in protest and brought the country to a standstill on 23
April 1918, the largest strike to date in Irish history –
but one which, uniquely, was fully endorsed by both the
employers and the Catholic Church. Everywhere outside
Belfast, the country lurched to a halt; transport, even the

munitions factories set up for the war, ceased work for the day. Cumann na mBan, the Republican women's movement, also called a day of protest, *Lá na mBan* ('The Day of Women') in which they urged women not to take the jobs of men conscripted for the Army.

Éamon de Valera, addressing a meeting in Dublin, made the case not only against conscription but against British rule in Ireland: 'We deny the right of the British Government or any other external authority to impose compulsory military service in Ireland against the expressed will of the Irish people... The passing of the Conscription Bill by the British House of Commons must be regarded as a declaration of War on the Irish people'.[368]

The Volunteers, who saw their numbers swell from less than 10,000 to over 100,000,[369] drew up plans for a new insurrection should conscription be introduced. Every police station was to be seized and its arms taken, every road was to be blocked and communications severed. Anyone siding with or representing the government was to be shot. So argued Ernest Blythe in a pamphlet entitled *Ruthless Warfare*.[370] In Kerry, where he had returned after imprisonment, he told his company of Volunteers 'about the necessity of fighting with whatever weapons were available if an attempt were made to apply conscription, and said it was better to die fighting for our freedom and for Ireland than to be led out like dogs on a chain to die for England on the Continent'.[371]

Against this mass movement, the authorities had only repression. Public fairs and sporting meetings were banned along with political rallies. In May 1918, alleging a 'German plot' between the 'Sinn Féiners' and their enemies in Europe, the British issued arrest warrants for hundreds of leading separatists. While there had been contact between the Germans and Irish Republicans since Easter 1916, the charge was essentially an excuse to round up militant leaders after mass protests against conscription. Edward Shortt, the new Chief Secretary, all but admitted as much: 'We do not pretend that each individual has been in personal active communication with German agents, but we know that someone has'. Some seventy suspects, including Éamon de Valera, were arrested, but many more, including Michael Collins, evaded capture.[372]

By mid-1918, the British Government decided that more troops would be needed to impose conscription on Ireland than would be gained from it, and quietly dropped the Bill. Sinn Féin emerged from the episode as national saviours. The conscription crisis did not quite develop into a shooting war, but in many ways it marks the start of the subsequent conflict. There may have been few deaths, but of arrests, beatings and riots there were plenty. The young Volunteers who marched in defiance of a post-Easter-Rising ban on military assembly found themselves baton-charged, bayoneted and imprisoned under emergency wartime legislation.

Armistice Day, at the end of the war, was the scene of national jubilation in most of the United Kingdom. In Dublin, while it did see celebrations by Unionists and families of serving soldiers (who indeed attacked Sinn Féin offices on the night), it also saw vicious rioting between troops and separatists. Michael Collins reported: 'As a result of various encounters, there were 125 cases of wounded soldiers treated at Dublin Hospitals that night... Before morning, three soldiers and one officer had ceased to need any attention and another died the following day'.[373] 'Ruthless warfare' had not been averted, only postponed.

The 1918 election

In December 1918, a month after the end of the Great War, the United Kingdom held its first ever general election with almost universal adult suffrage. Every man over 21 and every woman over 30 was entitled to vote, though some property restrictions remained in place for women. Sinn Féin, running on a promise to withdraw from the British Parliament and set up a rival Irish one, buried the Irish Parliamentary Party. The separatists won 73 seats out of 105 and just under 50 per cent of the vote.[374] In many constituencies, the IPP did not even field candidates.

In West Cavan, for instance, Paul Galligan, although interned in Reading Jail for the 'German Plot', was elected unopposed, as was Arthur Griffith in East Cavan. Ernest Blythe was returned for Monaghan alongside Eoin O'Duffy, who was likewise in prison for holding a rally with hurling sticks during the conscription crisis.

In Kerry, the IPP candidate Tom O'Donnell withdrew to wait for the 'whirlwind of political insanity' to pass. Of Sinn Féin, he said that 'I think the Sinn Féin policy, devoid of reason and sanity, has ruined and will further ruin my country... the storm will pass, leaving the stable, honest Irishman untouched'.[375] In fact, the storm was to blow his generation of Irish politicians into oblivion.

The fact that so many Sinn Féin candidates were elected unopposed seems to modern eyes to partially discredit their victory in 1918, but in fact it had been the most democratic election in Irish history to date. In 1910, 64 out of 103 constituencies were uncontested, compared to 27 out of 105 in 1918.[376] Under the new franchise the electorate was almost tripled, from 700,000 to over two million, and in contested constituencies there was a turnout of around 68 per cent.[377] Sinn Féin had received a resounding endorsement of their policy of abstentionism and independence.

The newly formed Irish Labour Party and the All For Ireland League stood aside for Sinn Féin in order for the election to be a straightforward exercise in self-determination. In the north, the nationalists divided the vote between them so as not to let the Unionists in. Nevertheless, the Unionists in the nine northern counties won more than twice as many votes as Sinn Féin (234,376 to 110,032), and in the six counties that would later make up Northern Ireland, the Unionist majority was still larger.

Elsewhere, however, where the rival nationalists clashed, the election battle was often a literal as well as metaphorical fight.

In Waterford city, for instance, where the Redmondites held onto the seat, a Republican activist reported that 'Redmondite mobs, mainly composed of ex-British soldiers and their wives... carried on in a most blackguardly fashion. Anybody connected with Sinn Féin was brutally assaulted with sticks, bottles etc'.[378] In Clare, where Sinn Féin had Éamon de Valera elected, it was the same story: according to one Republican, the ex-British soldiers were 'like lunatics, attacking with knives and heavy sticks'. Shots were also fired at Sinn Féin election workers.[379]

Both sides used impersonation and intimidation, but it was the Republicans who had the edge in militancy and enthusiasm. Street fighting and trickery had long been a staple of Irish elections, and was certainly not something Sinn Féin brought to bear for the first time in 1918. In Cork city elections in 1910 and 1914, for instance, eleven people were shot, two fatally, in confrontations between the rival nationalists of the Irish Party and the All For Ireland League.[380] The Volunteers and Sinn Féin in 1918 certainly gave as good as they got in brawls with Hibernians and ex-servicemen, but street violence was no worse than usual at election time, and certainly was not the reason for their victory. From this point until 1922 at least, though, it was Sinn Féin and the Volunteers who would be the leaders of nationalist Ireland.

1918 and the birth of a Republic

Before 1914, British rule in Ireland had not been characterised by systematic repression, but after the War it never quite managed to emerge from authoritarianism back into peacetime governance. It had, in short, lost its ability to govern normally, even by the standards that applied prior to the war.

Much more than the Rising of 1916, which for all its drama had been over in a week and which had made no real attempt either to take power or to win popular support, the years of 1917–18 mark the start of the revolution in Ireland. By the end of 1918, British rule in Ireland was in serious crisis. It had explicitly lost its legitimacy to govern and had to resort to prolonged use of coercive measures that it never would have contemplated in the rest of the United Kingdom. The Irish electorate had rejected it in the December 1918 election – and in voting for Sinn Féin had voted for independence. The Sinn Féin MPs had withdrawn from the British political system altogether and proclaimed an Irish Republic.

What was more, behind them they now had thousands of dedicated activists, agrarian agitators long schooled in the arts of rural revolt, a friendly trade union movement which could, as it had proved in April 1918, bring the country to a standstill, and a swelling and militant paramilitary formation, the Volunteers – or, as they would soon come to call themselves, the Irish Republican Army or IRA.

Revolution has been defined as a situation where competing bodies within a state battle for legitimate sovereignty. Or in simpler terms, they fight for who can make the law and have it accepted by the populace. Liam Lynch, one of the new firebrand Volunteer leaders, described the attitude of his generation most succinctly in early 1919: 'We have declared for an Irish Republic, and will not live under any other law'.[381]

Chapter 7:

The War for Independence

The First Dáil and Soloheadbeg: a watershed

In January 1919, after their election triumph, Sinn Féin formed an Irish Parliament – the Dáil – which met on 21 January in Dublin's Mansion House. Out of 73 Sinn Féin members (*Teachta Dála*, or TDs), only 27 were present. Some 35 deputies were described as being 'imprisoned by the foreigners' (*fé ghlas ag Gallaibh*). Another four were listed as being 'deported by the foreigners' (*ar díbirt ag Gallaibh*) in the records of the new Parliament. The Volunteers in January 1919 administered an oath to their members, in which they swore to be loyal to the Irish Republic and the Dáil; thereafter they were increasingly known as the Irish Republican Army or IRA.[382]

On the same day as the first meeting of the Dáil, two RIC policemen were escorting a consignment of gelignite explosives at Soloheadbeg in County Tipperary when they were ambushed by a party of Volunteers led by Dan Breen, Seán Treacy and Seamus Robinson. The two policemen were shot dead, their weapons and explosives seized.

This was far from the first attack on the RIC since the Easter Rising; two Volunteers had died raiding an

RIC post in Kerry the previous year and many others had successfully disarmed policemen and taken their guns since then without taking life.[383] No one in the Dáil – or even in the Volunteer leadership – had ordered the attack at Soloheadbeg, and the Volunteer Chief of Staff Richard Mulcahy even condemned it as murder.[384]

Breen later explained his and his comrades' motives in launching the attack. They as Volunteers were not mere political activists but soldiers of the Irish Republic. 'We felt there was a grave danger that the Volunteer organisation would degenerate and was degenerating into a purely political body, such as was the AOH or the UIL, and we wished to get it back to its original purpose'.

They made a decision to shoot the policemen as well as taking their arms: 'We felt that such a demonstration must have the effect of bringing about similar action in other parts of the country. The only regret we had, following the ambush, was that there were only two policemen in it instead of the six we expected, because we felt that six dead policemen would have impressed the country more than a mere two'.[385]

Both at the time and since, the Soloheadbeg incident has been used to show that the Volunteers began the subsequent war and that they felt compelled to use force when civil resistance was possible. However, in terms of violence, not much differentiated 1919, with its 18 deaths due to political violence, from 1918, which had seen a similar number.[386] IRA General Headquarters (GHQ) and particularly Richard Mulcahy were most unhappy with the ambush and advised Breen and Treacy to leave the country, though Collins quietly approved of the shootings. The operation was, as yet, most untypical of Volunteer actions, which generally still consisted of open parades, theft of weapons and bloody, but not generally lethal, riots with the RIC.

Nevertheless, the symbolism of the events of 21 January 1919 was impossible to miss. A rebel Parliament had proclaimed a republic in Dublin, and young men, claiming to be the Army of that republic, had made a premeditated and ruthless attack on the existing state's instrument of coercion.

Assassinations

In 1919, notwithstanding the ambush at Soloheadbeg, Volunteer attacks were generally reactive. With so many activists being arrested, Michael Collins, the Director of Intelligence, sought to incapacitate the police detectives who co-ordinated such arrests. The first target was G Division; detectives of the Dublin Metropolitan Police who were first threatened and told to resign and then marked down for assassination.

Collins' first step towards carrying this out was to form a small group of assassins in Dublin known as 'the Squad'. Such cold-blooded killing was a far cry from the 'stand up fight' of 1916, and some Dublin Volunteers who had fought in 1916 refused to get involved. However, Collins did assemble his killers, a small group of young men, mostly from working-class Dublin but supplemented when necessary by trusted gunmen from elsewhere, such as the Soloheadbeg ambushers Breen and Treacy.[387]

Detective Sergeant Patrick Smyth was their first victim, in July 1919; a long-standing thorn in the side of Republicans in Dublin. Four assassins waited for him as he got off the tram in the north Dublin suburb of Drumcondra and shot him several times outside his front door as his two sons looked on. Smyth died five weeks later. Such ruthlessness at first shocked the general Irish public. For the gunmen though, the lessons were more prosaic. Alarmed at their target's survival, they decided to use heavier .45 pistols instead of their .38s in future.[388] The Squad men, backed up by an intelligence unit which planned the assassinations, soon grew into highly efficient killers.

Four days later Collins' men shot dead another detective in Dublin. Two more would die there by the end of the year, and another five in early 1920. By such ruthless action the Metropolitan Police detectives (the main intelligence arm of the authorities) were effectively put out of action as a counter-insurgency force.

The Squad and Intelligence Department functioned effectively as Collins' personal Praetorian Guard. Outside of that, he along with Richard Mulcahy kept as tight a grip as possible on the local Volunteer units through the Irish Republican Brotherhood, which they used to appoint reliable officers. This created some problems. At Cabinet level, several senior figures such as Ernest Blythe and Éamon de Valera thought that the continued existence of the IRB was 'improper' now that the Irish Republic had openly elected representatives.[389] Nevertheless, its influence in the Volunteers remained. At one point the Sligo commandant wrote to Collins asking what the official position of the Brotherhood relative to the Volunteers was. Collins replied evasively, 'You will notice that there is no difference between the aims and methods of the Irish Volunteers Organisation and the other one you mention'.[390]

A state within a state

One of the first acts of the First Dáil was to send representatives to the Peace Conference at Versailles, where they hoped to be recognised as a legitimate government. Arthur Griffith put much hope in Woodrow Wilson's promise of self-determination for small nations, but in fact the Irish representatives were treated rather coldly; unsurprising given that Britain was one of the foremost victorious powers at the conference.

The Irish had more success at the Socialist Second International at Berne, where the Irish Labour Party persuaded the Socialist and Labour Parties of Europe to recognise the fledgling Republic.[391] In return for Labour's help, the Republicans adopted a 'Democratic Programme', written by Labour leader Tom Johnson, which promised that every citizen was entitled to 'an adequate share of the produce of the nation's labour'.[392]

In Ireland itself, considerable progress was made in making the Irish Republic a reality on the ground. In theory, the Republic was now an existing fact, but as Ernest Blythe, the Minister for Trade, recalled, 'Like most of the Ministries, except Local Government and Defence, the work of the Department of Trade and Commerce was mostly pretence, having no value except a propagandist value'.[393]

Blythe was perhaps being too harsh. If a state is defined by its ability to make and execute law, then from early 1919 until mid-1920, sovereignty in Ireland was seeping away from the British administration and towards the separatist para-state. The Dáil set up its own courts and police; usually local Volunteers, but also another body called the Irish Republican Police.

The first Republican courts were National Arbitration Courts, which were legal, voluntary bodies that handled civil cases. However, the law and order situation deteriorated as the political violence worsened and the RIC withdrew from the countryside in early 1920, forcing the Republicans to take over more state functions. In June 1920 Republican, or Dáil, Courts were launched to replace completely the existing justice system. The profile of Republican judges was quite egalitarian; many were young men, some were trade unionists and some were even women, but also many were also Catholic priests.[394]

The system was a curious mixture of the revolutionary and the conservative. The boycott and replacement of the British justice system was a bold strategy, but the law used was almost exclusively British Common Law, and the right to private property was rigorously upheld. Efforts were also made to include the existing legal profession. The Republican Chief Justice, Conor Maguire, remembered that 'solicitors, even those with no sympathy for Sinn Féin, found it necessary if they were to retain their business, to practice in the Courts'.[395]

The IRA and Republican Police started to take up policing, for example of fairs and markets. In Cork, Volunteers caught a gang who had stolen £15,000 in Millstreet, deported the thieves from the country and returned the money.[396]

In County Cavan, Seán Sheridan remembered, 'The Volunteers had the co-operation of the vast majority of the people, something the RIC could never get. There had always been a void between the people and the RIC, and since the rise of Sinn Féin this had become accentuated'. Petty criminals were arrested and made to work for farmers in another battalion area, while others were made to pay compensation to their victims.[397] At the same time, the Volunteers enforced a boycott of the RIC. Some locals in Cavan who took Sinn Féin to the British courts over their occupation of a hall got a visit from members of the Bailieboro Volunteers which 'compelled them to withdraw proceedings'.[398]

Industrial disputes were also dealt with by the Dáil Courts. Though some Republicans sympathised with

Labour, the priority of the movement was national unity, which sometimes created tensions between class and national aims. In September 1920, for instance, at a creamery strike in Cork city, workers refused arbitration and the IRA was called in to escort milk through the picket line. The problem was that many of the strikers were also IRA members. An open split was avoided when an agreement was patched up by the ITGWU and IRA, and arbitration of the Dáil Courts reluctantly accepted.[399]

By mid-1920, regular courts were finding that they had no cases to deal with. Charles P. Crane, a magistrate in Kerry, found on entering his court in February 1920 no-one there except a young man smoking a cigarette, in an 'insolent' way. He ordered him to leave, only to find nobody to carry out his orders. 'I could do no more than adjourn'. A month later, after receiving a death threat for jailing Volunteers for military drilling, he quit and returned to England.[400]

In the summer of 1920, assizes, or the local courts system, failed all over Ireland. In County Cork, only 12 of 296 jurors attended sessions and Cork Corporation, dominated by Sinn Féin, banned the British District Courts from using the city courthouse.[401] The collapse of the regular courts was a sign of the nationalist public's disillusion with British rule, compromised as it was by the First World War and the accompanying repression since 1916, but it was also a product of Sinn Féin's agitation on other issues: above all, the land question.

Land and loans

Rising food prices, the suspension of land reform and land hunger prompted an upsurge in 'cattle driving' and land occupations in 1917–18. With the police's authority undermined by the Republican 'counter-state', 1919–20 saw an even greater wave of agrarian agitation in the west of Ireland. In many cases, Sinn Féin and Volunteer activists were involved, and indeed some of the Volunteers' early actions in some areas were attacks on landlords, rent collectors or 'land grabbers'.

However, while this economic conflict helped the nationalist revolution up to a point by undermining the existing law and order, it also threatened to destroy not only the remaining great landlords but also prosperous Irish nationalist farmers. Sinn Féin activist Kevin O'Shiel described the unrest as a 'prairie fire over Connaught', 'sparing neither ranch nor medium farm'. The Volunteers as a result issued a directive forbidding their men from engaging in cattle drives or land grabs.[402] O'Shiel was put in charge of the Dáil Eireann Land Commission, an arbitration body set up mid-1920 to deal with land disputes, which proved quite successful at clamping down on cattle driving and land occupations. However, while in the short term Volunteers were now policing land agitation, it was popularly held in the Sinn Féin heartlands of the west and north midlands that an independent Ireland, when it came, would also mean substantial land reform.

Notwithstanding the relative success of the Land Commission, there remained the difficult problem of enforcing its verdicts, which, if arbitration was not accepted, had to be done by force. The Republic had no prisons, so more creative methods of punishment had to found. In County Galway, for instance, a land case was settled when tenants occupying farmland and demanding its redistribution were ordered to leave it because the land was too poor to be divided. When the claimants refused to accept the verdict, a Volunteer unit rowed them out to an island on Lough Corrib and left them there until they agreed to accept the ruling.[403]

The British initially had mixed feelings about the operation of the Dáil Courts. While they were regularly harassed, and their participants arrested at times, the British military also wrote approvingly of their success at keeping order in rural areas where RIC and regular courts no longer functioned.[404]

However, by July 1920, both the RIC and British Army were pressing for the suppression of Dáil Courts, claiming they were undermining the 'King's writ'. A government crackdown began in the autumn of 1920. The Dáil Courts were driven underground and reduced to hearing cases in farms, barns, creameries and the like. The Courts and the Land Commission recorded a two-thirds fall in activity by early 1921. Prime Minister Lloyd George told Parliament that the 'Sinn Féin Courts have disappeared into the cellars'.[405]

At the same time as it was establishing its own justice system, the Republic also began to raise its own finances. Michael Collins as Minister for Finance raised some £380,000 in Ireland itself via loans, and over $5 million was raised in Irish America.[406] Alan Bell, a magistrate who tried to investigate the Dáil loan scheme and to seize its funds, became one of the first victims of Collins' Squad. He was taken off a tram in Dublin and shot dead in March 1920.[407]

In June 1920, the Republic received further endorsement from the electorate when Sinn Féin gained control of 338 out of 393 county councils in the local elections. This raised practical problems for the new administrations, however, as the British promptly cut off funding to Sinn Féin-controlled local authorities and seized their existing funds. In Dublin the IRA 'stole' the Corporation's funds (with the connivance of that body) to stop them being confiscated.

W. T. Cosgrave, Sinn Féiner and Easter Rising veteran, was the Republic's Minister for Local Government. He had to find a way of staving off bankruptcy for the local authorities, who had to pay for vital services such as hospitals, water and roads. After trudging around several of the major banks in Dublin, looking for loans and being met by 'blank refusals', he finally secured a loan to keep local government afloat from the Bank of Ireland.[408] This episode is all the more interesting, since the board of the Bank, which included the Guinness and Jameson families, had always been staunch Unionists. That the banks were beginning to put their money on the separatists was a sure sign that British rule in Ireland was withering.

All of this, however, happened in parallel with the collapse of the existing state institutions. And this happened, not of its own accord, or by democratic means, but as the result of a violent assault on the state and its police by the Volunteers, or as they were now becoming known, the Irish Republican Army or IRA. It is to this that we must now turn.

Guerrilla war begins, 1919–1920

The guerrilla war developed haphazardly due to local circumstances. Throughout 1918 and 1919, the Volunteers tried to arm themselves by raiding the RIC and sometimes the British Army. A soldier was shot dead in 1919 in Fermoy, Cork, for example, by an IRA party led by Liam Lynch, the enraged soldiers in response shooting up the small town and burning down several local buildings.

Shots were exchanged and two RIC constables died in Limerick when the local Volunteers attempted to rescue a prisoner, Robert Byrne, who also died in the shootout. In response to the subsequent military curfew, the city's Trades Council called a general strike and the unions took over the city for a week in an episode nicknamed 'the Limerick Soviet'.[409]

Ernie O'Malley, who was making a name for himself as one of the most energetic and effective IRA organisers, took to pulling his revolver when stopped by the police. On several occasions, he and the RIC exchanged shots as he travelled the country.[410]

In the early days, therefore, there were deaths, but they were relatively few and they were usually incidental to arms raids, arrests, or riots. As yet, in 1919, with the exception of the odd targeted assassination, the protagonists rarely set out to kill one another. Moreover, as they were still poorly armed and inexperienced, the Volunteers tended to come off the worst in the early clashes, either through death, or more commonly, arrest, beating or bayonet wounds. The balance of terror at this stage still lay with the Crown forces.

As of late 1919 and especially from January 1920, this would all change. The fledgling IRA would hit back at the state, primarily in the form of the RIC, and knock away its foundations – in the process inaugurating a much deadlier phase of the conflict.

In November 1919, the British banned the Dáil, Sinn Féin and a host of other nationalist organisations. Most of the Republican political leadership was now in prison. Éamon de Valera, the President of the Republic, was in America. Peaceful means appeared to have run into a wall of repression. This left the way open for Michael Collins and Richard Mulcahy, who had positioned themselves strategically at the head of both the Volunteers and the IRB, to launch a guerrilla war. Collins had always been convinced that such an eventuality would be necessary. 'All ordinary peaceful methods are ended and we shall be taking the only alternative actions in a short while now', he said in late 1919.[411]

In December 1919, Collins ordered the assassination of Lord French, the Lord Lieutenant, who was ambushed on his way back to his residence in the Phoenix Park. In the event, the only person to die was one of the ambushers, Martin Savage. French got away, but the message was clear. This was not to be a state of civil disturbance or mass unarmed struggle, this was war. [412]

Barracks attacks

In January 1920, in response to urgings from Collins and Mulcahy at GHQ, the IRA around the country began attacking rural RIC barracks. Typically, several hundred Volunteers would muster at night and surround the police barracks, normally guarded by five or six policemen. The guerrillas would then open fire and try to either set fire to the building or detonate a home-made bomb against its walls. Quite often, the police surrendered and gave up their arms. The Volunteers would then take their arms and burn the barracks.

These attacks often involved large numbers of Volunteers, but rarely resulted in casualties. The attack on Kilmallock Barracks in May 1920 was one of the larger-scale actions, where several hundred Volunteers attacked and burned the police post. It was unusual in that two RIC men and one Volunteer were killed.[413] Ernie O'Malley, sent from Dublin to co-ordinate the actions, was involved in many such raids and was badly burned by petrol he poured onto the roof of a barracks at Rearcross, Tipperary.[414]

Although their body count was generally low, the barracks attacks rapidly changed the situation in much of rural Ireland. Many barracks were destroyed. The RIC withdrew from its smaller rural posts altogether, and about 400 of these were burned all around the country on Easter Sunday 1920. This came as a brutal shock to both the police and the British military, who had never imagined that the rebels were capable of such a level of co-ordination. Not only that, but the withdrawal of the RIC from the countryside made the everyday running of the British administration stagger. Income tax could not be collected; district courts could not sit. It was in these circumstances that the Republican counter-state rushed in to fill the vacuum.

In the front rank of the institutions that defended the British state in Ireland were Irish Catholics: civil servants in Dublin Castle, and above all, policemen in the RIC. Hundreds of these men died upholding British rule in Ireland. The writer Seán O'Faoláin, who served as a junior IRA member but whose father was an RIC man, wrote, 'men like my father were dragged out, in those years, and shot down as traitors to their country. Shot for cruel necessity – so be it. Shot to inspire necessary terror – so be it. But they were not traitors. They had their loyalties and they stuck to them'.[415]

The RIC, in places where the Volunteers had armed themselves, were now at the mercy of the guerrillas. Nationalist accounts of the period always refer to the RIC as a paramilitary force and note that it was armed, unlike police in the rest of the United Kingdom, and that it was trained in military drill. And all of this was true. The RIC had cut its teeth in the nineteenth century putting down rural land agitation and keeping an eye on militant nationalists.

However, by the second decade of the twentieth century, it was also substantially a normal police force. It was manned by lower-middle-class Catholics, mostly of rural origin, and it patrolled rural areas in ones and twos by bicycle. While it did play a political role in dealing with nationalist agitation, it was most unsuited to a counter-insurgency campaign. Its 'barracks', at the start of the conflict, were usually simply converted houses and were in no condition to withstand a determined attack by committed guerrillas. Hapless policemen in Kerry approached local IRA men the morning after a barracks attack, saying, 'You burned us out last night, young man. For God's sake don't shoot us, we're only doing our jobs'.[416] As of April 1919, the Dáil had also called for a boycott of the police. In certain areas, they were now ostracised and reduced to buying food at gunpoint.

If that was not enough to demoralise the embattled police, much of their will to combat the IRA was destroyed when most of the Republican prisoners who had been held up to that point were released after a mass hunger strike in April 1920.[417] The hunger strike episode was also an example of mass mobilisation in favour of the Republican prisoners. At Mountjoy Gaol, where most of them were being held, crowds of up to 40,000 demonstrated outside for their release. Women were especially prominent, many saying the Catholic rosary. Troops at Mountjoy stood nervously behind coils of barbed wire with bayonets fixed, while in an effort to intimidate the crowd, Royal Air Force aeroplanes flew towards them at rooftop height.[418]

For the second time in two years the trade unions, again led by William O'Brien's ITGWU, brought Ireland to a standstill with a two-day general strike in support of the hunger strikers. In many areas, workers' committees, often termed 'Soviets', took over food supply during the strike. According to a Republican source, 'not a train or a tram is running, not a shop is open, not a public house nor a tobacconist, even the public lavatories are closed'.[419] After two days of the strike, from 12–13 April, the British caved in and released the Republican prisoners.

Railway workers also helped to paralyse the co-ordination of British military movements when, in May 1920, they began a boycott on moving either British troops or military supplies in Ireland, restricting the military to the use of roads, which were constantly being trenched and blocked by IRA guerrillas.[420]

By the summer of 1920, it was the IRA which was in the ascendancy. The RIC was demoralised and badly hit by resignations. The guerrillas in rural areas and after dark could do as they liked. An RIC report of County Kerry in August 1920 read:

> All of the able-bodied men in the region have adopted the most aggressive attitude and have arranged with very short notice to attack on the return journey any military police or military transport... There is hostility to the police everywhere in the county... Almost all local magistrates have resigned their commissions through fear of terrorism, which is rampant... It may be taken for granted that nearly all the young people are Sinn Féin and that a large proportion of the young men are Volunteers. Between them these two organisations are controlling the whole life and action of the county.[421]

Those RIC men who remained either became quiescent or else locked in a vendetta with the local IRA. Sinn Féin and Volunteer leaders were sent an anonymous letter in response to the death of a policeman stating: 'an eye for an eye, therefore a life for a life'. In Cork, the RIC reported that 'the feeling is growing... that the only way to stop these murders is by way of reprisals or retaliation'.[422] Not long afterwards, in revenge for the killing of one Constable

Murtagh in Cork city, a squad of RIC men broke into the home of Thomas MacCurtain, Sinn Féin Mayor of Cork and head of the local Volunteers, and shot him dead.[423]

The cycle of revenge killings would come to define the conflict. Moreover, the assassination of MacCurtain and of another RIC officer named Smyth set in motion a series of events that broadened the violence beyond the nationalist south and west of Ireland.

The conflict spreads to the north

Gerard Smyth was a Divisional Commissioner of the RIC in Munster, but came from solidly Protestant and Unionist Banbridge in County Down. In mid-1920, in an effort to inspire demoralised and frightened policemen in Kerry to resume patrolling the area around Listowel, he gave a speech telling the local RIC that they could shoot anyone who approached them and who disobeyed an order to halt.

'Sinn Féin has had all the sport up to the present', he told the assembled policemen, 'we are going to have sport now... No man will get into trouble for shooting'. Smyth succeeded, not in reinvigorating the RIC, but in provoking a mutiny. The police, led by a constable named Jeremiah Mee, who had been used to ordinary policing rather than counter-insurgency, simply refused to follow his orders. Mee deserted and publicised the incident. Smyth was later tracked down and shot in Cork.[424]

In the north-east, where Unionists had been looking on appalled by the insurgency spreading through the south, Smyth's death unleashed deadly sectarian tensions built up over the previous two years. In his native Banbridge and surrounding towns, Catholic homes were burned in revenge.[425] Vicious rioting broke out in Derry, and over twenty people were killed in exchanges of fire between Catholics and Protestants.[426]

In Belfast, loyalists (many of them unemployed ex-servicemen) marched on the city's shipyards to expel Catholic workers and 'rotten Prods' – or left-wingers who were assumed not to be sufficiently anti-Catholic. Thousands were chased from their jobs amidst a hail of rivets and bolts – 'Belfast confetti', as it came to be known. A great many suffered severe beatings, and some were thrown into the River Lagan. In the little slum streets of west and central Belfast, volleys of shots and stones were exchanged, twenty-two people were killed and hundreds wounded.[427]

Just over a month later, on 22 August, the south-west and the north-east again exchanged reprisals. The RIC's assassination of Thomas MacCurtain, Sinn Féin Mayor of Cork, was avenged by the killing of Oswald Swanzy, another RIC inspector and a native of Lisburn, a small town just outside Belfast. Swanzy had been blamed by a Cork jury for the killing of the city's mayor. Michael Collins managed to track Swanzy back to his native Lisburn and, as he was leaving church, two Cork IRA men shot him in the head. The assassins got away, followed by an enraged mob, in a taxi with Belfast IRA men. Almost the entire Catholic population of Lisburn were driven out in revenge for the killing and over three hundred of their homes went up in smoke.[428] There followed another ten days of sectarian violence in Belfast, with another thirty-three deaths.[429]

Crossroads, summer 1920 – missed opportunity

By the summer of 1920, Ireland teetered on the brink. Much of the southern two-thirds of Ireland was already outside of effective government control. The north-east, with its Unionist majority, faced a descent into sectarian mob violence, in which the state could not be counted upon to be neutral.

The British Government, headed by David Lloyd George, was still trying to put back together the world order blown asunder by the First World War. In Ireland, they publicly refused to have anything to do with Sinn Féin, the Dáil and the IRA 'murder gang' (although in practice, secret contacts were maintained with Sinn Féin throughout the conflict). What they came up with was a two-part solution. The first part was political. Under the Government of Ireland Act of 1920, Ireland was to be partitioned into two parts: Northern Ireland (the six north-eastern counties) and Southern Ireland (the rest), both to be given autonomy.

Even at the time, top civil servants sent to Ireland, particularly the trio of Alfred Cope, Warren Fisher and John Anderson, told the government that there was virtually no support for the Government of Ireland Act in the south and recommended offering 'dominion status' – the same autonomy enjoyed by Canada and Australia – to Sinn Féin instead. On the Irish side, the indications are that even at this stage, Arthur Griffith and Michael Collins in particular would have accepted this offer.[430] However, the idea was not accepted at Cabinet level. It would not be until late 1921 and after a radical escalation of violence that such a proposal would be offered in earnest by the British side.

Secondly, parallel to 'Home Rule all around', as Lloyd George called his scheme of two new parliaments in Ireland, a security solution was proposed. This was particularly backed by a rival faction in Dublin Castle to the Anderson–Fisher–Cope group, led by Hamar Greenwood, the Chief Secretary for Ireland, and Henry Tudor, the head of the police. On 9 August 1920 the British Parliament passed the Restoration of Order in Ireland Act, which suspended all coroners' courts and replaced them with 'military courts of inquiry'. Military courts-martial were extended to cover the whole population and were empowered to use the death penalty and internment without trial. Finally, government payments to local governments in Sinn Féin hands were suspended.[431]

Loath to deploy the British Army (which in any case had many commitments elsewhere) in greater numbers, and with the regular RIC in disarray, they instead unleashed a series of new 'police' units on the country. The first of these was the 'Black and Tans'. These were ex-soldiers recruited mostly from Britain (but also, though this was not acknowledged until recently, from Ireland).[432] Recruiting for the new force began as early as January 1920, and the first of these recruits for the RIC arrived in March, but it was in the summer that their presence began to be felt as they were deployed. Their name came from their combination of 'black' RIC uniforms (actually dark green) and military khaki. The Black and Tans were viewed very differently from the old RIC, but in theory they did not form a separate organisation.

The RIC Auxiliary Division, set up in July 1920, was another story. From the start, they were to be separate from either the police or the military. Recruited from ex-officers, well armed and deployed in companies around the country, they were a dedicated counter-insurgency corps. Though often confused with the Black and Tans in popular memory, the Auxiliaries were much better motivated and more aggressive, and were at the forefront of the British state's attempt to wrest control of the country back from the IRA.

Finally, in the north, a third paramilitary police group, the Ulster Special Constabulary, was set up, partly at the request of the Unionists, but with British Government approval. The USC was a part-time armed force to be called out in times of emergency. In effect, given the time and place, it amounted to a Protestant militia, a guarantee against the northern Unionists being either overrun or 'sold out'.

In a sense, the proliferation of armed state forces created in the summer of 1920 –Auxiliaries, Black and Tans, USC – represented the worst possible solution. The new formations were undisciplined, outside the control of either police or military, and for the most part unfamiliar with the country they were entering or its politics.

British counterstroke, August–December 1920

On the arrival of the new police recruits, the balance of terror now shifted the other way. IRA activists found themselves arrested, beaten and shot.

One of those arrested was Paul Galligan, IRA commandant and TD for Cavan. Ten armed Black and Tans burst into his father's house. His father wrote, 'Paul was in the kitchen just after our tea. Paul rushed out the back door pursued by four armed soldiers who fired several shots at him at short range. He got as far as McCann's garden gate and while in the act of opening the gate a rifle bullet went right through his arm... Such savagery I never witnessed. They wouldn't give me time to have his wound dressed or allow him into the house but dragged him into the motor and drove to Cavan'. [433]

The Black and Tans and Auxiliaries were not police, and had no training in normal police work. One regular RIC man remembered:

... they knew absolutely nothing about police duties. On one occasion there was a county inspector in the barracks... and he asked this fellow what was his power of arrest, and he said he didn't know. He tried to make it simpler for him. He said, 'If you see a man on the street and asked his name and address and he refused, what would you do?' And the Black and Tan said... 'I would lift him under the jaw and the next thing I would use my bayonet. That is what I would do to the man'.[434]

Lloyd George said in Parliament, 'We struck the terrorists and now the terrorists are complaining of terror'.[435] With exact symmetry, Cork IRA leader Tom Barry later wrote that he told his men: 'The Auxiliaries were killers without mercy... the alternative now was to kill or be killed; see to it that those terrorists die and are broken'.[436] The new arrivals took out their reprisals not only on Republican activists, as the RIC had already been doing, but on the population at large. In September 1920, Head Constable Peter Burke of the RIC was shot dead near the police depot in Gormanstown, County Meath. It didn't take long for the Black and Tans to take revenge, rolling that afternoon out of the depot to the nearby town of Balbriggan, where they set fire to most of the main street and shot dead two IRA members. Trim, also in County Meath, was hit by the burners in the summer of 1920, as was Tuam in Galway.[437] At this stage, such actions were not the policy of Crown forces, but they were not stopped either and certainly not punished. It is difficult in hindsight not to regard them as a kind of tacit state policy to 'terrorise the terrorists'.

In Lixnaw in Kerry in late September, all the local men were taken from a Catholic church during local Mass and searched. At Abbeydorney, the Crown forces burned the local creamery and beat its manager with rifle butts. In

Tralee, they threw a hand grenade into the family home of two prominent Sinn Féiners, which, though it exploded, did not injure the only occupant, the Republican brothers' mother.[438] In Lixnaw on 25 October a patrol of masked police, exacting retribution for Republicans' cutting the hair of a local woman who was friendly to the police, publicly stripped two young men naked and beat them before cutting off their sister's hair and, as at Abbeydorney, setting fire to the local creamery.[439]

The burning of a creamery sounds like a rather mild form of repression, but in fact it was one of the worst forms of collective punishment possible in rural Ireland. Creameries were co-operatives where the local dairy farmers would deposit their milk for it to be turned into cream and butter and sold on to markets further afield. Not only would a large number of people work at a creamery, but much of the local population depended on it for their income and would also have to bear the costs of rebuilding it.

The 'Sack of Balbriggan' and similar incidents were reported across the English-speaking world, but many civilians suffered daily low-level terror, and sometimes straightforward robbery, at the hands of the paramilitary police. For instance, the following are a list of cases heard in a single hearing at Carrick-on-Shannon, County Leitrim in early 1922 regarding compensation for damage caused by Crown forces in 1920–21: the Ryan family was awarded £103 for having been robbed at gunpoint by Auxiliary policemen; Michael Flynn of Annaghbradigan was beaten by Auxiliaries, who also took £96 from his home; Thomas Moran, a vintner, was robbed and threatened at gunpoint and robbed of £25; Michael Murphy of Kilternan was beaten and stabbed with a bayonet prior to being arrested and interned. He was awarded £75.[440] County Leitrim, in one corner of which all of these events occurred, was one of the least violent localities in Ireland.

Did it work, this indiscriminate lashing out at the general population? In many areas of the country, across a great swathe of the east and midlands and in much of the west, IRA activity was very low-key throughout the conflict. Perhaps there, the guerrillas were successfully 'terrorised'. In Galway city, for example, the IRA commander tried to halt actions for fear of reprisals.[441] Mass mobilisation, such as strikes and mass protests, also fizzled out as state forces grew more violent. The railway boycott on carrying the British military was broken by widespread sackings in December 1920. But in the heartlands of the revolt, the southern province of Munster, Dublin city and parts of the north and west, the arrival of the Black and Tans and Auxiliaries only escalated the violence.

For one thing, the IRA was forced to develop 'flying columns', or full-time guerrilla units who could not go home for fear of arrest. This was ordered by Collins and Mulcahy at the IRA GHQ in Autumn 1920, but also arrived at on the ground out of necessity. The columns formed a small hard core, capable of mounting regular attacks on British forces.

In County Longford, for example, the Volunteers had in the region of 1,000 members, but the IRA flying column, led by Seán MacEoin, consisted of only thirty men. Nonetheless, they managed to hurt the Crown forces. The small column assassinated two RIC men in early November and then held off a reprisal assault on the village of Ballinalee by several hundred police and troops.[442]

This process of streamlining and hardening the IRA went furthest in County Cork, which had three active

'Brigades' and another 'Squad' in Cork city. Attacking well-defended and fortified barracks was no longer an option, but vulnerable patrols could be hit in ambushes. By itself, County Cork was the scene of between a third and a quarter of all deaths in the war.[443]

The conflict now involved smaller groups of more dedicated fighters, but paradoxically became much more lethal. Equally importantly in this form of political warfare, if the British forces were going to treat all civilians – a lot of whom had their doubts about the Republican use of violence – as potential rebels, they were going to help to make this a reality.

A cycle of escalation

A good example of how the dynamic of escalation was going to work was seen at Rineen in Clare in September 1920. The local IRA ambushed an RIC lorry, blasting it at close range with rifles and shotguns. Five of the officers were killed on the spot; another was chased across a field and shot down. Five were Irishmen ('old' RIC Constables), and one a Black and Tan. British troops coming upon the scene found the bodies and the burning lorry, but the ambushers escaped into the hills after a scattered exchange of shots.[444]

Earlier in the day a magistrate, Alan Lendrum, had disappeared (in fact he had been shot and dumped in a lake). There was no way for the state forces to hit back at the IRA directly. What they could do, however, was make the local population pay. A horde of enraged (and largely drunk) policemen and soldiers raided three local villages, Miltown Malbay, Lahinch and Ennistymon, where they burned sixteen houses and shops and shot dead or bayoneted five civilians.[445]

Perhaps the state forces were purging themselves of the fear and frustration they felt at grappling with an invisible enemy. Perhaps they thought that they were restoring the balance of fear in their favour. But in fact, their actions only strengthened those who argued that the British state had no right to be in Ireland. Later in the month, Clare County Council formally transferred its allegiance to the Dáil.[446]

The conflict had been transformed into something much more vicious than before. British forces, and particularly the Auxiliaries, not only arrested Republicans but quite regularly shot them dead after arrest. Formal executions of captured IRA men also began. The IRA in return became much more ruthless, increasingly setting out not to capture arms or barracks, or necessarily to take on British forces in combat, but simply to kill and hit back. November 1920 gave three chilling examples of what this would mean.

On 1 November, Kevin Barry, an 18-year-old IRA member, was hanged for his role in an arms raid in Dublin that had left three British soldiers dead. IRA GHQ issued orders to units around the country to hit back at anyone in the uniform of the Crown. In some places, County Kildare, for instance, the IRA received the orders but just refused to carry them out.[447] In any case, the orders were rescinded when tempers in Dublin had cooled.

Word of this, however, never reached Kerry, where ten people would lose their lives within twenty-four hours. Eight of them were RIC men, two of whom were abducted and 'disappeared'; their bodies were never found. Two more were local civilians killed by the police in reprisals. The RIC and Black and Tans occupied the town of Tralee for over a week, preventing all food entering until the missing RIC men were found. They also burned the homes and businesses of Sinn Féin activists, and over the next few days shot dead three more people, two of them IRA men. The 'siege' was finally lifted after a storm was raised in the British press.[448]

No sooner was this cycle of atrocities over than another broke out in Dublin. Michael Collins had been alarmed by the growth of British intelligence networks in the city and, with hair-raising ruthlessness, drew up a list to wipe it out. Early on the morning of Sunday, 21 November 1920, teams of killers from Collins' own 'Squad' and the IRA Dublin Brigade visited over a dozen private addresses, mainly in the south of the city. By the time the city had woken up, fourteen people were dead, eight of them British officers, of whom six were confirmed intelligence agents, two Auxiliaries, and the rest either bystanders or civilian informers[449].

There was nothing heroic about this action. The victims had been helpless, in many cases sleeping beside their wives, when they were shot. But as an act of terror – that is, to frighten the British administration and those who collaborated with it – it had no equal. Agents could be seen over the following days under military escort, moving into Dublin Castle, away from hostile eyes and hidden revolvers.[450]

At the time, the British memory of the day was of Irish 'savagery'. The dead officers were given state funerals in Westminster and barricades were placed around the Prime Minister's residence.[451] Had this been the end of the day's events, Irish memories of the day might be tinged with some regret. But the British forces' reaction ensured that 'Bloody Sunday' would be remembered not as a cold-blooded assassination but as a British atrocity. A mixed force of RIC and Auxiliaries raided a Gaelic football match at Croke Park – only a couple of miles across the city from the morning's killings – looking for suspects. For some reason, once inside the ground, they opened fire and killed another fourteen people, one of them a player.[452]

Only a week later at Kilmichael in Cork, an IRA flying column under Tom Barry, a former British soldier, wiped out a patrol of eighteen Auxiliaries. The Auxiliary company based at Macroom had dominated the area since their arrival in September, raiding the countryside, arresting suspects and shooting at least one civilian. Barry planned the ambush not to capture, or seize arms, but to kill.[453] In a carefully planned attack, the two Auxiliary lorries were swept with fire at close range.

In recent years, controversy has surrounded the action – did Barry kill prisoners and finish off wounded Auxiliaries? Was there a false surrender on the part of the Auxiliaries?[454] Regardless, taken together with the previous events of November, the course the conflict was taking was clear. The new militarised police forces had tried to terrorise the guerrillas and their supporters. The IRA, in those areas where it had strong and determined units, fought back with a terror of its own. Barry later wrote that he had 'gone down into the mire' to fight British forces. In the absence of a political solution, both sides could only up the violence by an ever-widening targeting of enemies. The distinctions between armed and unarmed, on-duty and off-duty, civilian or combatant, were all to become much hazier in the months ahead.

In the same month, Terence MacSwiney, Mayor of Cork, the man who had been so determined to wipe out the shame of having surrendered his Volunteers in Cork in 1916 without firing a shot, died on hunger strike. British forces in Galway abducted and murdered a priest, Michael Griffin, suspected of Republican sympathies.[455] On 11 December, the Auxiliaries burned out the centre of Cork city in reprisal for an ambush in the city, and for good measure assassinated two IRA suspects in their beds.[456]

By the end of the month, martial law had been declared all across the south of the country. This included official sanction for reprisals, whereby houses of Republicans, their families and supporters could now be burnt in retaliation for IRA actions. It is impossible to list all of the killings and reprisals of late 1920, but suffice it to say that they could do nothing but destroy whatever confidence the nationalist population still had in British rule.

It is therefore something of a tragic irony that concrete proposals were already on the table in December 1920, not dissimilar to those that would end the war six months later.

Secret talks, carried out via an intermediary, between Lloyd George and Arthur Griffith had produced the bones of a deal. Griffith presented the terms to Collins and the Dáil Cabinet, who reacted favourably. A truce was scuppered by Hamar Greenwood, the hard-line Chief Secretary for Ireland, who threatened to resign if there was a truce before the IRA surrendered its weapons.[457] As a result, the two sides would butt heads for six more bloody months.

A bloody spiral, January–June 1921

By early 1921, what existed in parts of Ireland was a war. It was not, of course, a matter of territory held or captured. Nor, by and large, was it a case of combat between large forces. But a thousand people would die between January and July; an average of forty per week.[458]

In the 'martial law area' of the south, the British Army was deployed in ever greater numbers, and it was here that most of the violence took place. The formation of flying columns initially meant larger and more regular engagements between the guerrillas and British forces. In Cork, for example, Tom Barry's column, around 100 strong, was almost trapped by a British 'sweep' of over 1,000 men at a townland named Crossbarry. It fought its way clear, killing ten British soldiers. In neighbouring Kerry in

March, an ambush on a train carrying troops at Headford Junction killed another nine and wounded twenty-five.[459]

But the flying columns also gave the British the opportunity to hunt down and trap relatively large bodies of guerrillas, and when they did, they were often ruthless. At Clonmult, for example, in north County Cork, a whole IRA column of some twenty men was surrounded in a farmhouse. Five were killed in combat, before the rest, with the house burning around them, surrendered. According to one of those captured, 'We were lined up alongside an outhouse with our hands up. The Tans came along and shot every man, with the exception of three who were saved from the Tans by an officer in charge of the military party'. Seven of the captured IRA men were summarily shot dead before the officer's intervention.[460]

Barry's West Cork column lost eleven of its Volunteers killed during 4–6 February. Three were killed in an abortive ambush at Upton train station, one in an accidental shooting, the remainder arrested and murdered by British troops.[461]

By March 1921, the British commander-in-chief General Neville Macready would write that 'the rebels in the martial law area carry out operations [which]… frequently resemble a minor military engagement as distinct from small ambushes formed by men who shot and ran away'.[462] However, this phase of the conflict did not last. The British deployed more troops and resources to Cork, including armoured trucks, aircraft and tanks (though the latter seem to have been mainly used for demolishing houses in urban areas). They also changed their tactics, deploying small 'active service platoons' to hunt the flying columns, using aerial reconnaissance and mounting huge 'drives' of thousands of troops across the countryside.

These methods effectively neutralised the Cork flying columns. The celebrated West Cork Brigade Flying

Column fought its last large action against British troops
– the Crossbarry ambush – in March 1921. It spent the
remaining three months trying to avoid British 'drives' and
shooting suspected 'spies' who might betray their presence.

The war in Dublin

Dublin, apart from the events of Bloody Sunday and the
Squad's assassinations, saw little enough guerrilla warfare
until early 1921.

After this, however, the city saw its daily life torn apart
by ambushes, house searches, arrests and assassinations. An
Active Service Unit (ASU) was set up in January 1921,
comprising of roughly twenty men in each of the city's
four IRA battalions. They were dedicated to mounting at
least three attacks per day on British forces in the capital.
Usually this meant throwing an improvised grenade at
troops, a volley of revolver shots and a quick getaway. Ernie
O'Malley, who had been picked up by Auxiliaries and
badly beaten in Dublin Castle, but who had escaped with
the help of a friendly soldier, left us this account of a street
ambush on Stephen's Green:

> Eggs [grenades] shattered in a tearing smash, one
> burst above the lancia [truck]; automatics shot
> quickly, rifle reply came more slowly, then the rifles
> merged with the swaying thresh of the machine
> gun. The passers by ran or threw themselves on the
> pavement... A man flattened on his blood on the
> cobbled street, two soldiers lay loosely against each
> other in the corner of the lancia; up on the street
> men tried to stop the red stains on woman's white
> blouse. Women beside me were moaning and pray-
> ing 'oh Sacred Heart of Jesus help us'.[463]

There were no more than 2,000 men enrolled in the Dublin Brigade, and fewer than 100 of these were active in the Active Service Units.[464] Against them, the city was garrisoned by no less than 10,084 British troops and 1,600 police.[465] Of these, the 400 Auxiliaries were the most visible, flying through the streets in their tender lorries, weapons sticking out the sides. In any given operation they were the rapid-response unit, the first to arrive at the scene of an ambush or shooting. The IRA could do nothing of a truly militarily significant nature, given such a disparity of forces. But every day brought news of a new attack in the streets, generally the IRA volunteers flinging a home-made hand grenade at troops or police, firing a few pistol shots and disappearing into the back streets.

On 12 May, for example, there were three attacks. A squad of British troops was 'bombed' on Grafton Street, killing none of them but wounding fifteen civilians. Another patrol was ambushed in the northside suburb of Clontarf, while at the North Wall an RIC supply lorry was held up and its contents (food rations) thrown into the sea.[466] Three days later, an IRA party led by Emmet Dalton seized a British armoured car and used it to try to break Longford IRA leader Seán MacEoin out of Mountjoy Prison. May 17 and 18 saw two grenade attacks, killing a British soldier and a civilian and wounding eight more bystanders.[467] By the time of the truce that ended the war in July 1921, these pinprick attacks had killed dozens of police and soldiers, but also forty-six civilians and wounded hundreds more in the capital.[468] The British responded by cordoning off large areas of the city and conducting house-to-house searches.

The month of May also saw five civilians shot dead in Dublin as alleged informers; all, *The Irish Times* reported, ex-soldiers. June would see ten more killed and dumped on the streets of Dublin with the label attached: 'Spies and informers beware. IRA'.[469]

Dublin was primarily important for its symbolic and propaganda value, and Éamon de Valera, President of the Irish Republic, was particularly keen for a spectacular show of force with which to enter negotiations. At a meeting of the Dáil Cabinet, he had proposed an assault on either Beggars Bush Barracks, where the Auxiliaries were based in Dublin, or on the Customs House, the centre of local government. The Beggars Bush operation was clearly impossible, so it was decided instead to burn the Customs House, which did not have a military or police guard. Michael Collins, for one, who had seen much more of the conflict in the city up close than de Valera, tried to keep the Squad, whom he had assembled painstakingly over the previous three years, out of the attack, only to be overruled by Tom Ennis, who had been put in charge of the operation.[470]

The operation was mounted on 25 May, involving over 100 lightly armed Volunteers. It was a propaganda success for the Republicans; the building, an icon of the city designed by the famous architect James Gandon in 1781, was all but completely destroyed. It burned for three days. A watching Dubliner wrote in his diary: 'Towards midday, [the tower] took fire and spurted out flame. The copper dome held out till the afternoon, when the flames burst out underneath it and caused it to belly out like the sails of ship. Finally the sheeting gave way disclosing the pedestal of the statue of hope. Huge crowds [are] watching the fire.[471]

The *Irish Bulletin* declared:

A detachment of the Dublin Brigade of the Irish Army was ordered to carry out the destruction of the Customs House in accordance with a decision arrived at after due deliberation of the ministry of Dáil Eireann. We in common with the rest of the nation regret the destruction of historical buildings. But the lives of four million people are a more cherished charge than any architectural masterpiece.[472]

But the operation also led to the capture of over eighty IRA men and the death of five, after the Custom House was surrounded by well-armed troops and Auxiliaries (three civilians were also killed in the firing). The Squad and the Active Service Units of the Dublin IRA had to be amalgamated into a single 'Dublin Guard', such was the shortage of reliable manpower in Dublin after the affair. Nevertheless, the violence there went on. The Dublin Brigade's attacks fell from 107 in May and ninety-three in June, showing that the IRA was damaged by the losses at the Customs House, but not fatally so.[473]

The west and north

In the west, guerrilla activity took off in the spring, with successful IRA ambushes at Tourmakeady and Carrowkennedy in Mayo, but also failures such as at Kilmeena, where seven IRA members died in a failed attack on a patrol.

In the north, the IRA, the RIC and the Ulster Special Constabulary exchanged reprisals, sometimes on each other, but more often on civilians of the 'opposing' religion. In Belfast, a city in the 1920s dominated by Protestants, Catholics were regularly subjected to sectarian assault.

Along the rural Ulster borderland, the IRA and the Special Constabulary formed, in practice, rival sectarian militias. IRA leader Frank Aiken, for instance, operating in the south Armagh/northern Louth area, took a Protestant church congregation hostage at Creggan to draw a USC patrol to an ambush where one of them was killed. The local 'Specials', for their part, burned Aiken's family house and those of ten of his relatives, as well as half the Catholic village of Camlough.[474]

The village of Rosslea on the border between Fermanagh and Monaghan was similarly subjected to waves of raids and counter-raids by the IRA and the Specials, in many cases causing civilians alternately Catholic and Protestant to flee to 'safer' territory.[475]

Terror and counter-terror

By the late spring of 1921, the British forces rarely travelled in convoys of fewer than two lorries, sometimes accompanied by an armoured car. Their barracks were also by now formidably defended.

The IRA simply could not take on these forces in combat. But what they could do was take revenge for the British assassination of their men with assassinations of their own. In February 1921 in County Clare, for instance, three British soldiers were found unarmed, apparently having deserted. With little hesitation, the local IRA men shot them and dumped them on the roadside.[476]

The increasing use of executions by the British brought its own dark logic. In Cork city on 28 February, six IRA men were shot by firing squad. The following day, in a welter of shootings in the city, twelve off-duty British soldiers were shot, and six killed.[477]

Ernie O'Malley, whom we first met as a medical student turned Volunteer activist back in 1917, left us the most evocative account of these reprisal executions. By spring 1921, he was a senior figure in the IRA, in command of the First Southern Division, and based in his own little republic in the hills of Tipperary, where the British rarely ventured and never left the roads.

Three unlucky British officers fell into his hands just as the British were executing prisoners in Dublin. O'Malley informed them, 'Any officers we capture are to be shot until such time as you cease shooting your prisoners. This is not a personal question... my mind is made up about it. You are to be shot at dawn tomorrow'. He had the three shot by firing squad the following morning.[478]

In all of Ireland, the IRA, honed down to about 3,000 fighters, came under tremendous pressure through British arrests, raids, assassinations and counter-ambushes. British repression certainly took its toll on the IRA, but it also brutalised and alienated the general Irish population. After the shooting of a police inspector in Kerry in March 1921, for example, 1,000 soldiers and armed police surrounded Ballymacelligot, arrested 240 men and marched them to Tralee for questioning, where many of them got a beating for good measure.[479]

Another typical such operation was mounted in County Monaghan in late June of 1921. The local newspaper reported that over 2,000 troops, including cavalry and aircraft, 'rounded up hundreds of local men, Protestant and Catholic, Sinn Féiner and Hibernian, there was no distinction made'. In the following week another 215 men were arrested, sent to Belfast and imprisoned.[480] Such methods did get some results. The British had generally failed to penetrate the IRA with informers and develop 'covert intelligence' on the guerrillas, but they were gradually amassing, through wholesale arrests and interrogation, what they called 'overt intelligence': files of names, movements and the probable whereabouts of IRA suspects.[481]

The cost of such a policy was the alienation of much of the Irish population. Many British officers by 1921 frankly

viewed the whole population as being one of 'rebels'.
One, Major General Wimberly, remembered, 'I think I
regarded all civilians as "Shinners". It never bothered me
one bit how many houses were burnt'.[482] The extreme
unpopularity of British forces by the summer of 1921 and
the polarising effect violence could have is illustrated by a
dispute between two women, neighbours in County Cavan,
which came before Cavan Petty Sessions in July 1921. One
woman insisted on referring to the RIC as 'constables'; the
other was equally insistent on the derogatory term 'Black
and Tans'. Doubtless the latter had seen relatives or friends
dragged away by the police and their property burnt.
From this war of words the Republican-minded woman
eventually threatened her neighbour that 'she would get
the house burned over her' that night. The frightened
women fled to the nearest barracks for protection. The
woman who issued the threat was eventually fined £2.[483]
Such was the intimate nature of the conflict.

The shooting of spies and informers

In April 1921 Richard Mulcahy and IRA GHQ issued
the following General Order: 'The communication to the
Enemy of information concerning the work or personnel
of the Army or the Civil Administration of the Republic is
an offence against the life of the nation and in the ultimate
is punishable by death'.[484]

The IRA ruthlessly stamped on anyone helping
the British, shooting at least 180 civilians as 'spies and
informers'. Almost all of these shootings occurred in the
first six months of 1921 as the conflict became increasingly
brutal. Local and national newspapers filed weekly reports
of bodies dumped on the roadside with labels such as
'Convicted Spy, IRA', or 'Spies and Informers beware'. Such

killings were not gratuitous. They cut off any intelligence the state forces had. They also terrorised the IRA's enemies and emboldened their friends.

County Cork saw by far the greatest number of alleged informers killed, raising fears in the IRA command of many being shot there on flimsy evidence. Other areas such as County Mayo, on the other hand, were highly reluctant to shoot any, and County Clare saw just three such deaths. In Dublin, where violence was more tightly controlled, there were few informers shot until May and June 1921, when fifteen were shot in quick succession.[485]

Who was killed in these shootings of informers? No fewer than eighty-two were Irish ex-soldiers in the British Army – a fact constantly reiterated at the time by the authorities and the Unionist press, who suggested a concerted campaign against ex-soldiers.[486] There had, throughout the years of the Great War, been intense hostility between the Volunteers and the families of servicemen. However, the number of Irish veterans of the War was well over 100,000 and the number of these who were shot was less than 0.1 per cent of the total. Some former soldiers actually joined the IRA, famously Tom Barry; however, a considerable number were also to be found in the Auxiliaries and Black and Tans. So unless they were actually friendly, ex-soldiers were immediate targets of suspicion for the IRA when they suspected the presence of an informer, an attitude that helps to explain the over-representation of ex-soldiers among the IRA's civilian victims. Another target was tramps and travellers, who were considered to be unreliable and easily bribed.[487]

According to Tom Barry, however, the most dangerous of all were those who informed on the IRA out of conviction, believing they were British and that their loyalty was to the Empire. Barry recorded that his column shot fifteen spies: nine Catholics and six Protestants.[488] He remembered that one Protestant informer told him before his execution that he had helped the British because the King of England was the head of his Church and the IRA were fighting to drive out the Protestant religion.[489] Barry may have been misremembering the numbers, however. According to a recent study, eight out of ten informers shot by Barry's IRA Brigade in January and February 1921 alone were Protestants – well out of line with their share of the population (about 16 per cent) in West Cork.[490] Though it seems that these men were killed for their actions in aiding Crown forces rather than their religion, inevitably violence of this sort added a sectarian dimension to the war.

The question of sectarian conflict continues to be one of the most bitterly contested in the history of the struggle. In some respects, against the background of escalating conflict, some sectarian rancour was inevitable. But loyalties in Ireland were far from straightforward in 1921, and communal barriers were riddled with contradiction.

In Cork and elsewhere, where Republican property was destroyed by British forces, loyalist (in practice mostly Protestant) homes were burned in reprisal.[491] Other loyalists were forced to billet guerrilla 'flying columns'. When the IRA raided private houses for arms, they inevitably raided the Unionist, generally Protestant, houses first. If not sectarian, such actions were certainly collective reprisals on political enemies. Protestants in the south were too small a minority to form a combatant force; however, some did aid Crown forces by passing information to them. In such rural areas, where it was strong, the IRA could (had it been so inclined) have killed and driven out isolated Protestant communities. By and large, however, it did not do this. Where Protestants did help state forces though, they were targeted as 'enemies of the Republic', and there is some evidence that the IRA was more likely to shoot Protestant than Catholic alleged informers.

A particularly troubling killing for IRA GHQ was that of Mrs Lindsay, an elderly and wealthy Protestant loyalist, who was abducted after she and her chauffeur gave away an IRA ambush at Mourne Abbey in Cork, at which three Volunteers were killed and eight captured, of whom three were later hanged. In reprisal for their deaths, and despite orders to the contrary from Mulcahy in Dublin, Lindsay and her chauffeur were shot and secretly buried by the North Cork IRA Brigade.[492]

Republican ideology was officially non-sectarian, and along with Ernest Blythe, who spent the period as a clandestine Minister of Trade for the Republic, a list of Protestant separatists can easily be reeled off: Robert Barton, Minister for Agriculture; George Gilmore, a Portadown-born member of the IRA Dublin Brigade; Erskine Childers, the Republican propagandist, and so on. The fact remained, however, that on the ground, many Irish Protestants did feel a duty of loyalty to the Crown. This was particularly pronounced in Ulster, where the conflict was essentially sectarian, but also existed in places such as West Cork. And there were indeed some incidents of IRA killing which were seen by all sides as the product simply of local sectarian rancour.

In County Cavan on 12 June, twenty armed men raided the home of 79-year-old retired Protestant cleric Dean Finlay. Finlay was, depending on different reports, either shot in the head or bludgeoned to death. His house was then burnt down. Judge Brown, in the local County Sessions, remarked: 'It passes belief that Cavan men could find it in their hearts to commit such an unspeakable crime against an inoffensive, charitable and highly esteemed old gentleman... Why was he singled out for attack? One cannot come to any other conclusion than that behind the trigger was a feeling of sectarian animosity'.[493]

Incidents like the Finlay killing were all the more shocking, however, because they were so rare. The incident was condemned by local Republicans and the Catholic clergy. Nevertheless, such incidents also demonstrate the gathering pace of brutalisation the conflict was causing.

The young leaders of the IRA, increasingly hardened by guerrilla warfare, showed little tolerance for political dissent from the Republican struggle, regardless of religious affiliation, and targets included rival nationalists on occasion, as well as loyalists. The great majority of people shot by the IRA as informers were in fact Catholics.

In Belfast, the IRA targeted Hibernians, with whom they still vied for the support of the Catholic population, in numerous beatings, arson attacks and shootings. In Monaghan, Eoin O'Duffy executed at least two Hibernians on rather flimsy charges of spying; many others had their homes raided. Nine Hibernians were killed in Ulster by the IRA.[494]

However, the single-minded ruthlessness that was growing within the IRA could have had dangerous consequences for the Protestant minority. Ernie O'Malley and Liam Lynch, commanders of the IRA in Munster, after discussing the issue of collaborators and informers in a rural dugout in June 1921, decided that 'The people of this country would have to give allegiance to it, or if they wanted to support the Empire, they would have to clear out and support the Empire elsewhere'.[495] In May 1921 Liam Lynch proposed to Richard Mulcahy that with the British stepping up executions of their men, the IRA should shoot a local loyalist in response to each execution. While there is no indication that Lynch meant this proposal to be sectarian, the fact was that most of those identified as 'loyalists' in Lynch's command area in Cork were Protestants. The proposal, if implemented, would have seen dozens of civilians, many of them inevitably from the Protestant minority, shot by the IRA. Perhaps fortunately, Mulcahy rejected the proposal.[496]

An abrupt end

Such a hardening of attitudes may eventually have brought the conflict to much greater depths of brutality than it actually reached. However, in July 1921 it came to an abrupt halt.

Whether the guerrilla campaign would have broken British will or been crushed remains a contentious issue. A captured IRA report of May 1921 indeed highlighted the organisation's weakness. It was down to 2,000 active fighters in the field, who possessed between them no more than 569 rifles and 477 revolvers with a mere twenty rifle rounds per weapon.[497] Though efforts were underway to import weapons and ammunition, including a batch of Thompson sub-machine guns which arrived in July, there is no doubt that by the summer of 1921 the IRA was fatally short of ammunition, and its military capacity was diminishing. Its resolve, however, was not, and it was already showing signs of adapting to the new conditions by increased use of explosives. In May and June 1921, for instance, the Cork Brigades killed seven military bandsmen with a bomb at Youghal, and two Auxiliaries with a mine near Banteer. A train bringing cavalry to a parade by King George V in Belfast to open the new Northern Ireland Parliament was bombed near Newry, killing four soldiers, two drivers and sixty-three horses. As outlined above, some (including Liam Lynch, head of the Second Southern Division) contemplated the systematic killing of civilian enemies in reprisal for escalating executions of Republicans. The IRA could perhaps not have kept up the classic 'flying column' tactics through late 1921, but they could certainly have ramped up assassinations, bombings, kidnappings and targeting of hostile civilians.

The British military asserted that they were on the verge of putting down the guerrillas. Their official report of their Dublin command on the 'Irish Rebellion' argued that by July 'the rebels had again begun to realise how hopeless was force. They had been driven to resort from one method to another and in the final stages to adopt the least dangerous methods to themselves'. Nevertheless, the same report concluded that 'we were compelled to remain on the defensive... [owing to] congestion of prisoners and later through lack of troops'.[498] General Macready, the overall commander of the British military in Ireland, told the Cabinet that it was time to 'go all out' – deploy twenty more battalions, declare martial law all over the country, have up to one hundred executions per month, and to intern tens of thousands of suspects – or 'get out'.[499] But even if they had done this, it would have been at the price of permanently alienating most of the population. Macready himself argued that a policy of military repression did not guarantee any long-term settlement, as support for British rule in southern Ireland was dead. Moreover, British public opinion would not accept it. The Labour Party, an increasing force in British politics since the extension of the franchise in 1918, had been highly critical of repression in Ireland, as had much of the press, and supportive of Irish self-determination. There was little appetite in Britain for a war of extermination in Ireland. For all of these reasons, after several months of backchannel talks, a truce was agreed for 11 July 1921.

On 9 July 1921 a Dublin Volunteer, Paddy O'Connor, made his way to the hills around Donohill, South Tipperary. He was a messenger, and had come all the way from Dublin with an urgent message for Ernie O'Malley, the second-in-command of the IRA's Second Southern Division: the Republican Army had been reorganised into divisions to make it more decentralised and thus more difficult to decapitate. When O'Malley returned to his safe house, O'Connor, who had refused to discuss his business with any of O'Malley's subordinates, handed him a message from Richard Mulcahy, IRA Chief of Staff. It read: 'In view of the conversations now being entered into by our Government with the Government of Great Britain, and in pursuance of mutual conversations, active operations by our forces will be suspended as from noon, Monday, 11 July'.

O'Malley wrote later that he was 'bewildered' by the order. The first senior IRA officers had heard of the truce was this 'bald message'. Nevertheless, he had orders typed out and sent to the five IRA Brigades under his command across Munster.[500]

In many places, the IRA had a final crack at their enemies just before the truce came into effect. On 10 July, just a day before the truce that ended the war, the Bailieboro Volunteers in County Cavan, who had done little enough during the conflict, attacked the RIC barracks in that town, which was thirty strong, armed only with shotguns. The attack was beaten off, with two IRA wounded and two more captured.[501] In County Cork, in the twenty-four hours before noon on 11 July, the IRA ambushed two military parties and shot two policemen and one suspected informer. Four off-duty soldiers were also snatched in Cork city and found on the morning of the truce, lying blindfolded in a field, shot in the head.[502]

In neighbouring Kerry, nine men (four British soldiers and five IRA Volunteers) died in a bloody gun battle in the village of Castleisland on the morning of 11 July.[503]

In Belfast, the day before the truce was a day of carnage, known at the time as 'Belfast's Bloody Sunday'. Loyalists, incensed by an IRA ambush in the city the previous day, attacked the Catholic enclaves in the centre and west of the city. Loyalist groups, the police and IRA blazed away at each other from rooftops, windows and street corners with rifles, machine guns and grenades. By the time the day was out, 16 civilians were dead and 161 houses destroyed. The sectarian body count was heavily in the Protestants' favour – 11 Catholics for 5 Protestants and 150 Catholic houses destroyed for 11 Protestant.[504]

For all that, as of noon on Monday, 11 July, most of the guns did indeed fall silent. Ernie O'Malley concluded his memoir of those years: 'And so for us ended what we called "the scrap"; the people "the trouble" and others, fond of labels, "the revolution"'.[505] The conflict was also variously called at the time the 'Terror' by the British military, the 'Irish Rebellion', and later the 'Anglo-Irish War' or the 'Irish War of Independence'. But the revolution, as O'Malley well knew, was not over; it was simply entering another phase.

The cost

The conflict, if we take it from the start of 1917 up to December 1921, had produced 2,141 fatalities.[506] Of these, the vast majority were inflicted in south Munster, above all in County Cork, and elsewhere deaths were concentrated in the cities of Dublin and Belfast. County Cork had some 495 killed and another 513 wounded.[507] Dublin had seen 309 people lose their lives, and in Belfast, long ignored in the history of the conflict, over 200 were killed, though its troubles were not over. At the other end of the spectrum, County Wicklow saw only seven people killed and County Cavan only ten.[508]

Of the dead, 467 were IRA Volunteers, of whom another 4,500 were interned and over 2,000 more convicted and imprisoned.[509] Another 514 were police (from the DMP, RIC, Black and Tans, Auxiliaries and Ulster Special Constabulary) and 262 were British soldiers.[510] The civilian cost was 898 killed, of whom 281 were killed by the IRA, 381 by Crown forces, and another 236 in the crossfire, in rioting, or by loyalist groups in the North.[511]

The majority of the dead were not killed in battle, but assassinated or executed, either by the state forces or the guerrillas. At the time, neither side was exactly sure how to describe what was happening. The British Army's official history called it 'a strange atmosphere between war and peace'.[512] A Republican, Todd Andrews, thought it was not a war but 'terror and tyranny tempered by assassination'.[513]

While the mythologising of the heroes of the guerrilla struggle had already begun even before the war was over, many areas were relieved to have been spared the full brunt of 'the Terror'. Paul Galligan, when released from prison in late 1921, told a rally in Cavan that while he 'regretted it has been said of Cavan that that it did not take its place in the fighting movement... [it] might have been for the best'.[514]

The incidence of violence, however, which had its own dynamics of retaliation and revenge, should not be confused with the intensity of nationalist sentiment, or even politicisation, in a given locality. County Cavan, which had the second-lowest number of dead of any county, had one of the highest rates of Sinn Féin membership, was one of the first to elect Sinn Féin MPs and one of the first places to institute the Dáil Courts.

The total casualties of the war were, in comparison with other conflicts that followed the First World War, fairly modest. However, it is not only in raw statistics that the impact of the conflict should be measured. Localities where fatalities were relatively low had still lived in terror due to state forces kicking in doors and dragging away suspects, or from hooded IRA men at night looking for 'spies and informers'. Hundreds of houses and businesses were burned, and thousands of people had to flee their homes after threats from one side or the other.

The *Dundalk Democrat* (which had remained loyal to the Irish Parliamentary Party), wrote in mid-1921, just after the truce:

> From January to June [1921] over a thousand human lives were taken in the prosecution of the night-time war. Some of the victims were men who took their lives in their hands as combatants. Many were harmless and innocent people... Men were shot down on the country roads, in city streets, in their homes, in railway trains, on the threshold of the house of God. Every such shooting was the prelude to a bloody reprisal... In such conditions, mere suspicion seals many a death warrant. Nor is it improbable that private vengeance exacted its toll under the cover of civil turmoil.[515]

Unlike the Rising of 1916, the War of Independence saw much violence that was difficult to mythologise. The British military rarely, as it did in 1916, voiced any respect for the insurgents of 1919–21, who, it alleged, had carried out an 'unmanly' and cowardly 'murder campaign'. On the Irish side, great publicity was generated with those engagements which could show the IRA as an Irish Army taking on an occupier, such as those at Crossbarry and Kilmichael – but such incidents were not typical of its operations. And yet, quite unlike the Easter Rising, the armed campaign of 1920–21 was highly effective in destabilising British rule, in preventing attempts to put down the separatist movement and in avoiding defeat.

By late 1921 the fighting had mostly ceased. It was now time for hard negotiations, the results of which would eventually set off another phase of armed conflict.

Chapter 8:

Truce, Treaty and Border War

On the ground, nobody thought at the beginning that the truce would be permanent. In Monaghan, one Volunteer later admitted to mixed feelings. 'To say that we were jubilant would be untrue. It was more bewilderment. Through the years of struggle, the hangings and executions and sufferings had generated in us something unchristian. Our lust to kill had not been satisfied'.[516]

However, for all their misgivings, it was the IRA that benefited most from the cessation of hostilities. New Volunteers flooded into its ranks. It was given official recognition, the ability to train in public and given the status – effectively if not in theory – of a national Army. Throughout the second half of 1921, negotiations took place between British and Irish teams in London for a final settlement.

The Treaty negotiations

Éamon de Valera, the President of the Irish Republic, engaged in preliminary negotiations with the British, but decided not to take part in the final talks that would thrash out a settlement. Perhaps, as has often been alleged, he did not want to take responsibility for a settlement short of the

Republic. His thinking was as follows: 'We will have proposals brought back to us [the Cabinet] that cannot satisfy everybody... when such a time comes, I will be in a position... to come forward with such proposals as we think just and right'.[517]

In his place he sent Michael Collins as head of the Irish negotiating team. With him went Arthur Griffith, founder of the Sinn Féin movement, Eamon Duggan, Charles Gavan Duffy and Robert Barton. Erskine Childers went as secretary to the delegation.

Collins was not keen on leading the negotiating team, citing both his lack of experience in matters of state and his vulnerability in exposing himself should hostilities resume. In spite of this, Collins followed the orders of his 'Chief' and went to London. It was a decision that de Valera would later have cause to regret.

The negotiations that led to the Treaty essentially concerned three vital points. First, the unity of Ireland; second, the degree of independence an Irish government would have; and third, the relationship of an Irish state to the British Empire.

The first of these points had already been decided before negotiations started. Northern Ireland, limited to the six north-eastern counties of Ireland with a Protestant and Unionist majority, was up and running by late 1921. By the time of the Treaty negotiations, the partition of Ireland was therefore an established fact and no longer up for negotiation. Thus the Unionists, under James Craig, did not even take part in the Treaty talks. Northern Ireland as a whole was given the option of uniting with the southern state after a year.

There would also be a 'Boundary Commission' set up to arbitrate on how the border could be changed to reflect the wishes of the local population. It was the hope of the

Irish delegation that Northern Ireland's viability would eventually be undermined by the defection of much of its Catholic-populated western and southern territory to the southern state. Nevertheless, the Treaty confirmed the partition of Ireland in the short term.[518]

Perhaps more important to the Irish delegation, which was almost entirely composed of southerners, was the question of the independence of the southern state. The British had determined ahead of the talks that they would not grant the Irish an independent republic. Nor would the new state be allowed to secede completely from the British Commonwealth.[519] The British would retain three deep-water naval ports: Lough Swilly in the north, and Berehaven and Cobh in the south. Irish citizens retained the right to appeal to the British High Court.

The symbolic head of the state would be the British monarch, to whom elected representatives would have to swear an Oath of Allegiance and who would be represented in Ireland by a Governor General. The British also made sure that the new state would have what they considered a responsible administration by insisting on the retention of the existing civil service and committing the Irish to pay the pensions of those, such as the RIC police, who were dispensed with.

Outside of these areas, the British conceded quite a lot – making the southern Irish state much more independent than the Northern one. The Irish were given leave to choose any name short of 'republic', for their state. What Collins came up with was the 'Irish Free State', taken from the Irish-language term 'Saorstáit' which the nationalist movement had been using.[520] British troops were to be withdrawn from the country, which was to have its own armed forces and a new police force. It was also to have full control over its fiscal policy, tariffs and customs.

These terms were a considerable improvement on either the Home Rule Bill of 1912, or the 1920 Government of Ireland Act in terms of Irish independence. Nevertheless, they were still far from the independent Irish Republic. The Irish team was divided. Childers and Barton later ended up fighting against the Treaty, and Childers died for his opposition.

The negotiating team brought back the terms for the Dáil Cabinet's perusal on 3 December 1921. In a bad-tempered all-day meeting, Cathal Brugha, the Minister for Defence, all but accused Collins and Griffith of treachery; 'the British government selected its men', he remarked acidly. De Valera told the negotiators that he might have been willing to compromise on either Irish unity or on unconditional independence, but 'you have got neither this nor that'. The meeting was brought to an end when Griffith proposed that they should not sign the document in London but bring it back for the Dáil to vote on its acceptance.[521]

Late that evening, the negotiating team sailed back to Britain, but so divided were they that they took different boats; Barton, Childers and Duffy leaving via Dublin's North Wall, with Collins, Griffith and Duggan sailing from Kingstown (Dun Laoghaire).

But back in London on 4 December, Lloyd George told them that it was either immediate signature or war, and that he had to know by the next day. Lloyd George's threat may have been bluff – he was under pressure from his shaky coalition of Liberals and Conservatives – but it worked. Collins and Griffith impressed on Barton, the last dissenter, that if he did not sign, he alone would be responsible for 'Irish homes laid waste and the youth of Ireland butchered'. Barton caved in at about 11 p.m. on 5 December 1921. The Treaty was signed in the early morning of 6 December 1921.[522]

In an oft-repeated exchange, F. E. Smith, Lord Birkenhead, one of the British negotiators, told Collins, 'I may have signed my political death warrant'. 'I may have signed my actual death warrant', Collins replied.[523] Nine months later he was dead.

Debating the Treaty

The Irish team brought back an already-signed Treaty to the Dáil for them to approve or reject, but with the threat of war looming should they take the latter option. De Valera was furious that the negotiators had signed the deal without first consulting him or his Cabinet, as had been his plan. However, his actual position remained somewhat vague, proposing that the Free State would have 'external association' rather than membership of the British Commonwealth. 'We are not Republican doctrinaires', he had told the Dáil in August 1921.[524]

After a stormy debate, the Dáil narrowly passed the Treaty on 7 January 1922, by sixty-four votes to fifty-seven. The pro-Treaty case was almost purely pragmatic. The Treaty was the best that could be obtained in the circumstances. Collins defended the Treaty as a 'stepping stone' to ultimate independence. Eoin MacNeill, who had led the calls for the foundation of the Irish Volunteers back in 1913, maintained, 'it is just as unpalatable to me as it is to the most uncompromising man here, I do not like a single item of it'.[525] Ernest Blythe, similarly, was initially a reluctant supporter of the settlement.

Only Arthur Griffith, the founder of the original Sinn Féin party, defended the Treaty on its merits, arguing that 'we have brought back the flag, we have brought back the evacuation of Ireland after 700 years by British troops and the formation of an Irish Army. We have brought back to Ireland her full rights of fiscal control'.[526] Regarding partition, Collins argued that the Treaty 'will lead very rapidly to goodwill and the entry of the north-east under the Irish Parliament'.[527] The other key aspect of the pro-Treaty case was that 'the people' wanted peace and the Treaty and 'the will of the people' must be respected.

On the other side, the admission of British sovereignty over Ireland, even in symbolic form, was too much for some to take. Mary MacSwiney, sister of Terence MacSwiney, the late Mayor of Cork who had died on hunger strike in protest against his imprisonment by the British, asked the Dáil 'in the name of the dead to unite against this Treaty and let us take the consequences'. Liam Mellows asserted, 'The delegates had no right to sign away the rights of Ireland and the Irish republic'[528].

Southern Unionists generally supported the Treaty without enthusiasm as a means of restoring law and order. Some, however, remained opposed to Irish self-rule. Edward Carson, who had hoped to use Ulster Unionist muscle to block Home Rule back in 1912, declared, 'I never thought I would live to see a day of such abject humiliation for Great Britain'.[529]

On the Treaty's ratification, de Valera resigned as President of the Republic and failed to be re-elected by a vote of sixty to fifty-eight. Two other Cabinet members, Cathal Brugha and Austin Stack, also resigned in protest. A provisional government headed by Michael Collins and Arthur Griffith was set up to transfer power from the British administration to the Irish Free State. Over the following nine months, they attempted to create the nascent institutions of the new state around an uneasy balance of the old British regime and elements of the revolutionary Republican 'counter-state' built up in 1918–21.

The IRA split

Much has always been made of the part played by de Valera in helping to ignite the Civil War, and certainly his subsequent actions were divisive, even irresponsible. However, he was not, and had never been, in control of the armed Republican guerrillas. It was the IRA, above all, who could impede, accept, or perhaps enforce the birth of the new state. Since the truce of July 1921, the IRA had been massively expanded, from about 3,000 fighters up to 72,000 by early 1922. Training camps had sprung up around the country, more arms imported and military demonstrations had been performed for the benefit of the world's press.

With British troops confined to barracks and the old RIC officially disbanded as of August 1922 (but in reality defunct much earlier), the IRA was in effective occupation of the country, providing what law and order there was in early 1922. Within this force, it was the influence of a small cadre of officers, the most committed and the most active during the War of Independence, who would determine whether the IRA as a whole would accept or reject the Treaty.

Collins took most of his IRA headquarters staff, including their chief Richard Mulcahy, with him. The Dublin IRA was split, but many of the most experienced and ruthless fighters, the old 'Squad' and the Active Service Units, which had done most of the urban guerrilla work in the capital and were now grouped together in the 'Dublin Guard', accepted the Treaty out of personal loyalty to Michael Collins. Similarly, the IRA in Longford followed Seán MacEoin to the Free State side, as did much of the Clare IRA under Michael Brennan and Eoin O'Duffy's Monaghan Brigade. Some activists, for instance Seán O'Hegarty and Florrie O'Donoghue in Cork, opposed the Treaty but ultimately refused to take up arms against the new Irish Government. Paul Galligan, as TD for Cavan, voted for the Treaty but later, bitterly disillusioned by the infighting over the Treaty, withdrew from politics and from the IRA altogether.

The Irish Republican Brotherhood was split by the Treaty, with senior members such as Liam Lynch and Liam Mellows coming out against it. However, Collins and Mulcahy, along with Eoin O'Duffy and Seán O'Muirthile, controlled the Supreme Council of the IRB, which was an important factor in having the Treaty accepted. Cathal Brugha alleged that up to forty TDs voted for the Treaty as result of their IRB affiliation.[530] Seamus McKenna, a Belfast IRA man, for instance, supported the Treaty as a result of the advice of his IRB centre, Pat Casey. He later regretted this choice and pondered, 'I am sure that many other IRB men accepted that ill-fated Treaty on the advice of their officers in that organisation'.[531]

The northern IRA, despite the Treaty copper-fastening partition in the short term, paradoxically went pro-Treaty, with the exception of Belfast commander Joe McKelvey. This was mainly a result of Collins having made the partition issue his own, through his public championing of the northerners' cause and arming of the IRA in the six counties. He also seems to have assured them that partition would be temporary. However, a great swathe of the country south of a line from Waterford to Limerick was occupied by IRA units who rejected what they saw as the betrayal of the Republican ideal. Among them were many of the most dedicated and effective guerrilla leaders. Ernie O'Malley remembered his reaction to the Treaty: 'I cursed long and loud, so this was what we had fought and died for, what we had worn ourselves out for during the truce'.[532] Another IRA man, Todd Andrews, on reading of the Oath of Allegiance, ports being retained by the

British and the Irish state 'paying the pensions of the hated RIC', 'thought there must be something wrong with the newspaper report, Collins would never have agreed to this'. He felt sick 'with rage and disappointment'.[533] Tom Barry, whose flying column in West Cork had been perhaps the most effective in the War of Independence, also rejected it.

These IRA commanders were young and had been forged on the anvil of guerrilla war between 1919 and 1921. O'Malley, for instance, aged 25 in 1922, had dropped out of university to join the Movement in 1917. He had been a full-time organiser for the IRA, had killed and seen friends killed, had been captured and beaten, but had escaped from British custody. For him the world was still black and white; he later wrote in his memoirs that there was 'a certain hardness in our idealism, it made us aloof from ordinary living as if we were above it'.[534] As Mary MacSwiney put it in the Treaty debates, 'it is not a matter of war or peace, but of right or wrong'.[535] The women of Cumann na mBan were, indeed, more than any other Republican organisation, almost unanimous in rejecting the Treaty. Such men and women would accept no compromise short of the 'Republic'. The purist Republicans were not ideologically sophisticated, and expressed themselves badly politically, but their conviction was simple enough. They had fought for an Irish Republic, sworn an oath to uphold it and would never again accept the sovereignty of a British king.

From January to July 1922, there existed side by side two parallel armies in the country. One was the National Army, built around the pro-Treaty IRA loyal to the government in Dublin, being slowly armed and uniformed through the British. The other, the anti-Treaty IRA, occupied much of the provinces and supported itself with compulsory levies on the civilian population, which were often much resented, and sometimes by robberies of banks and post offices.[536]

In March 1922 the anti-Treaty IRA officers held an Army Convention in the Mansion House in Dublin, in which they repudiated the right of the Dáil to abolish the Republic. They went on to elect their own sixteen-man Army Executive, led by Rory O'Connor, who had been the IRA's Head of Engineering, and Liam Mellows, who had led the Easter Rising in Galway back in 1916. Emerging from the Mansion House, having proposed a military council as temporary head of government, O'Connor was asked by a journalist if this meant 'we are to have a military dictatorship?' O'Connor replied gruffly, 'You can take it that way if you want'.[537]

Pro-Treaty invective at the time, and a trend in recent historical writing, has been to paint the anti-Treaty IRA as anti-democratic militarists.[538] No doubt there is some truth in this; they were to show little respect for democratic norms in the months ahead. When Michael Collins and his supporters tried to organise rallies in favour of the Treaty around the country in the spring of 1922, they faced harassment, threats and at times attacks from anti-Treaty Volunteers. On the other hand, the anti-Treaty IRA never proposed to overthrow Irish democracy, nor did they, Rory O'Connor's intemperate remark notwithstanding, put forward an authoritarian alternative.[539] Rather, what they argued in early 1922 was that the people had been 'stampeded' into accepting the Treaty by fear of the British threat of war and that there could be no real democratic decision until the British threat of force had been removed. Far from joining the contemporary European fashion for authoritarian nationalist movements, many of the anti-Treatyites of 1922 went on to participate in and then run the democratic institutions of the Irish state in the following years. In any case, whatever militaristic tendencies existed in the anti-Treaty IRA, there were no plans for a military coup. Todd Andrews, for one, thought, 'I did not see anything wrong with an IRA military dictatorship... but it began to appear that the IRA leadership had not merely not envisaged a dictatorship but had not considered any alternative policy'.[540] It is more helpful to see the anti-Treatyites as impatient young men and women (few were over 30), flushed with the belief that they had taken on the British Empire and fought it to a standstill. 'The People' might be celebrated when they provided aid for the guerrillas, but sometimes they needed a good hard shove back onto the true path of revolutionary Republicanism. Ernie O'Malley summed up this attitude best: 'If we had consulted the people in the first place, we would never have fired a shot, give them a good strong lead and they will follow'.[541]

January–June 1922: Settling old scores and new ones

British forces began evacuating from the south of Ireland in early 1922. In Cork, they not only took down the Union Jack, but sawed down the flagpole to prevent the hoisting of the rebel tricolour in its place.[542]

The IRA, by now much more numerous and better armed than it had been during hostilities, triumphantly took over the British posts. In several places, the newly ascendant guerrillas had a final go at the departing British forces. In Ennistymon in Clare, the RIC threw a grenade at a taunting crowd, wounding six people, but were immediately penned back inside their barracks by rifle fire from enraged IRA men. Two Black and Tans were later seized and shot.[543] In Tralee in Kerry, a shooting incident led to hundreds of well-armed IRA fighters besieging the police in their barracks with a storm of bullets.[544]

Elsewhere, several ex-RIC men were hunted down and killed – old scores were being settled with the police – in the early months of 1922. In addition, the period that we know as 'the truce' saw the killing of many informers. In Cork in April, thirteen men – all Protestants – were killed around Dunmanway after the shooting of an IRA officer by a local loyalist. Debate continues to rage over whether this was a straightforward sectarian reprisal or whether the dead had already been on a Republican blacklist as informers.[545] Between January and June, twenty-three RIC men, eight British soldiers and at least eighteen civilians were killed in southern Ireland by the IRA.[546]

Mere anarchy?

In the same few days as the killings in West Cork, other elements of the IRA carried out two major robberies elsewhere in the country. At Clonmel, County Tipperary, armed men seized the Customs and Excise duties, and at Leixlip in Kildare a paymaster of the Great Western Railway was held up and robbed of £1,839.[547] A total of 323 Post Offices had been held up in the previous month.[548] Taken together, this indicates the degree to which IRA units on the ground were out of the control of civilian authorities in the months leading up to the outbreak of civil war.

One anecdote told by Todd Andrews is especially revealing of the lack of restraints on IRA men in these months. Andrews recalled that he, Ernie O'Malley and Seán MacBride, all IRA officers in Dublin, 'commandeered' a car 'from some harmless citizen', and went for a spin in the mountains, where they practised some pistol shooting. Back in the city, they accidentally careered into a British troop tender. The car was a 'write-off', and the three soldiers of the Republic mingled into the crowds when the British produced a machine gun. 'Such', Andrews remembered, 'was our thinking at the time'.[549]

Elsewhere, in the absence of effective state authority, social conflicts took on a violent intensity. Late 1921 saw a revolt all across the north midlands by farmers who had not purchased their land in previous Land Acts. It began on the Portland Estate in County Monaghan, property of one Captain Maxwell, where tenants demanded an 85 per cent reduction of rents and warned of 'defensive action' if their offer was rejected, or there was any attempt to collect rent. By late February the rent strike had spread to dozens of estates across Counties Monaghan, Longford and Cavan.[550] While the same farmers' unions voted to approve the passing of the Treaty, it was also clear that they expected Irish independence to mean the end of landlordism. They argued that 'each person should get an equal chance in a free Ireland to compete for a decent living at least', and called on the Dáil to 'make completion of land purchase the first act of the Irish parliament'.[551] In the rural west and north midlands, attacks on landlords and 'ranchers' spiralled.

At the same time, while one type of rural class conflict (farmers against landlords) threatend to boil over, so did another kind: farmers against labourers. The context to this unrest was an international economic recession, in which the value of agricultural exports had fallen by as much as 50 per cent. In Leitrim it was reported that 1922 was the 'worst year for farmers since '47 [the famine year]'. In that county £20,000 in rates went uncollected.[552] Farmers' falling profits meant downward pressures on labourers' wages, leading, in the absence of effective policing, to a potentially murderous series of disputes. The Monaghan Farmers' Union reported that 'the farmer goes to work with a revolver in one hand for the time to come'. In the south, 'houses have been burnt, farm produce has been burnt'. The farmers urged the new Irish Government to 'fight their battles for them'. 'Farmers may have to fight labour', they warned.[553] In an echo of 1920, 'Soviets' were formed around the country as workers protested against falling wages. In the south-east, workers occupied agricultural co-operatives and raised the red flag.[554]

Particularly vulnerable to the breakdown of law and order was the southern Protestant minority, whether because of their religion, their political allegiances, or their relative wealth. A deputation of panicked southern loyalists told Winston Churchill that 'the last relic of government had collapsed and there was no effective police, it was possible for any man who was armed to rob whom he pleases... there is nothing to prevent the peasants expropriating every Protestant and every loyalist'.[555]

However, at the same time that class conflict was sharpening, the link between the Republicans and labour, forged in 1917–18, was being broken. In April 1922, in protest at the IRA's rejection of the vote of the Dáil, the unions, which had declared general strikes against the British in 1918 and 1920, called one against 'militarism' (understood to mean primarily the anti-Treatyites). Only a small rump of socialists led by James Connolly's son Roddy, in the newly formed Communist Party of Ireland, publicly backed the Republicans.[556]

The anti-Treaty units of the IRA were by now mounting, if not yet a military campaign against the new government, then certainly armed defiance of it. In February 1922 Ernie O'Malley seized the RIC barracks in Clonmel, taking forty policemen prisoner and carrying off 600 rifles and thousands of rounds of ammunition. In an even more flagrant breach of the truce, on 29 March an IRA unit under Seán Hegarty raided the British warship

Upnor, which was docked off Cork, again taking a large quantity of arms and ammunition. Rory O'Connor had the newspaper the *Freeman's Journal* closed for its pro-Treaty stance, and Seamus Robinson did the same with the *Clonmel Nationalist*. In Cork city, the *Cork Examiner* was merely censored.

In March, fighting almost broke out over whether pro- or anti-Treaty troops would occupy Limerick. Bloodshed between 700 fighters was narrowly averted when the city's mayor brokered a deal in which each side would occupy two of the four vacated British Army barracks.[557] Similar standoffs took place in various other barracks all around the country, including Athlone, where a pro-Treaty Brigadier General, Adamson (a veteran of both the First World War and of the IRA in the war against the British), was shot dead by anti-Treaty Volunteers[558].

Mossie Hartnett, an IRA Volunteer in West Limerick, recalled that after the split over the Treaty 'it was difficult to keep the peace between our troops and the... Free Staters'. The latter he described as 'poor needy labourers and ex-British soldiers' who were 'paid their keep of 25 shillings a week'.[559] The Republicans' contrast between themselves, the Volunteer soldiers and the slum-dwelling mercenaries of the Free State Army was to be an enduring theme.

Most seriously of all, the anti-Treaty IRA was challenging the government's authority in its own capital. On 14 April, around 200 IRA men under Rory O'Connor occupied the Four Courts in central Dublin, centre of the Irish legal system, as well as several other public buildings. The same week there were prolonged gun attacks in the city on government soldiers stationed at the Provisional Government headquarters in Merrion Square, the Bank of Ireland on College Green, the telephone exchange,

City Hall, and various barracks, in which eight people were wounded.[560]

On 2 May Republicans took over the centre of Kilkenny, including the city's barracks and the medieval castle. Collins hastily dispatched 200 government troops by train from Dublin to dislodge them, provoking a day of fighting in the city centre before a truce was reached with, again, each side agreeing to garrison different posts.[561] By the end of May, eight combatants had been killed in clashes between pro- and anti-Treaty IRA fighters, and forty-nine had been injured.[562]

At one level, therefore, the coming civil war was simply the inevitable effort of the Free State to put down the disparate armed groups that opposed it and to establish itself as the monopoly on armed force within its territory. No state hoping to be viable could have acted any differently. However, what gave the conflict a wider resonance was the backing of a considerable sector of the nationalist elite for what the Provisional Government termed the 'Irregulars'. In the spring of 1922, Éamon de Valera went on a speaking tour of Republican-held Munster, in which he made two notorious speeches often interpreted as incitements to civil war. On 17 March in Dungarvan, he said: 'If the Treaty were accepted, the fight for freedom would still go on, and the Irish people, instead of fighting foreign soldiers, will have to fight the Irish soldiers of an Irish government set up by Irishmen'. At Thurles, several days later, he added that the IRA 'would have to wade through the blood of the soldiers of the Irish Government, and perhaps through that of some members of the Irish Government to get their freedom'.[563]

In spite of such violent rhetoric, de Valera's position was to remain hard to pin down. The anti-Treaty IRA recognised only their own executive as a legitimate authority and, while they respected de Valera as a symbolic leader, they never took orders from him. De Valera himself had, moreover, indicated a willingness to accept a settlement short of the Republic, making him suspect in the eyes of the true believers. His speeches should therefore be read partly as an attempt to regain his influence over the young men with guns.

To the beleaguered Collins and Griffith in Dublin, it was apparent that the country was teetering on the verge of civil war, or perhaps mere anarchy. At the same time, the British, with around 6,000 troops still stationed in Dublin, were pressuring the Provisional Government to establish control, by force if necessary, over their territory. Griffith argued from the start for the removal of the anti-Treaty units occupying the Four Courts in central Dublin. Collins, who remained at heart a Republican conspirator, opted instead for conciliation of the hardliners.

Ernest Blythe, a member of the Cabinet, recalled:

> ...incidents of all sorts occurred which indicated that a civil war was steadily becoming next thing to inevitable. Griffith seemed to me to have made up his mind at a comparatively early stage that the conflict was ineluctable. Collins was much slower in coming to such a conclusion. Occasionally, when some incident occurred which made him angry, he indicated that he was prepared to fight those who were challenging the majority decision, but in a day or two he would cool off.[564]

On 3 May, the day after the fighting in Kilkenny, a truce was arranged between pro- and anti-Treaty IRA factions. Collins, in tandem with Liam Lynch (now the anti-Treaty IRA's Chief of Staff), organised an 'Army Reunification

Committee' with the intention of healing the breach caused by the Treaty. The supposedly reunified Army was temporarily diverted into a murky and short-lived assault on Northern Ireland. Collins agreed with Liam Lynch that IRA units would be moved to the border and rearmed with weapons from the government stockpile.[565]

Northern Ireland, January–June 1922

Northern Ireland, created in mid-1920, had its existence confirmed under the Treaty, effectively as a homeland for the Ulster Protestant Unionists within the United Kingdom. In theory, Northern Ireland was given the option of a year to decide if it wanted to be incorporated into the Free State, but as all parties knew, the Unionists had no intention of doing this. More hope was placed in the Border Commission, which was to redraw the border in accordance with the wishes of local populations and was expected to hand over large, nationalist areas of Northern Ireland to the southern state.

However, one thing about which both pro- and anti-Treaty wings of the IRA could agree was that partition of Ireland was unacceptable. For this reason, the leadership of both the Provisional Government under Michael Collins, and of the anti-Treaty IRA under Liam Lynch, co-operated in attacking the Northern state in early 1922.

The truce had never really applied in the North. The day before its coming into force, Belfast had its own 'Bloody Sunday' where sixteen people died in clashes along the sectarian 'frontier' in the west of the city and 161 houses were destroyed. The main victims of the violence in the Northern conflict were invariably civilians of the 'opposing' religion. Out of over 500 people killed in the North between 1920 and 1922, only twelve were IRA volunteers and eighty members of the State forces.[566]

Violence there had died down a little in the autumn of 1921, but flared up again that December, when power over security was transferred to James Craig and the Northern Ireland Government. In early 1922 there were numerous clashes along the new border. An IRA party posing as Monaghan Gaelic footballers were arrested in Derry, and, in reprisal, Eoin O'Duffy had forty prominent Unionists abducted and held in Athlone in southern territory as security for the lives of the IRA prisoners. In February, four Ulster Special Constables were killed in a gun battle after crossing in a train into southern territory at Clones. Almost forty people died in the two days of ferocious street fighting that followed in the Catholic slums of west and central Belfast. Six of the dead were Catholic schoolchildren killed by a bomb thrown into a school playground by loyalist paramilitaries.[567] By April the local press in Cavan and Monaghan was reporting that farm work along the border was at a standstill due to the fighting, and that Protestants were fleeing north – and Catholics south – of the new border.[568]

Perhaps the most disturbing feature of the violence, from the point of view of the northern Catholic minority, was the role of Northern Irish state forces in it. In one week between March and April, there were two instances of a police 'murder gang' randomly targeting Catholics in reprisal for the deaths of policemen. On 23 March, uniformed policemen all but wiped out the male members of the McMahon family (they missed one adolescent boy) in revenge for the shooting of two of their colleagues. Owen McMahon, a prosperous publican, had no connection with the IRA and was in fact an Irish Parliamentary Party supporter.[569]

A week later, what was probably the same group – constables from Brown Street Barracks – broke into houses along Arnon Street and killed six more Catholics at random.[570] Unsurprisingly, in Belfast Catholic folk memory, the period is known as the 'pogrom'. The picture of defenceless Catholics being shot down by fascistic sectarian police is not the full story, however. The IRA in the north killed hundreds of Protestant civilians in reprisal attacks. Trams taking Protestant workers to the shipyards, from where the Catholics had been driven out in 1920, were bombed.[571] Frank Aiken, commander of the IRA in south Armagh, led a night-time raid on Protestant farms around Altnaveigh in June, killing six Protestants in revenge for the murder of Catholics the previous day.[572]

In military terms the northern campaign of the IRA was ineffectual. It reached its high point in May, which was supposed to see co-ordinated uprisings by IRA divisions massed around the border. For some reason Collins called it off at the last minute, but the month did see a wave of burnings across the six counties, the assassination of a Unionist MP, William Twaddell, and numerous isolated skirmishes.

At three villages along the border – Pettigo, Belleek and Belcoo – clashes between the IRA garrisons (both pro- and anti-Treaty) and the Ulster Special Constabulary led to the British Army being mobilised to dislodge the IRA. A full-scale battle, including an artillery bombardment and infantry assault, in which seven IRA men were killed, ensued at Pettigo (incidentally, on the Free State side of the border) before the IRA made it back into friendly territory.[573]

Many questions remain about the undeclared war between north and south in early 1922. Michael Collins appears to have orchestrated IRA involvement, but whether he was simply using the issue to reunite the IRA, rather than to achieve Irish unification, remains under debate. The engagement at Pettigo showed that the IRA could not simply have marched over the border and hoisted the tricolour over City Hall in Belfast – it remained a guerrilla Army, capable of only small-scale actions. The Belfast IRA in particular was all but finished after the failed May offensive. Hundreds of their men were interned by the Northern Government, and some 500 more fled south to avoid arrest. It is difficult to see what more, beyond limited harassing attacks, the IRA could have done in the six counties.

In any case, southern attention was distracted by the conflict over the Treaty. The Northern Ireland Government ruthlessly rounded up and interned active Republicans (some of whom they flogged under new emergency legislation) in its jurisdiction and then slowly, haltingly, some loyalist militants as well. By October 1922, the northern conflict had petered out.

The 'pact' election and the outbreak of civil war

While the 'joint northern offensive' was fizzling out, on the civilian side Collins pursued a similar policy of trying to win over the Republican opposition. He formed an election 'pact' with de Valera on 20 May, so that they would campaign jointly in the Free State's first general election in June 1922. He also attempted to eliminate those parts of the Treaty most objectionable to Republicans in his proposals for the Free State's new constitution. One of the more emotive elements of these was the Oath of Allegiance that members of the new Free State Parliament (TDs) would have to take to the British monarch.

Collins proposed a Republican-type document without mention of the British monarchy; a compromise that Liam Lynch, head of the anti-Treaty IRA, agreed to in principle. However, the British vetoed the proposal, insisting that the constitution acknowledge the authority of the Crown, include the oath, and recognise Northern Ireland.[574]

Winston Churchill told the House of Commons that 'in the event of such a Republic [being declared], it will be the intention of the [British] Government to hold Dublin as one of the preliminary essential steps to military operations'.[575] Collins, whose primary aim was the withdrawal of the British military from the country, had no choice but to withdraw the proposed constitution.

This exploded the Collins/de Valera pact, and as a result two mutually hostile Sinn Féin parties, respectively pro- and anti-Treaty, contested the General Election on 18 June. The result, effectively a referendum on the Treaty, was a triumph for Collins. His pro-Treaty Sinn Féin won 239,193 votes to 135,864 for their anti-Treaty opponents. A further 247,226 people voted for other parties, all of whom supported the Treaty.[576] The largest of these was Labour, which polled only 3,000 votes fewer than anti-Treaty Sinn Féin, and indeed topped the poll in Cork city.[577] Labour's policy was, in theory, based on the pursuit of a notional Workers' Republic, but in practice was for the pragmatic acceptance of the Treaty.

The election result left the Provisional Government, complete with a democratic mandate, with the unavoidable and intolerable fact that it was in control of only portions of its national territory. Within ten days, the inevitable would happen and civil war would finally break out, but not before a final twist.

On 22 May, retired Field Marshal Sir Henry Wilson, who had been the military advisor to the Northern Ireland Government, was assassinated in London by two IRA men.

Churchill understandably assumed that the anti-Treaty IRA were responsible and ordered the British garrison in Dublin to attack the Republicans ensconced in the Four Courts.[578] On the urgings of Macready, the British commander in Dublin, the plan was cancelled at the last minute and Collins' Government was given an ultimatum to retake the Four Courts or have British troops do it. The irony, or perhaps tragedy, of this is that it now seems that Collins himself may have ordered the killing of Wilson, in reprisal for attacks on Catholics in the north. Alternatively, the London IRA may have carried out the attack on their own initiative. What seems certain is that the Four Courts garrison knew nothing about it. [579]

Regardless, the British response to the shooting left Collins no more wriggle room. He could not afford to be seen attacking fellow Republicans on the orders of the British, but fortunately for him, the Four Courts garrison gave him the excuse he needed by kidnapping a National Army general, J. J. 'Ginger' O'Connell in retaliation for the arrest of one of their men, Leo Henderson. Collins gave the Four Courts garrison a final opportunity to hand back O'Connell. When it ran out on 28 June, the Provisional Government's troops opened fire on the Four Courts with two 18-pounder field guns borrowed from the British. The Civil War had begun.

Chapter 9:

Civil War

The anti-Treaty IRA, particularly the faction in the Four Courts, had done much to provoke civil war. Arguably they had put the Provisional Government in an impossible position and made open conflict unavoidable. But this had never been their intention; with hindsight, they almost sleepwalked into civil war. In the run-up to the outbreak of fighting, the Four Courts leadership was unsure of what to do, resolving neither to abandon their positions for the sake of unity nor to stage a coup and oust the Provisional Government, nor even to restart the war against the British. In the last meeting of the IRA Army Executive on 14 June, they resolved to 'maintain the Republic against British aggression', but not to attack the Provisional Government or its troops.[580]

Ernie O'Malley, second in command of the Republican fighters in the Four Courts, recalled, 'there was no attempt to define a clear cut policy. Words ran into phrases, sentences followed sentences. At times I sat holding my head in my hands, dulled, wishing I could let out a few wild yells to relieve my feelings... a drifting policy [was] discussed endlessly in a shipwrecked way'[581]. They had sat in their position for three months without deciding on what exactly it was they were trying to achieve. Tom Barry advised marching the veteran anti-Treaty units to Dublin while the Provisional Government was weak, taking over the capital and restarting the war with the British. It was better, he said, to get it out of the way.[582] However, the anti-Treatyites took no such action.

With a grasp of the symbolic, but not of military realities, the anti-Treaty fighters were ordered not to fire first, so that the Free State side, who were thus permitted to surround the complex, would be seen to be the aggressors.[583] At the last minute, Rory O'Connor and the Four Courts garrison had fallen out even with Liam Lynch over the kidnapping of O'Connell. They faced the Provisional Government's attack all alone.

An air of unreality pervaded the fighting that followed. Men on both sides were reluctant to fight each other; one National Army unit simply refused to participate in the attack,[584] while some others passed ammunition to the anti-Treaty fighters inside the Four Courts.[585] The National Army's first attempts at bombardment came to grief and Paddy Daly, in command of the assault, had to find some ex-British soldiers, who realised the guns' carriages had to be fixed in position to prevent the recoil from causing the cannon to hit the gunners. After the first day's bombardment had made little impression on the Four Courts' thick walls, the British donated two more artillery pieces and more high-explosive shells. Churchill also offered a 60-pounder howitzer and to bomb the Four Courts from the air, but Collins turned him down, fearing heavy civilian casualties in the densely populated inner-city area.[586] The following day, National Army troops stormed the eastern wing of the Four Courts. Three National Army soldiers were killed and fourteen wounded, and thirty-three Republicans were taken prisoner.

Less than a kilometre away, in O'Connell Street, the main thoroughfare of the Irish capital, Oscar Traynor, who was head of the anti-Treaty IRA's Dublin Brigade, occupied the north-eastern part of the street in order to try and distract Free State troops from the assault on the Four Courts. Traynor led roughly 500 men throughout the city, opposed by around 4,000 Provisional Government troops. As with the occupation of the Four Courts, there seems to have been little military planning on Traynor's part. The intention was simply to make a stand and to show that the attack on their Republican comrades was being resisted. His command was based in 'the Block', a series of buildings on the corner of Parnell Street and O'Connell Street through which the anti-Treaty fighters had burrowed connecting tunnels. They had also taken over the Gresham, Crown, Granville and Hammam Hotels. Despite several attempts to relieve Rory O'Connor's men, which were repulsed with casualties, they never reached the Four Courts.

On 30 June the Four Courts, now commanded by Ernie O'Malley, surrendered. The building had been badly damaged by shellfire, and fires were raging throughout the complex. Casualties had been fairly low, however; only three of the 180 defenders had died during the siege.[587]

Rory O'Connor, Liam Mellows and Joe McKelvey, all members of the anti-Treaty IRA's Army Executive, were captured. Ernie O'Malley, along with Seán Lemass, slipped away after the surrender. O'Malley asked a National Army soldier he knew to let them go, and in an act of generosity that would be unthinkable several months later, he did. 'It's terrible to see them fighting among themselves', O'Malley heard a bystander say as he and Lemass walked away through the backstreets.[588]

Just before the surrender, a massive explosion destroyed the western wing of the Four Courts, in the process blowing to pieces the Irish Public Records Office (which contained much of Ireland's historical archives), severely injuring

forty advancing Free State soldiers and sending a massive
mushroom cloud skywards over the Dublin quays. Debate
rages to this day over whether the explosion was caused by
a deliberate booby trap bomb, as the government claimed,
or the accidental ignition of the Republicans' ammunition
dump, as they maintained.[589] Winston Churchill, much
relieved by the course events were taking, quipped, 'better a
state without an archive than an archive without a state'.[590]

Within five days, the remainder of the Republican
positions in the capital had been captured. General Tom
Ennis first took the outlying anti-Treaty outposts on
Harcourt and Aungier Streets, south of the River Liffey,
before moving on to the main concentration on O'Connell
Street. Using artillery, his troops forced the Republicans to
abandon their position on Gardiner and Parnell Streets,
giving them a clear field of fire on 'the Block'.[591]

Field guns were placed on Henry Street, behind
armoured cars for protection, to bombard the remaining
positions at point-blank range, while a barrage of small arms
fire kept the anti-Treatyites pinned down. Oscar Traynor's
positions finally became untenable when National Army
troops planted incendiary bombs inside the buildings of
the Block, setting them ablaze. There was, however, to be
no final assault. Traynor ordered his remaining 100 fighters
(seventy men and thirty women) to mingle into civilian
crowds and make their way to Blessington, a village about
thirty kilometres south of Dublin. Most of them got there
by tram.

Left behind were fifteen men led by Cathal Brugha.
Brugha was known for his difficult personality – he had
fallen out repeatedly with both Collins and Mulcahy –
but also for his personal bravery. When the heat from
the fires in the Hamman Hotel became unbearable, he
ordered his men to surrender but emerged alone from the

hotel, revolver in hand, to confront the Free State troops. He was hit in the thigh, and died later of blood loss from a severed artery.

The fighting in Dublin was over. Oscar Traynor had appealed for help from the rest of the country, but only a small column from Tipperary had responded, and they reached Blessington too late to take part. Sixty-five people (nineteen government, twelve insurgents and at least twenty-two civilians) were dead, and around three hundred injured.[592] A further four hundred Republicans had been taken prisoner.

The fighting had been confused and confusing. Much of the city centre had been sealed off, and although troops had had to mount cordons to keep curious crowds back, neither the press nor the general population seemed to know fully what was happening until it was over. Todd Andrews, who spent the week exchanging fire with Free State troops across O'Connell Street, remembered, 'it was strange to see a sizable crowd of spectators, indifferent to any danger from stray bullets. They behaved as if they were rubber-necking a traffic accident... Even more curious was the occasional pedestrian strolling down O'Connell Street'.[593]

Ernie O'Malley, whose brother had been killed in the fighting, got away over the Dublin Mountains, where he was asked by an old man what all the trouble was about. He recalled saying, 'It's hard to tell you in a few words but I think they think they're fighting for a younger generation'.[594] It is difficult to find a better summing up of the muddled but quite determined stance of the anti-Treaty fighters in the Civil War.

Strange as it may seem, for most Republicans the attack on the Four Courts was completely unexpected. They had envisioned fighting a war against the British, not, despite the tensions of the previous months, against other Irish nationalists. For Todd Andrews, 'I never thought it could happen that IRA men would kill fellow IRA men'.[595] Mossie Hartnett in Limerick thought that 'We underestimated them [the Free State] and the public support they received'. The outbreak of the Civil War 'took us by surprise, we did not seriously believe that they really meant it'.[596]

Several Free State units deserted after the attack on the Four Courts. The garrison in Waterford defected, for example, as did some recruits, such as 17-year-old Frank Sherwin, who deserted from the military camp at the Curragh when he heard that his brother, an anti-Treaty Volunteer, had been arrested in the Dublin fighting.[597]

A daunting task

For Collins and the Provisional Government, the outcome of the battle for Dublin was a major relief. The capital was firmly in their hands, and British intervention had been averted. Collins expressed the hope that it would also mark the end of the fighting, and to this end released Liam Lynch, on the understanding that he would prevent the spread of the war to the provinces. Lynch, however, would do nothing of the sort.

Fighting had already broken out around the country. A firefight in the centre of Drogheda had seen three people killed, and the anti-Treaty side taking control of the town. They blew up the railway bridge to prevent the arrival of Free State reinforcements. Republicans had also taken over Skibbereen in County Cork and Tipperary town. In Listowel, County Kerry, an entire National Army garrison had surrendered its arms when attacked by local Republicans.

In Wexford, the anti-Treaty fighters who had dispersed from Dublin took a string of towns. In the south, Liam Lynch announced that his anti-Treaty IRA would hold the 'Munster Republic'; a notional entity stretching across the south of Ireland from Limerick in the west to Waterford in the east. Starting from Dublin, the Provisional Government would have to reconquer its own territory.

This proposition looked daunting on paper. The Free State had only four thousand troops at its disposal in Dublin and several other garrisons scattered around the country. The anti-Treaty side, whom the government would name and instruct the press to call 'the Irregulars', had, according to Richard Mulcahy's estimate, around 15,000 men under arms; enough, in theory, to overwhelm the nascent Free State.

However, in practice the Free State side had considerable advantages. For one thing, it had in its hands the apparatus of the state, and with it the means to raise and equip a regular Army. It also had a powerful patron in Britain, which throughout the war supplied the Free State with arms, uniforms and supplies, including armour and artillery and even aircraft. There was also a pool of tens of thousands of Irish First World War veterans on hand, many of whom had faced intimidation by the IRA in 1919–21 and had little love for the Republicans. By the end of August, the National Army had 14,127 men. By the end of the war it would be over 58,000 strong.[598] Also, in the final analysis, the Free State was backed up by British armed force. The fact was that, had the war gone against them, British garrisons would have been rapidly redeployed to southern Ireland to enforce the Treaty.

By contrast, the Republicans had only around 6,000 rifles, a handful of commandeered armoured cars and no artillery of any kind. One of their most effective weapons would be the home-made 'mine' – a tin filled with gelignite and placed along a roadside or beside a barracks. Though more than twice as well armed as the IRA had been against the British, the Republicans were in no position to wage a conventional war.

Perhaps even more importantly, Collins and his Cabinet had a unified strategy: to retake the national territory and consolidate the existence of the new state. The Republicans had no such clarity of purpose. Their forces were in reality a series of local militias, most reluctant to operate outside of their home areas, and in any case very difficult to co-ordinate. Moreover, Liam Lynch offered no military plan except to hold what territory he had and impede the establishment of the Free State. The civilian anti-Treaty leadership was sidelined. Éamon de Valera enrolled in the anti-Treaty IRA as an ordinary Volunteer, and spent most of the war being shunted from safe house to safe house.

A civil war is not decided on the battlefield alone, however. A great many people wanted law and order restored, which the government promised to do. The pro-Treaty side also had the support of not only a majority of the population, but also its most powerful sectors. These elites, including the strong farmers, business, finance and the media, all threw their weight behind the Free State.

The Republicans were aware of this, and made some noises about social revolution. Ernie O'Malley approvingly quoted a programme, originally devised by the Communist Party of Ireland (who imagined that they had growing influence among the Republicans) that 'under the Republic all industry will be controlled by the state for the workers' and farmers' benefit… all banks will be operated by the state… the lands of the aristocracy will be seized and divided'.[599] Liam Mellows, the imprisoned Republican leader, also voiced his approval. But no such programme was adopted, and although class conflict is part of the story of 1922–23, it was essentially parallel to, rather than part of, the Civil War.

As for the Communist Party, a small number of IRA men including Seán McLoughlin (the young man who took command of the Volunteers in Moore Street in 1916) and Peadar O'Donnell (a member of the anti-Treaty IRA executive) were attracted to them, and a small number of Communists, including the writer Liam O'Flaherty, fought in the Civil War on the Republican side. However, aside from a botched mission by Roddy Connolly to buy arms for the IRA from German Communists, their influence was negligible.[600]

The Catholic Church, which had never been comfortable with the use of political violence, even though it broadly supported Irish independence, threw its enormous moral authority behind the new government.

The first steps

The first step for Collins was to secure the counties around Dublin and the midlands and to re-establish contact with the Free State garrisons in provinces. On 4 July a Free State force equipped with artillery and mortars pounded the anti-Treaty fighters in Drogheda into surrender. The Republicans in Wexford, who had occupied several towns such as New Ross and Enniscorthy, simply melted away when a Free State expeditionary force equipped with a field gun and four armoured cars arrived in the county.

There was some fighting in Queen's County (now Laois), including a four-hour gun battle in the streets of Maryborough (now Portlaoise) before National Army troops secured the county. Galway fell to Free State troops on 7 July with minimal loss of life (one anti-Treaty officer and two Free State privates were killed) as the Republicans fled their position and burnt the barracks they had been occupying.

In the north-west, things initially went badly for the Free State. An ambush near Coolooney in County Sligo on 11 July left five Free State soldiers dead and the anti-Treaty side in possession of the town. However, only four days later a 400-strong National Army force under Seán McEoin, complete with an 18-pounder artillery piece, retook the village after a bombardment and a protracted firefight. The fighting at Coolooney lasted the better part of a day, involved hundreds of fighters firing thousands of rounds and an artillery barrage, but produced only one fatality, an anti-Treaty IRA Volunteer.[601] This surprising lack of casualties was to be a feature of the subsequent fighting. By the end of July, Seán McEoin was able to report that 'in the midlands divisions all posts and positions of military value are in our hands'.[602] The same was true of most of the north, east and west. The real challenge lay to the south.

Limerick

Liam Lynch made his headquarters in Limerick, the western stronghold of what he termed 'the Munster Republic'. Notionally, this was defended at its eastern extremity by Waterford and in between by a string of Republican-held towns. Its 'capital' was Cork. In reality, there was nothing like a continuous defensive line from Waterford to Limerick; rather a series of locally held positions.

Still, the elimination of the 'Republic' posed a serious problem for the Provisional Government. Fighting in Limerick itself broke out on 7 July, but was temporarily halted when Lynch agreed to a truce with the local Free State commander Michael Brennan. The city's four military and police barracks had been divided evenly between the National Army and Republican forces back in March, and as the fighting in Dublin developed they eyed each other nervously. Both sides busied themselves building barricades in the streets. On 11 July, while building a barricade on Nelson Street, a Free State soldier was fatally wounded by a sniper's bullet and fighting broke out throughout the city.[603]

The battle got underway in earnest when Free State reinforcements arrived from Dublin. On 15 July, National Army troops made assaults on both the Strand and Castle Barracks, resulting in six dead and more wounded.[604] In urban fighting, however, artillery was the decisive weapon, knocking down walls that bullets could not breach and reducing otherwise impregnable strongholds to heaps of rubble. The Free State had this weapon and the Republicans did not, a blunt fact that essentially decided the conventional phase of the Irish Civil War.

On 17 July, Eoin O'Duffy (by now a National Army general) arrived in Limerick city with 150 reinforcements, three armoured cars and a field gun. The walls of the Strand Barracks were breached. Republican attempts to come to the aid of the Strand Barracks by advancing down O'Connell Street were caught in a crossfire of Free State machine guns, killing at least five of them and wounding many more.[605] A final assault on the breach was led by a small squad of twelve National Army soldiers, hurling grenades in front of them. Two of the attackers were cut down by Thompson sub-machine guns and the attack stalled, but it convinced the Republican commander, Connie Mackey, that it was time to surrender the barracks. As he called his headquarters to tell them of his decision, the telephone was shot out of his hand by a Free State sniper in the surrounding buildings.[606]

In an indication of the almost amicable nature of the early hostilities, Michael Brennan, commander of the National Army troops, complimented Mackey on his defence and offered him a command in the National Army should he change sides. Mackey turned him down and instead was imprisoned.[607]

After the surrender of Strand Barracks, the Republican position in Limerick collapsed very quickly. Lynch had already left the city, moving his headquarters south to Clonmel. The Castle Barracks was evacuated after coming under artillery fire and subsequently was set alight by the Republicans, who retreated to the south. O'Duffy's troops, amidst clouds of black smoke from burning buildings, were left in possession of the city.

The fighting had seen much of the civilian population flee the city to the surrounding countryside, and food run scarce. The local paper reported that 'rashers were as rare as rubies'.[608] Looting also broke out wherever the fighting died down. The week's combat had left nineteen bodies in the city morgue, twelve of whom were civilians and the remainder Free State soldiers. Another eighty-seven people were wounded. The Republican dead were reported in the press as thirty killed, but they themselves recorded just five.[609] The jail, built to accommodate 120, was soon filled with 700 Republican prisoners.[610]

The Republican stand in Limerick was a foretaste of how they would fare in the war's conventional phase. They had failed to co-ordinate their forces while they had an advantage in numbers, and when faced with larger forces supported by artillery and armour had rapidly abandoned their positions. Kerry anti-Treaty Volunteers asked their commander, Tom McEllistrim, 'What's the use of carrying on a fight when we ran away in Limerick?'[611]

Waterford

On the other side of the country in Waterford city, the eastern stronghold of the Republican-held south, fighting began when a Free State column arrived from Kilkenny on 18 July. Waterford was held by 200 men under Pax Whelan and George Lennon, respectively commanders of the Waterford IRA Brigade and Flying Column. Also in the area were Cork IRA men led by Seán Moylan and a Tipperary unit led by Dennis 'Dinny' Lacey.

The Waterford men had actually been part of the National Army up to the outbreak of fighting in Dublin, when they decided that their sympathies lay with the Republicans. They had been paid by the government and uniformed in the Free State's dark green uniforms, which they were still wearing during the fighting in Waterford. To distinguish themselves, they had thrown away their Army caps and donned civilian ones.[612] During their occupation of the barracks in Waterford, Lennon had had to 'act on my own as a kind of military governor', and put down a strike by local agricultural labourers – something that troubled his conscience greatly. He later wrote that it was almost a relief finally to be attacked by the Free State forces.[613]

In command of the National Army troops was General John T. Prout, a veteran of the US Army in the First World War and subsequently an IRA Intelligence officer. In the Civil War he would gain a reputation as an efficient and relatively humane soldier. No prisoners were killed in custody under his command in the south-east (and only two officially executed), a leniency that Republicans put down to his restraining influence.[614] Prout's second was Paddy Paul, who had been the Waterford IRA's commander but had fallen out with them over the Treaty. Dragged by horses from Kilkenny was a single 18-pounder gun; here, as elsewhere, this would make all the difference.

Waterford city clings to the south side of the River Suir and is overlooked to its north by a low hill known as Mount Misery. The Republicans for some reason chose not to defend the heights that could fire down onto the city and instead occupied the barracks, prison and post office along the river bank, with the city's bridge raised. Their plan was for the Cork and Tipperary IRA columns to attack the rear of the Free State positions on Mount Misery once the government troops were engaged in fighting. As was often the case, their 'command and control' – that is, the ability to link up the movement of several different forces – proved wanting.

The National Army force arrived on Mount Misery on 18 July, seen from the city as a stream of infantrymen emerging over the hill. A general fusillade was opened up along the river bank. Free State soldiers manhandled the field gun into place, with bullets pinging off its armoured shield. As in Dublin, civilians lined the quays to watch on the first day of the fighting, as if it were a spectator sport. As the fighting intensified, though, they were soon fleeing Waterford in special trains to the seaside resort of Tramore. A further stream of refugees on foot was reported on the Cork Road, where they provided 'a pathetic spectacle'.[615]

The Free State bombardment forced the abandonment the following day of the military barracks, which had caught fire. Looters, from a city with terrible poverty and high unemployment, swarmed over the building in spite of the fires and the ongoing fighting, stripping it of valuables. Two of them were cut down in the crossfire. On 20 July a small party of 100 Free State soldiers led by Ned O'Brien, a 21-year-old from Waterford, crossed the river in small boats into the city. With his troops across the Suir, General Prout ordered his artillery piece brought down to the riverside to blast the Republicans out of their remaining position in the post office.

The end was not long in coming. The Republicans set fire to their positions and streamed south out of the city. The end of the fighting was the signal for the mass looting of the city's public buildings, several more looters being shot dead in the final exchanges of fire. Five civilians, two Free State troops and only one Republican fighter had been killed.[616]

The Republican attack from the rear had never materialised; the Tipperary men had retreated after a skirmish with the Free State supply column. Many of the Waterford fighters, including their leader, George Lennon, on being instructed to hold another imaginary line from Dungarven to Congreve, simply gave up and went home. One told Liam Lynch plaintively, 'I've had enough and want no more trouble'.[617] In Waterford itself, Prout found that his greatest challenge was policing the restive civilian population and recovering property looted during the fighting.[618]

Prout's Free State column went on to take the towns of Tipperary, Golden, Carrick-on-Suir and Clonmel, effectively securing the south midlands for the Free State. Ned O'Brien, who had led Free State troops across the Suir, was assassinated a month later on the streets of Waterford.

The fighting at Kilmallock

The only really determined Republican stand was south of Limerick, in the area around Kilmallock. Here, the best troops of the anti-Treaty side – veteran Cork, Kerry and Limerick IRA units complete with four armoured cars, commanded by Liam Deasy – held a string of hilltop towns: Bruff, Bruree, and Kilmallock itself. They were faced initially by 700 Free State troops under Eoin O'Duffy; largely raw recruits, badly armed and without artillery.

On 23 July, National Army troops under W. R. E. Murphy, an ex-British Army officer, took the town of Bruff, only to lose it again the following day. On the advance of the Republicans, the inexperienced Free State soldiers simply took to their heels and seventy-six of them were captured. The fighting there highlighted how ramshackle the National Army still was. Certainly their commander, O'Duffy, was far from impressed: 'We had to get work out of a disgruntled, undisciplined and cowardly crowd. Arms were handed over wholesale to the enemy, sentries were drunk at their posts and... a whole garrison had to be put in the clink for insubordination'.[619]

The combat at the Kilmallock line consisted in large part of a furious exchange of fire from behind hedgerows but with few casualties. Dan Sandow O'Donovan's Cork city IRA unit fired 'five thousands [rounds of] .303 [ammunition] a day and I couldn't stop men firing'.[620] Liam Lynch received a report from Deasy that 'any time his forces met them [Free State forces] in this area, the enemy ran away'.[621] The stark reality was that when not possessed of an overwhelming advantage in firepower, the Free State was relying on quite a small nucleus, mostly of ex-IRA men, to do the hard fighting. The most prominent in this nucleus were the Dublin Guard, a unit built around a hard core of the Dublin IRA's 'Squad' and Active Service Unit, and also Northern IRA men from Belfast who had fled south to escape internment.

The Dublin Guard, by now backed up by artillery and armoured cars, took Bruree on 30 July, but in one week's fighting had thirteen men killed and many wounded, compared to nine dead anti-Treaty fighters.[622] By the standards of the fighting elsewhere, these were considerable casualties. The death toll around Kilmallock could have been higher still, had the town itself been defended. As it was, many of Deasy's units from Cork and Kerry had returned home after Free State troops landed by sea in their home counties on 2 and 5 August respectively. O'Duffy's troops rolled almost unopposed into Kilmallock on 5 August.

One of the anti-Treaty prisoners taken in the fighting, a First World War veteran, later bemoaned his experiences to his comrades in a Free State internment camp: 'We had Limerick and we ran away, we had Bruree and we gave it up to a pack of bastards. At Kilmallock... I saw one man with three guns... and two bandoliers of ammunition – about 1,000 rounds, and we ran away'.[623]

The Cork and Kerry landings

While the anti-Treaty fighters were still defending their positions around Kilmallock, the 'Munster Republic' had been outflanked by a series of Free State naval landings on Ireland's south coast. The plan to cut into the heart of anti-Treaty-held territory by sea was proposed by Emmet Dalton and enthusiastically taken up by Collins. On 2 August, five hundred Free State troops, spearheaded by the Dublin Guard under Paddy Daly, landed at Fenit in Kerry.

The landing, according to one participant on the Free State side, 'could have been our Gallipoli'.[624] As it was, however, two employees of the harbour commission at Fenit disconnected a landmine that would have destroyed the pier, and, in all likelihood, have inflicted horrific casualties on the landing Free State troops. Following scattered resistance on the way, the Free State column took Tralee from its surprised Republican garrison after some hard fighting that left nine pro-Treaty and two anti-Treaty fighters dead, with a further twenty to thirty Free State wounded.[625]

One well-placed Lewis machine gun in a mill overlooking a crossroads alone had killed seven of the National Army soldiers in Tralee: proof of how much bloodier such encounters might have been had Republican resistance been better organised. The Free State troops, using mortars and armoured cars, eventually stormed the mill and put the anti-Treaty fighters into retreat.

Five days later, another force under Emmet Dalton landed at Passage West near Cork city. Two more landings disembarked Free State troops at Youghal and Glandore, putting up to one thousand National Army troops into the heart of the 'Munster Republic'. Taken utterly by surprise, the Republicans gave only patchy opposition.

Most of the Cork IRA fighters had been at either Limerick or Waterford, and had to race back to Cork when the landings took place. One, Mick Murphy, recalled that 'I commandeered a train [from Waterford] and we brought the train back to Cork... we threw our crowd in front of the Staters but we couldn't stem them, we had about eighty men'.[626] Between Rochestown and Douglas, in the hills south of Cork city, the more determined fighters made a stand and some sharp fighting ensued. Both sides used machine guns and armoured cars in an all-day battle. It was not until the Free State troops managed to outflank the Republicans' positions, and not before nine National Army solders and seven Republicans were killed and many more wounded, that the government troops could resume their advance.[627]

The following day the anti-Treaty force abandoned their barracks in Cork. Several hundred fighters, who had been ensconced in strong positions and were heavily armed, scattered into the countryside, leaving (as in Waterford and

Limerick) the military barracks in Cork city and Charles Fort at Kinsale Harbour in flames, with smoke covering the city so that it seemed as if all of Cork were on fire. Emmet Dalton, in command of the Free State forces, wrote that 'it is hard to credit the extent of the disorder and disorganisation displayed in the retreat'.[628] One eyewitness saw them 'marching raggedly, no military precision about them... they had not been properly fed and had slept rough... they were a rabble and they knew it'.[629]

The following day, Liam Lynch, from his final fixed headquarters in Fermoy, issued orders that all IRA units were to abandon their fixed positions, burn them to deny them to the enemy, and form guerrilla columns.

That might have been the end of the war. Many Republicans would later argue that it should have been.[630] There was now no hope of them displacing by force of arms the Provisional Government, which was backed by a popular vote and in possession of all the country's main towns. The Republican forces were scattered and demoralised. They had failed, in the brief period when they had had the chance, to defeat the government's makeshift Army. It would only get stronger now as they got weaker. Michael Collins certainly hoped that the war was over. He said of the anti-Treaty side that they were 'misguided, but practically all of them are sincere'. They must 'accept the people's verdict' on the Treaty, but could then 'go home without their arms. We don't ask for any surrender of their principles'. He argued that the Provisional Government was upholding 'the people's rights' and would continue to do so. 'We want to avoid any possible unnecessary destruction and loss of life. We do not want to mitigate their weakness by resolute action beyond what is required'. But if Republicans did not accept his terms, 'further blood is on their shoulders'.[631]

Guerrilla war

Conventional military victory may now have been out of reach, but Liam Lynch hoped to make the new and fragile state collapse by making the country ungovernable. He instructed his forces to 'attack and destroy if possible small enemy outposts, concentrate on destroying enemy intelligence service, attack [the] enemy when he leaves his base, destroy road and rail communications, intensify campaign in cities and towns'.[632]

Opposition to the Treaty might be explicable, as might resistance to the armed dispersal of their forces after the attack on the Four Courts. But the subsequent long, drawn-out guerrilla campaign waged by the Republicans against the Free State is more puzzling.

The Free State issued numerous amnesties for anti-Treaty IRA fighters throughout the war, where they could surrender without consequence and go home, but many thousands of young men stuck out the guerrilla campaign for months, risking ill-health, capture, execution or death in action. Considering the gravity of the consequences, from where did they muster this determination to resist the new Irish state? By the end of the war some 13,000 of them had been locked up, and around 500 killed. So why did they do it? Hostile observers such as Lady Fingall thought that the Civil War was 'an escape from the dullness of Irish rural life... before they went back to the hard work on the farm and the parental tyranny that existed to a peculiar extent in Irish country life'.[633] Members of the government, Collins aside, tended to see it similarly; Kevin O'Higgins wrote in September 1922, 'It is becoming less and less a question of war and more and more a question of armed crime'.[634]

But probably closer to the truth is Todd Andrews' recollection that, on the outbreak of the conflict, 'My place was with my friends in the Four Courts' and 'it never even occurred to me to accept the terms of the amnesty and go home'.[635] The anti-Treaty IRA consisted, in the main, of small groups of closely bonded young men and women. They stuck together out of loyalty to each other and to vindicate the sacrifices they had already made, which would somehow be sullied by surrender and compromise.

At their head was Liam Lynch, a 29-year-old former hardware store clerk from Cork who was determined that there would be no compromise short of victory. 'Views of political people are not to be too seriously considered. Our aim and course are now clearly defined and cut and dried. It is certain that many influences will constantly be brought to bear to deflect us from them, but these will be brushed aside'.[636] It was this kind of intransigence that had sustained the guerrillas against the British. It would now prolong, agonisingly, the Civil War.

August and September 1922, instead of seeing an orderly end to the fighting, plunged the Free State into a new crisis. By September, General Macready was reporting back to London that it was a question of 'when, not if' British military intervention would be needed.[637] Guerrilla attacks on Free State convoys and patrols were soon taking place throughout the countryside, as was the destruction of the country's infrastructure. National Army soldiers, in dozens of different incidents, died in twos and threes at various crossroads and byways. Railway tracks and roads were ripped up and railway bridges came crashing down.

August 1922 also saw the deaths of the two most important political leaders of the Free State. Arthur Griffith died of a stroke on 12 August, and Michael Collins was killed in an ambush in his native Cork on 22 August.

The death of Collins

Collins, who had seen the state through its uncertain birth, was still confident of using his personal contacts with Republican guerrillas to 'put an end to the damned thing [war]'. 'The three Toms', he said (Barry, Hales and Malone), 'will fix it'.[638] Partly with a view to making contact with the Republicans, partly to see for himself the recently secured areas, he travelled to west Cork with a small escort, though the region was filled with anti-Treaty fighters. Even more imprudently, driving between Cork and Bandon, he used the same route there and back. An improvised ambush party led by Liam Deasy opened up a fusillade on Collins and his party on their return journey at a place named Béal na mBláth. Collins, unwisely but with characteristic bravado, stopped to return fire and was hit in the forehead by a bullet fired by a local man named Dennis 'Sonny' O'Neill, dying instantly.[639]

Collins was not, as is sometimes maintained, assassinated. He died in an action that was no different from many others taking place around the country. For instance, the day before Collins' death, on the road between Clonmel and Kilkenny, a senior National Army commandant named Frank Thornton, like Collins unwisely using the same route twice, was badly wounded in an ambush and two of his men were killed.[640] Thornton, like Collins, had not been selected for death; he was simply the victim of an opportunistic attack by a local anti-Treaty IRA unit.

As it was, most Republicans regretted Collins' death. Lynch wrote that 'it is indeed a regrettable national position – which nothing could better illustrate – that makes the shooting of such leaders and with such a splendid previous record necessary'.[641] Liam Deasy recalled that 'his death caused nothing but the deepest sorrow and regret and brought about in many of us a real desire for the end of the war'.[642]

Power in the Free State passed to a young, relatively inexperienced, but, as it turned out, tough and ruthless leadership. Richard Mulcahy took over as Commander-in-Chief of the Army and W. T. Cosgrave, who had been Minister for Local Government, became the head of the government. Patrick Hogan, the Minister for Agriculture, and Kevin O'Higgins, the Minister for Justice, also rose to prominence in Collins' and Griffith's absence.

O'Higgins, a 30-year-old lawyer, who had worked under Cosgrave in the Dáil Ministry of Local Government, emerged as one of the most forceful personalities in the Cabinet. He famously described the new government, who along with their families lived under armed guard in government buildings, as 'eight young men in City Hall, standing in the ruins of one administration, with the foundation of another not yet laid, with the wild men screaming in through the key holes'.[643] Even some of their pro-Treaty colleagues, however, saw them in a less favourable light. Liam de Róiste, for instance, thought that 'they are narrow, petty... too much inclined to the mailed fist towards their own people yet displaying in many aspects a fear of the English government... [they] are not sure of their own ground either with the English government or with their own Sinn Féin supporters'.[644]

Gone completely was any thought of social revolution or even reform. The government could think of nothing now but its own survival. The wages of public servants were slashed at a time of 130 per cent inflation. In September 1922, postal workers took strike action in protest. J. J. Walsh, the Minister for Posts and Telegraphs, wrote to the British Government: 'Anticipate sectional strike of employees disloyal to Free State on 1st prox. Provisional Government determined to dispense with their services and substitute those of hundreds of loyal Irishmen in Great Britain seeking transfer'.

Walsh had to repudiate the telegram, but during the three-week dispute, the Army was used to break up pickets of postal workers, and its troops beat up and even shot at trade Unionists. Labour's Cathal O'Shannon told the Dáil that 'all the guns and all the power and all the force in Ireland is not going to make the whole working class in Ireland lie down when the right to strike is challenged'. But Kevin O'Higgins retorted that 'no State, with any regard for its own safety, can admit the right of the servants of the Executive to withdraw their labour at pleasure. They have the right to resign; they have no right to strike'. By the end of September the strike was broken.[645]

Republican successes

In the early guerrilla phase of the war, the Republicans were able to operate in large numbers and mount attacks on medium-sized towns, sometimes with success. On 14 August, Frank Aiken's anti-Treaty IRA unit blasted in the walls of the National Army barracks in Dundalk with improvised 'mines' and quickly subdued the garrison, five of whom were killed, fifteen wounded and 300 taken prisoner. Aiken's raid also freed 240 Republican prisoners held in the town.[646].

The Kerry IRA similarly took Kenmare on 9 September, taking 120 National Army prisoners and seizing their arms before dispersing. Unsuccessful but relatively large-scale attacks were also made on Bantry, Cork (30 August) and Killorglin, Kerry (30 September), both of which involved several hundred fighters and significant casualties.[647]

Cork, Kerry, and Tipperary in particular also saw a number of ambushes in September, where vulnerable National Army columns were badly shot up and only saved by the intervention of armoured cars. The use of mines proved a particularly effective tactic in attacking barracks or motorised columns. In one such attack at Fermoy, Cork, for instance, a mine blew an Army Crossley tender 'to fragments', killing three soldiers, and 'the right side of [the driver's] face was almost blown away'.[648]

In Kerry, *The Irish Times* reported that 'the National Army are pinned to their barracks and cannot leave in columns of less than one hundred men. Even in their barracks they are harassed by sniping or are subject to even more aggressive attacks, while [Republican] columns several hundred strong move along the hills with complete impunity'.[649]

In the west, in the rugged and inaccessible countryside of west Mayo and Connemara, Free State troops found it difficult to keep control. Up to fifteen National Army soldiers, including a brigadier, Joe Ring, were killed, wounded or captured in ambush in the Ox Mountains on 14 September by IRA men under Michael Kilroy.[650] The government troops had to evacuate their garrison in Newport towards the end of September due to the guerrillas cutting off the town from its supplies. As late as 29 October, Clifden in Connemara fell to the local anti-Treaty column.[651]

So while the National Army was lodged firmly in the towns, in parts of the south and west especially, their writ did not run in the countryside. On top of that, even in cities like Dublin and Cork, daily life was disrupted by regular, if small-scale, attacks. The very ease of the Free State's victory in the war's conventional phase had meant that the Republican guerrilla units had been left mostly intact, and their reduction would prove to be a most painstaking process. A National Army report in August 1922 noted ruefully how 'the Irregulars in Cork and Kerry are still more or less intact. Our forces have captured towns but they have not captured

Irregulars and arms in anything like a large scale. Until this is done, the Irregulars will be capable of guerrilla warfare'.[652]

The more perceptive Republican leaders, such as Ernie O'Malley, knew, however, that in this war, unlike that against the British, guerrilla warfare would not be enough. 'The Staters would recruit and train an Army [and] we would be worn down piecemeal... Slowly the resistance retrogressed back from semi-open fighting to a disintegrated guerrilla war in which smaller and smaller columns took part... control became increasingly difficult and co-ordination was impossible'.[653]

Reprisals

It was also quickly apparent, as the war took on the form of hit-and-run ambushes, shootings and sabotage, that the relatively 'clean fight' of the conventional phase was not going to last. The war was soon, in some parts of the country, to become a very nasty cycle of reprisal and counter-reprisal. From the onset of the guerrilla war, roughly from late August 1922, Free State troops, no doubt maddened by the increasingly common deaths of their comrades, began seeking revenge on the anti-Treaty guerrillas. How did a war initially characterised by a great reluctance among the combatants to kill each other become so embittered? The apparent futility of the anti-Treaty campaign deepened the frustration and bitterness of many on the Free State side. What was more, the methods used by the anti-Treaty guerrillas were far from chivalrous.

In some instances these included the use of mines, the weapon most hated by those in Free State uniform on the receiving end. On 12 September, for instance, a patrol of National Army troops led by one Captain Tom Keogh walked into a booby trap mine on the Cork-Kerry border. Keogh (a well-liked Dublin Guard and a former member of Collins' Squad) and eight of his men were, in the words of his fellow Free State officer Niall Harrington, 'blown to bits'.[654] In some other cases, though, pro-Treatyites died in revenge for what was considered their personal betrayal. In the Republican attack on Kenmare, for instance, two Free State officers, brothers Tom and John 'Scarteen' O'Connor, local IRA men who had taken the pro-Treaty side, were pulled from their beds and murdered.[655] On a number of occasions, Free State troops were attacked going to or from Mass, the ultimate taboo in Irish Catholic society. In Ballina, for example, on 12 September, Michael Kilroy's IRA column took over the town while its garrison was at a memorial service for soldiers killed in recent fighting.[656]

Moreover, the death of Collins, who had always seen the Republicans more as wayward comrades than real enemies, to some extent released Free State troops from effective restraint. In the weekend after he was killed, four Republicans were abducted by Free State troops in Dublin, shot and dumped in rural spots outside the city.[657] Collins had stated that 'I am against shooting unarmed men in any circumstances', whereas Patrick Hogan, the Minister for Agriculture, thought that 'the National Army is a little too courteous, a little too ready to take prisoners'.[658] Ernest Blythe thought that Collins' death 'had definitely a hardening effect on opinion everywhere... Moreover, we felt that in certain respects Mulcahy was less sentimental about old comrades than Collins had been'.[659]

In Kerry, there was a string of incidents in which National Army troops killed prisoners in reprisal for the deaths of Free State soldiers. Many of these reprisals were carried out by the former Dublin IRA Volunteers serving in the National Army. Paddy Daly, commanding the Dublin Guard in Kerry, put it bluntly: 'Nobody asked me to take kid gloves to Kerry and I didn't take them'.[660]

Similarly, in Cork the Dublin soldiers sought out Timothy Kenefick, a local Republican activist who had broken cover to go to his mother's funeral, and killed him in what Ernie O'Malley reported as 'a most brutal murder'.[661] Not long afterwards, in revenge for the death of another Dublin Guard officer in Kerry, the Free State troops beat a confession out of a prisoner, Bertie Murphy, in Tralee, shot him, and dumped him at a crossroads.[662]

David Robinson, a Republican commander in Kerry (and Erskine Childers' cousin), wrote to former friends in the Provisional Government appealing to them to stop such reprisals. 'You may imagine what the result will be if it goes on'.[663] Ultimately, though, the government did not have either the will or the capacity to discipline the wilder elements among its armed forces until well after the Civil War was over.

In Dublin itself, some of the Squad's former assassins wound up in the Criminal Investigation Department (CID), in theory a police unit, but which in fact was a counter-insurgency intelligence corps responsible directly to the Minister of Home Affairs.[664] Based in Oriel House in the city centre, the CID, in the words of one author, 'succeeded in its task of suppressing small-scale Republican activities in the Dublin area, not by the sophistication and efficiency of its intelligence work... but by the more direct method of striking terror into its opponents'.[665]

By mid-September, Ernie O'Malley, by now trying to co-ordinate the anti-Treaty campaign in Dublin, had been told of twelve assassinations of Republican militants in the city by what he called 'the murder gang'.[666] In one incident in October, a National Army Intelligence officer named Charlie Dalton arrested three youths putting up Republican posters in Dublin. The following day they were found shot dead at a quarry in Clondalkin, then a rural village west of the city.[667] There were in total around twenty-five such anonymous assassinations of Republicans in Dublin.

Those who were taken prisoner often received the most brutal treatment. Frank Sherwin, a 17-year-old Republican guerrilla, was picked up after an attack on a barracks in Dublin in November and beaten so badly that he never recovered the use of his right arm.[668] Another, Tom Derrig, had an eye shot out while in custody.[669] There is no reason to think that these were isolated cases.

The tide turns

It was thus in a climate of deepening bitterness that the Free State's young Cabinet attempted to get their new state off the ground. Fortunately for them, by the onset of the winter of 1922, the Republican guerrilla campaign was already running out of steam. One factor in this was several successes of National Army troops in the field at breaking up the larger guerrilla concentrations and capturing their leaders.

In Dublin, good intelligence led to the progressive weakening of the urban guerrillas there. Oscar Traynor, head of the IRA in the capital, was picked up in late July. In early August, over 100 IRA men were captured in Dublin while trying to destroy all the bridges leading into the city. Their intelligence officer Liam Clarke had told the National Army of the operation under interrogation.[670] In November, Ernie O'Malley's safe house in Dublin was tracked down and the leader of the anti-Treaty side's eastern command was captured, badly wounded after a gunfight. O'Malley, shouting 'No surrender here', killed a Free State soldier and was himself hit by no fewer than twenty bullets before being taken. Only the intervention of a soldier prevented him from being summarily executed, as many Republican fighters in his position would have been.[671]

Two cumbersome but nevertheless effective Free State operations in the west did much to break up the larger Republican columns there. In late September, Seán MacEoin led a sweep of northern Sligo to clear it of several anti-Treaty columns. Many of the Republicans were captured, and a party of six was wiped out as they fled up the slopes of Ben Bulben mountain. Four of them were found with bullet holes in the forehead, indicating a close-range execution. The Republican dead included Brian MacNeill, the son of Free State minister Eoin MacNeill.[672] Of the fifty-four people killed in County Sligo during the civil war, only eight died after September 1922 – indicating the success of MacEoin's operation[673].

In November, Free State troops under Tony Lawlor trudged on foot through Mayo and Connemara, in foul weather and fighting regular skirmishes with local guerrillas, before eventually retaking Newport and in the process capturing Michael Kilroy, who had led Republican resistance in the locality, and around fifty of his fighters. Lawlor's soldiers were exhausted by the effort, however, and suffered serious losses – five killed and nine wounded in action, but another thirty hospitalised due to illness caused by the forced marches through barren hillsides in cold and wet weather. In the future it would be found better to distribute small garrisons in the countryside rather than to sweep it searching for Republican fighters[674].

Elsewhere, it was attrition and lack of supplies that diminished anti-Treaty strength. By the closing days of 1922, many areas were reduced to columns of ten men or so, incapable of large-scale attacks on Free State troops. Moreover, in contrast to their experience against the British, they could not count on civilian support. It was only committed Republican houses that would offer them shelter and food while on the run. They were also faced with a hostile and censored press and the opposition of the Catholic Church, which issued a formal statement condemning the anti-Treaty campaign as 'a system of murder and assassination' against the 'legitimate, elected government'.[675]

In the media, the government successfully managed to have the conflict depoliticised – essentially portraying the anti-Treatyites as little better than criminals. General instructions sent to the press laid down that the Free State forces were to be called 'the Army', 'National forces' or 'troops', whereas their opponents were to be called 'Irregulars' in preference to 'Republicans', and 'bands' or 'bodies', rather than 'troops'. The guerrillas did not 'attack'; they 'fired on'. They did not 'arrest'; they 'kidnapped'. Ernie O'Malley remarked, 'the press was consistently hostile [to the Republicans]... there was strict censorship, but in the majority of cases, little additional pressure was required'.[676]

Another major success for the Free State was getting a new, unarmed police force up and running. The Civic Guard (later known by the Irish term Garda Síochána) had originally been an armed and semi-mutinous corps. It was disbanded and relaunched in September 1922 under Eoin O'Duffy, a former IRA and National Army commander. O'Duffy filled the new police force with former IRA members, restricting members of the old RIC to positions at Headquarters. O'Duffy sent the unarmed force out with orders to resist anti-Treaty attacks passively: 'Don't be alarmed at the sound of a shot... you [have] right on your side and the gunmen only might... only cowards come armed to unarmed people'.[677]

The strategy was highly risky. Over 200 police stations were attacked and burned, one guard was killed by the Republicans, and several more by armed robbers. However, O'Duffy's gamble that the IRA would not risk the public opprobrium of shooting unarmed men paid off. In December 1922 the anti-Treaty IRA issued a General Order not to target the guards.[678]

Occasionally, the anti-Treaty forces could still mount major operations. For instance, in December 1922, a 100-strong column of Cork IRA men under Tom Barry marauded across the south midlands, capturing three towns in Tipperary and Kilkenny, where the Free State troops simply surrendered and handed over their weapons. Barry, along with columns from Kerry, also made an assault on Millstreet in County Cork in January 1923, killing two soldiers and taking thirty-nine prisoner. But ultimately, such local successes made little difference. The Republicans had neither heavy weapons nor supplies to hold the towns, nor the means to hold prisoners, who had to be released.

It was a measure of the unreality of Republican thinking that de Valera, while in hiding, along with the anti-Treaty TDs, declared in October the formation of a Republican Government, to 'be temporarily the Supreme Executive of the Republic and the State, until such time as the elected Parliament of the Republic can freely assemble, or the people being rid of external aggression are at liberty to decide freely how they are to be governed'.[679]

Executions

By late 1922, the initial impetus of the guerrilla campaign was largely spent. The anti-Treaty side could neither defeat the National Army in the field nor even engage it in large-scale actions. Nevertheless, the Free State still had a very serious security situation on its hands. Normal life was disrupted by the destruction of roads and railways. Several thousand guerrillas still roamed the countryside. An undisciplined and inexperienced Army, scattered in small garrisons, was still taking casualties daily and carrying out occasionally murderous reprisals of its own. Taxes could not be collected. Business was at a standstill in the south and west.

Moreover, outside of the guerrilla war, social unrest, which had been a serious problem since early 1922, continued to flare in the countryside. O'Higgins cited over 500 seizures of land by tenant farmers, burning of landlords' property and a labour dispute in Kildare where shots had been exchanged between farmers and labourers.[680] If the Irish state were to be viable, the guerrilla opposition would have to be crushed for good, and the Cabinet intended to squash it with all the means at its disposal. W. T. Cosgrave declared icily, 'this will not be a draw with a replay in the autumn'.[681]

Towards the end of September 1922, the Dáil passed emergency legislation known as the Public Safety Bill, which allowed for the execution of those captured bearing arms against the State. Technically, the Provisional Government had no legal right under the Treaty to enact new legislation without royal assent, the King being represented in the person of the Governor General. And in theory, the Provisional Government's powers did not apply after the Treaty formally passed into law on 6 December 1922. So, technically speaking, the Public Safety Bill was not a law but simply a resolution passed in the Dáil. However, since there was as yet no Governor General who could give his assent, and as the government felt that the situation was too grave for legal niceties, the legislation setting up military courts was passed anyway. In August

1923, the Free State would pass an Act of Indemnity for all actions committed during the Civil War, and also passed new, formal special powers legislation – the Emergency Powers Act – retrospectively legalising what it had enacted in the autumn of 1922.[682]

In September 1922, however, the Public Safety legisation meant in effect passing the power of life and death over prisoners to the Army. Executions needed only the signatures of two National Army officers. Cosgrave told the Dáil, 'Although I have always objected to the death penalty, there is no other way that I know of in which ordered conditions can be restored in this country, or any security obtained for our troops, or to give our troops any confidence in us as a government'.[683] After an amnesty of two weeks, in which anti-Treaty fighters could surrender without consequences, the legislation came into force in mid-October.

Still, many Republicans did not believe that the government was serious. They would shortly find out that it was. On 17 November, four IRA men who had been captured in Dublin were shot by firing squad, and another three were executed two days later. By the end of the week, Erskine Childers, who had signed the Treaty but later organised Republican propaganda against it, was also dead. He had been captured at his home in Wicklow on 11 November in possession of a small pistol that Michael Collins had given him before he departed for London and the Treaty negotiations. He was sentenced and shot on 24 November. On 30 November another three Republican prisoners were executed in Dublin.

Republican and even international opinion was rocked by the severity of the government's actions. Liam Lynch ordered the killing of any TD who had voted for the 'Murder Bill' and also threatened hostile judges and newspaper editors. The war had entered its darkest phase, with all the malicious bitterness of a vendetta.

On 6 December 1922, the Free State was formally established by an Act of the British Parliament and the last six thousand British troops in Dublin were shipped back to Britain. The following day, 7 December, TDs Seán Hales of Cork and Pádraic Ó Máille of Mayo emerged from their lunch at a hotel on Ormonde Quay, ten minutes' walk along Dublin's River Liffey from the still-ruined Four Courts, for the short drive to the Dáil. Both had been active in Sinn Féin and the IRA in the struggle against the British, but had supported the Treaty. Hales had a brother, Tom, in the hills of west Cork fighting with the anti-Treaty IRA. As they were getting into the car that would drive them to Parliament, two gunmen opened fire on them, killing Hales and severely wounding Ó Máille, before disappearing into the backstreets behind the quays. A British Army lorry was passing as the shooting took place, and its soldiers, in what may have been the last actions ever by British soldiers in Dublin, fired some fleeting shots after the assassins as they ran in the direction of Capel Street.[684]

The assassination was revenge for the executions. A brutal exercise in reprisals had begun. The Cabinet met in an emergency session and decided, after an all-night debate, on retaliatory executions of four Republican leaders captured in the Four Courts back in July: Liam Mellows, Rory O'Connor, Dick Barrett and Joe McKelvey. The executions were no more and no less than a reprisal killing for the death of Seán Hales. The four had been captured months before the government had even proposed its emergency legislation. They were shot within hours of the Cabinet's decision. Defending the action in the Dáil from shocked Labour Party TDs, O'Higgins exclaimed, 'Personal spite! Great heavens! Vindictiveness! One of these men was a friend of mine!'[685] Rory O'Connor had not only been a friend of O'Higgins, but actually the best man at his wedding only six months earlier.

Before December was out, the State had executed nine more prisoners, including a batch of seven young IRA men from Kildare who had been captured ripping up railway tracks on 13 December and were shot six days later. In January 1923, a total of thirty-four official executions were carried out, spreading out from Dublin to Dundalk, Roscrea, Carlow, Birr and Portlaoise, Limerick, Tralee and Athlone. Before the end of the war, the firing squads would also be active in Cork, Kerry, Tuam and Ennis.[686] The ruthlessness of the government's thinking could be chilling. O'Higgins argued that the executions should be 'regionalised' so that every area where guerrillas were active would feel their impact.

Ruthless they may have been, but the executions worked, to a large degree. Paddy O'Connor, an ex-Dublin IRA Active Service Unit fighter and now National Army officer, told Ernie O'Malley later that, by December 1922, 'we were losing the support of the people, our men were war-weary and the going was too heavy for us. Our men had no grub, no uniforms and no pay, so don't think all the idealism was on your side... The executions broke your morale, there is no doubt about that'.[687] Republicans in the field knew that if they continued their campaign their imprisoned comrades would pay with their lives, and guerrilla activity trailed off dramatically from this point on. By the end of hostilities, a total of eighty-one judicial executions had taken place. Republicans claimed seventy-seven of the dead as their martyrs and guarded the memory bitterly for decades afterwards (the remaining four executed were unaligned gunmen).

Even though perhaps twice as many men were killed in 'unofficial' summary reprisals by Free State troops

(Todd Andrews put the figure at 153),[688] it was the official executions that Republicans would find hardest to forgive. That their former comrades could draw up legislation, try and execute their men in defence of a British idea of legality was impossible for them to swallow.

Soft targets

Not that the viciousness was one-sided. No more TDs were killed, but Dublin TD Seán McGarry's house was burned down with his seven-year-old son inside. Kevin O'Higgins' father was assassinated and his family home burned, as was that of W. T. Cosgrave, whose uncle was also murdered. A pro-Treaty politician, Seamus Dwyer, was gunned down on December 20 at his grocery business in Dublin.[689] Todd Andrews thought that 'except in one or two places we [the Republicans] were unable to mount a counter-terror campaign partly because we lacked the means and partly because we lacked the will and nerve. We also lacked an intelligence service'. For him a wholesale campaign of assassination would not have presented moral problems: 'We should have been able to find out who the counsellors [of the execution policy] were and eliminate them'.[690]

Instead, in the New Year Republicans embarked on a wholesale campaign of arson against the homes of Free State Senators. The Senate was the State's upper house, and many of its members were former Unionists and members of the old Protestant upper class. In early 1923 almost 200 mansions, which had once dominated the Irish countryside, went up in flames.[691] This was more than three times the number of 'big houses' burned by the IRA in 1919–21.

The Senators were a soft target, being outside the nationalist Catholic community, scattered around the country and difficult for the Free State to protect. Attacking them was less likely to attract public outrage than killing directly elected nationalist TDs. It was even popular among sections of a rural population who had traditionally seen the 'landlord' as an oppressive, alien ruling caste and who often came to loot the burnt-out mansions. After the burning of the 'big house' at Derreen in County Kerry, 'crowds of every description [came]... pulling, hauling, fighting for what they could take. The house is absolutely destroyed, the doors all smashed, every particle of furniture taken'. Similarly, at Glenfarne in County Leitrim, 'the people came with carts and carried away... everything that was portable... so that only the roof was left and the roof went eventually'.[692]

It was not only in rural areas that Free State supporters were attacked. In Dublin, for instance, over a single week in February 1923, the Free State's Chief Solicitor, M. A. Corrigan, had his house blown up with explosives, and there were attempts to do the same to the houses of Cosgrave's father-in-law and the Managing Director of the *Irish Independent*. Senator John Bagwell was kidnapped at gunpoint from his house in Howth.[693]

The campaign of intimidation caused at least one pro-Treaty TD, Frank Bulfin, to send in a letter of resignation. However, terror, as Bulfin soon discovered, could come from both sides. Ernest Blythe recalled that in response to Bulfin's resignation the government dispatched three plainclothes men, led by ex-Squad gunman Joe O'Reilly, to fetch him to Dublin to explain himself: 'They stopped the car and one of them proposed that they "shoot the oul' bastard and have no more trouble with him". Another agreed that it would be the simplest procedure, while a third, ostensibly more cautious, argued that Cosgrave would be so annoyed with them that they would be in endless trouble'. Bulfin withdrew his resignation and was housed under guard with other TDs in Buswell's hotel. 'We had', Blythe recalled, 'no other incidents of the kind. I suppose Frank's story got round amongst the TDs, but I must say that the incident made me feel very strongly that once civil war is started, all ordinary rules must go by the board'.[694] Both sides therefore targeted civilian as well as military opponents. And yet there were also restraints on the violence. The campaign against Senators and other pro-Treaty civilians, while undoubtedly traumatic for those affected, was largely limited to violence against property rather than people. There were no massacres of the civilian 'enemies of the Republic', no mass graves were filled, no wholesale displacement either of Free State supporters or of former loyalists took place. One memoirist recalled that his mother ordered the anti-Treaty fighters who burned their house to first rescue the valuables and the children's Christmas presents.[695]

In fact, civilians were killed far less frequently in the Civil War than in the War of Independence. The IRA had shot up to two hundred people as informers during the earlier conflict and, despite much more widespread public co-operation with the Free State forces than with the British, only a fraction of this number were killed as 'spies' in the Civil War. This seems to show that the anti-Treaty fighters were more reluctant to punish those who accepted the legitimacy of the Irish state than those supporting British rule.

The other target of Republicans was the railway system, against which they launched a 'blitz' in January and February 1923, destroying at least three stations and hundreds of miles of track, and derailing dozens of trains.[696] In Kerry this caused the death of two drivers, whose train crashed after its track had been derailed.[697] The Free State was ultimately forced to form a special section of the Army to protect the railways and build a network of blockhouses to keep the lines open. By March 1923, under heavy military guard, most lines were back up and running.

The bitter end

Victory in a guerrilla war can be hard to define. As long as some guerrillas have the will to remain in the field and to disrupt the operation of government, the war cannot be said to be over, even if the numbers and capabilities of the insurgent force have been greatly diminished. So it was in early 1923 in Ireland. Nevertheless, as February turned into March, it was clear that the anti-Treaty side's ability to obstruct the government of the Free State was weakening. The National Army, after an internal reorganisation in early 1923, was functioning better, while the Republicans increasingly avoided direct attacks on troops. Badly armed, badly fed and hunted from hiding place to hiding place, theirs was a miserable existence. One Cork IRA veteran recalled how 'we lived almost back with the foxes in the end and you got as wise as foxes too'.[698] In Waterford, Pax Whelan recalled that there were three columns of fifteen men on the run and 'the people had turned against them. They had no clothes, they had nothing, they were outcasts'. The Church's condemnation 'influenced womenfolk, except our own loyal followers'.[699]

Many guerrillas contracted the skin disease scabies, nicknamed the 'Republican itch', from living in cold, wet dugouts throughout the winter. Liam Deasy, on the run in the hills of Tipperary, described the condition thus: 'I was covered with broken skin from hips to toes, with blood and matter oozing from the skin breaks'.[700] In early January, Deasy was captured in Clonmel and kept in custody; he signed a document calling on all IRA men under his command to surrender. His detractors maintained that he did this merely to avoid execution, but Deasy maintained that he had become convinced, even before his capture, of the war's futility.[701]

In February 1923 another senior IRA figure, Dinny Lacey, who had been leading guerrilla activities in Tipperary, was killed, and most of his column captured, in the Glen of Aherlow. Towards the end of February, the Executive of the anti-Treaty IRA met in an isolated location named Ballingeary in Tipperary. Liam Lynch was told that the guerrilla Army was on the brink of collapse. Their 1st Southern Division reported that 'in a short time we would not have a man left owing to the great number of arrests and casualties'. The Cork units reported that they had suffered twenty-nine killed and an unknown number captured in recent actions and, 'if five men are arrested in each area, we are finished'.[702]

Lynch chose to continue the war. The Free State had suspended executions in early February, in the hope that it would help to speed the end of the conflict, and the meeting of the IRA leadership must have seemed like the ideal opportunity to call it off. For whatever reason – bloody-mindedness, fanaticism and idealism are among those attributed to him – Lynch refused.

The 'terror month'

The following month, March 1923, known among Kerry Republicans as the 'terror month', would demonstrate the cost in lives and bitterness of such a policy. Kerry had seen more violence in the guerrilla phase than almost anywhere else in Ireland. The local IRA had been almost entirely anti-Treaty, and after the landings in August of the previous year, Kerry had been occupied by sometimes brutal

National Army troops of the Dublin Guard. By March 1923, sixty-eight Free State soldiers had already been killed there and 157 wounded – a total of eighty-five would die there by the end of the war.[703] March 1923 would be the nadir of the Civil War in the county.

The month started in Kerry with an anti-Treaty attack on Cahirciveen. The Republicans were surprised before they could actually assault the town and dispersed, amid running fights, into the hills to get away. Three National Army and two Republican soldiers were killed and six IRA men captured.[704] The following day, acting on information from an informer, a party of National Army officers drove out of Tralee to a village named Knocknagoshel, where they expected to find a Republican dugout. As they entered the dugout, they triggered a booby-trap mine, which blasted the party and killed three Dublin Guard officers and two soldiers.

Two of the dead were close personal friends and ex-IRA comrades of Paddy Daly, in command of the Free State's Kerry forces. He announced that in future prisoners would clear mined roads. The day after the Knocknagoshel bomb, nine prisoners were taken from Ballymullen Gaol in Tralee to Ballyseedy crossroads, ostensibly for this purpose. The troops made sure that they were 'all fairly anonymous, no priests or nuns in the family, those that'll make the least noise'.[705]

Some of the prisoners had already been beaten by the time they arrived at Ballyseedy, where they were tied around a landmine and literally blown to smithereens. One man, Stephen Fuller, was not killed but blown clear by the blast, and lived to tell about the massacre. At the scene, the Free State troops shovelled the remains of the pulverised bodies into nine coffins and drove them back to Tralee with the story that they had been accidentally killed while clearing a mined road. A riot broke out in the town when the relatives of the dead tried to break open the coffins and identify the dead.[706]

If anyone believed that the explosion at Ballyseedy had been an accident, they would have trouble explaining the deaths of nine more Republican prisoners in the next four days. Four were blown to pieces in Killarney and another five at Cahirciveen, the last five having been first shot in the legs to stop them escaping.[707] Before the month was out, seven more prisoners were killed in Kerry, five judicially executed for their part in the action at Cahirciveen, and another two simply shot out of hand.[708] Perhaps the most sinister aspect of the incidents was the government response, which showed the extent to which they looked the other way at atrocities committed by their troops throughout the war. Richard Mulcahy defended Paddy Daly's story of 'accidental' deaths in the Dáil, and an Army inquiry cleared the soldiers concerned.[709] We now know, following the release of documents kept secret until December 2008, that not only did the government know that the prisoners had been murdered, they even knew who did it: a group of Dublin-based troops known as 'the Visiting Committee' in National Army circles.[710]

Before the month was out, there were two more long-remembered incidents of vicious revenge killings. In Wexford, which had been free of executions up this point, three Republican prisoners were shot on 13 March. Bob Lambert, the Wexford IRA commander, had three National Army soldiers captured and killed in retaliation.[711] The local Free State forces retaliated by assassinating at least two more local Republicans.

In Donegal, National Army troops responded to the death of a soldier by executing four prisoners who had been held in Drumboe Castle since January.[712] The IRA and the Republican 'government' proclaimed a period of national mourning for their dead and banned public entertainments and sporting events. An international boxing match in Dublin on 17 March had to be guarded by a battalion of Free State troops and was attacked with a mine and gunfire.[713] A Volunteer named Patrick O'Brien died, shot by Free State troops, trying to blow up a Dublin cinema.[714]

If the savagery of March 1923 was not reason enough for calling a halt to the war, then the Republicans had also the compelling reason of the collapse of their military effort. And yet even then they did not end their campaign. In a meeting in the Knockmealdown Mountains on 26 March, their Executive voted to continue the war by six votes to five. De Valera, by now urging the military leadership to end the fighting, was allowed to listen to their debate, but not given a vote.[715]

The end

By the middle of April, the National Army had cause to report to the government that the end was in sight. Sweeps of the Knockmealdown Mountains in early April, by troops led by General Prout and acting on intelligence extracted from prisoners in Dublin, captured a host of senior IRA figures including Todd Andrews, Dan Breen and Seán Gaynor, who had been in the area for the meeting of the IRA Executive.

Liam Lynch himself, the Republican Chief of Staff and the man who had done so much to prolong the conflict, was killed on 10 April. He and four other senior Republicans, armed only with revolvers, were spotted by a National Army patrol; fleeing up the hillside, Lynch was brought down by a rifle shot to the back. Grievously wounded, the troops took him to nearby Clonmel, where he died. Austin Stack, Lynch's Deputy Chief of Staff, was arrested four days later.

If the Republican head had been decapitated, the body was also dying of a thousand small cuts. Two examples from the last month of the war will give an idea of the many small tragedies that accompanied the war's sad, slow sputtering-out.

In Castleblake, County Kilkenny, National Army troops acting on good intelligence (as was now common) surrounded a Republican dugout in a ruined castle. Inside was a Republican column including two former National Army officers, Ned Somers and Theo English, who had defected to the Republicans the previous December. Had they been captured they would almost certainly been executed, as had a number of previous deserters. Thus, when a Free State Lieutenant named Kennedy called on the occupants to surrender they answered with a grenade, mortally wounding Kennedy. Free State troops then rushed the building, killing Somers and English and taking the rest prisoner.[716]

Four days later, an anti-Treaty IRA column in Kerry under Tim Lyons (known as 'Aeroplane') found itself surrounded by Free State troops in a cave near Kerry Head. Two Free State soldiers were killed when they tried to storm the cave. After three days' siege, explosives were lowered over the cave mouths and detonated, killing three Republicans. Lyons then tried to surrender and was hoisted up from the cave by a rope, which snapped (Republicans claimed it was deliberately cut). Lyons fell to his death on the rocks below. The remaining three IRA men surrendered, but were executed in Tralee a few days afterwards.[717]

On 30 April, Frank Aiken, who had taken over as IRA Chief of Staff after the death of Lynch, called a ceasefire. Aiken was from Armagh, which he had seen separated from the rest of the country by partition. While he had not liked the Treaty and its acceptance of the existence of Northern Ireland, he had never been in favour of the Civil War and had entered it only unwillingly, after he and his men had been arrested by Free State troops. In his attack on Dundalk back in August, he had managed to free most of his command, but his 4th Northern Division had taken only sporadic part in the fighting thereafter.

Now he made rapid moves to end the war. On 24 May he ordered the remaining guerrillas in the field to 'dump arms'. This was not the same as a surrender – the Civil War never formally ended – but it was effectively the end of the war.

The Irish Civil War had no clean finish. Even after the Republicans had given up, the Free State continued with its executions, 'round-ups' and even assassinations. Éamon de Valera was picked up at an election rally in August. Noel Lemass, brother of Seán, was abducted in Dublin in June 1923, and his decomposed body was found in the Wicklow Mountains four months later.

The other civil war

With the threat of guerrilla attacks fading, part of the National Army, organised in a 'Special Infantry Corps', was used to put down a wave of social disorder.[718]

In County Waterford there was a bitter farm labourers' strike in the creameries around Kilmacthomas. In May 1923, 1,500 labourers were sacked for refusing to accept a pay cut. Republican (and later Communist) activist Frank Edwards recalled that 'It was a localised civil war but a more logical one... the Free State Army had to convey the farm crops and stock to the towns'. The workers, whether former IRA members or simply union men with access to guns, sniped at the convoys, who returned fire.[719]

By the summer, 600 troops under General Prout were stationed in the county, which was put under martial law, and a curfew was put in place. A Labour TD was arrested and farmers formed their own self-styled 'White Guards', who beat up union activists and burned their cottages. By October, the workers were forced to cave in. The defeat cost the ITGWU the defection of almost all of its agricultural labourer members.[720] The wave of labour militancy that had done so much to carry along the nationalist revolution was over.

Elsewhere, state forces were used to collect unpaid rates, debts and even rents. From February 1923, the Special Infantry Corps was deployed to areas where farms had been illegally seized by the IRA and others, particularly in the west and in County Cork, to restore them to their owners. Cattle that had been grazing on occupied land were seized by the troops and sold off in Dublin. In Roscommon, Free State troops fired over the heads of a crowd trying to prevent the impounding of animals. A pro-Treaty TD for Cork lamented that 'these people gave us assistance when we were out in the hills fighting against an alien government. I think it is a very bad action for the government to seize cattle on these farms for arrears of rent due to English landlords'.[721]

Indeed, as the government well knew, collecting rents for landlords was a most hazardous thing for a nationalist government to do. In the north midlands, late 1921 and early 1922 had seen a peaceful revolt of farmers who still lived on landed estates, demanding compulsory purchase of their holdings by the new Irish state. At a meeting of these 'unpurchased tenants' in Ballybay, Monaghan, 100 delegates – representing farmers on rent strike since early 1922 – heard that the CID had been used to collect landlords' rent. One Father Maguire declared that, while there should not be 'armed resistance', it was 'terrible for the government to lift money for absentee landlords who never spend a penny in the country'.[722] It was against this background of what might be called the final 'land war'in Ireland that many of the 'Big Houses' belonging to the landlords were burnt in early 1923.

Mollifying the farming class, the bedrock of pro-Treaty support, was necessary for the survival of the Free State, especially as they had called a general election for August of 1923. In June, the Agriculture Minister Patrick Hogan tabled a Land Bill under which 70,000 tenancies, containing about 300,000 people, with a rental value of £800,000-£1,000,000 would be compulsorily purchased from the remaining landlords.[723] This was not a redistribution of land, as many agrarian radicals had hoped for; rather, it simply meant that existing farmers would be freed from paying rent.

As far as the pro-Treatyites were concerned, they had settled the national question, bringing self-government and now, in a similar, conservative, gradualist way, they were settling the land question too.

'They haven't much sense, the creatures'

The death toll of the Civil War was never calculated. Richard Mulcahy released two separate figures for National Army dead: 540 killed between the signing of the Treaty and the war's end and up to 800 Army deaths between January 1922 and April 1924.[724] The IRA death toll appears to be between 400 and 500, but there is still no hard figure.

The conflict varied widely in intensity: 180 were killed in Cork,[725] 185 in Kerry,[726] and around 200 in Dublin,[727] the localities most affected by the war. Another forty-eight died in Sligo,[728] and forty-five in Kildare[729] – areas of moderate violence – and only twenty-one were killed in a 'quiet' county like Offaly.[730] Even by the end of the war, there were still an estimated 500 guerrillas at large in the hills of Kerry, but in Longford the local 'flying column' was '15 men who cannot go home' for fear of arrest.[731] The total death toll was under 2,000 and probably closer to 1,500.

The war left appalling bitterness in its wake, but even in this respect, the animosity generated by revenge killings varied widely. Guerrillas in Kerry and Dublin had experienced state 'murder gangs', many executions, assassinations and torture of prisoners, and had of course also killed unarmed pro-Treatyites themselves. But in Cork there were few cases of Free State reprisal killings, and those there were had been mostly carried out by visiting Dublin troops rather than by native Corkmen. Waterford had no National Army reprisal killingss and only two executions. Some areas had none at all. Todd Andrews found in the internment camps that Volunteers from Dublin and Kerry 'regarded the Free Staters as traitors and murderers', but the Cork IRA men 'didn't share my resentment and bitterness... they frequently expressed regret at the death of Collins'.[732]

Moreover, it had been a war largely between combatants. Civilians were sometimes caught in the crossfire, or killed in raids on houses, but were rarely deliberately targeted. Unlike the War of Independence, this was a conflict *within* nationalist Ireland; there was no 'enemy community' to punish for the hurt caused to one's own side. How many civilians died? We still have no overall figure, but the number appears to be much lower than the 800 plus non-combatants killed in 1919–21. An intelligent guess puts the figure of civilian deaths in the Civil War at about 200; or about 10–15 per cent of the total dead, compared to 30–40 per cent in the war against the British.[733]

There is also considerable evidence that much of the civilian population took neither side during the Civil War.

Elections held just after the war in August 1923, in which the anti-Treaty side were allowed to participate (though many of their candidates and activists were imprisoned) showed that the belligerents of the war were indeed the two biggest parties: 409,876 pro-Treaty votes were cast to 288,794 anti-Treaty, but a third of the electorate of just over one million voted for non-aligned parties, or independents.[734]

The Republicans did much better than they expected in the election, given that the pro-Treaty Cumann na nGaedheal controlled the state and heavily censored the press. But their activists had no stomach for a return to armed resistance. Máire Comerford, who had been arrested for the attempted kidnap of W. T. Cosgrave during the war and was subsequently shot in the leg by a Free State soldier while in prison, was released just in time for the election. With all the male activists imprisoned, she was given a motorbike and told to organise the Sinn Féin campaign in County Cork. In the Sinn Féin office in Dublin, she found that Republicans in the United States had sent them cases of guns. 'They were the last thing we wanted to see... Sinn Féin was cleaning itself of its military reputation and trying to be political'.[735]

There was a widespread sense of disillusionment, both among former activists and the general public in the wake of the Civil War. The Farmers' Party leader Patrick McKenna, launching their election campaign in Moate, lamented that it was 'High time for the warring elements to have common sense. No more jail and bullet'. 'Why in god's name can't the parties to this miserable dispute settle the bloody conflict?'[736] The Farmers' Party emerged as the third-biggest party after the election, with over 127,000 votes.

Ernest Blythe, campaigning in Monaghan for pro-Treaty Cumann na nGaedheal, was unapologetic for his government's use of executions to put down 'the Irregulars':

> The people in a manner blame the government for the executions but it must be remembered that they were up against guerrilla warfare. It was almost magnifying it to call it a war at all. Except in one or two cases in Kerry, the Irregulars never put up a decent fight. They got behind a hedge and shot a man and came in the dead of the night and burned a house. They weren't around to fight the Black and Tans but suddenly they were great heroes. It became absolutely necessary for the government to show the fellow with the gun that he could not go out to shoot and burn with only the risk of being taken to prison... Any fellow who went out with the gun and petrol tin deserved the firing squad and none got it except who deserved it.[737]

For all the talk about 'settling the bloody conflict', there must have been a receptive audience for such belligerence, as Blythe was re-elected with over 11,500 votes.[738]

Ernie O'Malley, elected for Dublin North Central while still imprisoned, noted with a mixture of amusement and dismay that voters often gave their second preference votes across the Civil War divide. He had been elected with the help of transfers from voters who had given their first preference to Richard Mulcahy, the man who had nearly had him executed. 'How could one arrive at the point of view which gave him first preference and me second? Perhaps it was as the people once said when they talked of our marching and drilling as play-acting. "Musha God help them, they haven't much sense, the creatures"'.[739]

The Labour Party did respectably with 10 per cent of the vote and over 111,000 votes, though this was 20,000 votes down on its performance in 1922. Confusingly, given the leadership's *de facto* pro-Treaty position, it still campaigned on a platform of socialism and the Workers' Republic. But here too, the desire for peace was evident. In Cavan, their candidate told his listeners that he was a follower of James Connolly and would be still in Dundalk Gaol (presumably for IRA activities) 'if someone hadn't blown a hole in it' in July 1922. Nevertheless, his message was essentially pacifist: 'The spade produces, the gun does not. Muzzle the guns!'[740]

Around 13,000 anti-Treaty fighters and political activists were still imprisoned even after the election. More remained on the run to avoid arrest. The country remained under effective martial law, and was dotted with the charred remains of houses gutted by the Republican arson campaign. The prisoners held a mass hunger strike in October 1923, in which three of them died. Most were not released until mid-1924. Ugly scenes also accompanied the handover of the remains of the executed to their families. The reburials of the bodies were heavily policed, and in Dundalk shots were exchanged in the graveyard.[741]

Violence took some time to stutter out around the country, and the bitter enmities of the fratricidal strife of 1922–23 lingered for many years thereafter, but the Irish revolution was over.

Chapter 10:

Aftermath and Legacy

The aftermath

The Civil War bled much of the idealism out of the new Irish state. It emerged as a besieged entity, suspicious of its own people. The Cosgrave Government closed down a number of elected local governments for disloyalty or corruption, and effectively stripped the remainder of real powers. They were replaced with appointed 'county managers'. Even today, the Republic of Ireland remains one of the most centralised countries in Europe.[742] One of the abiding ironies of the Irish revolution is that the very local democracy that allowed Sinn Féin to undermine British rule so effectively was neutered upon their accession to power.

Though of course tragic in human terms, the demographic losses from revolutionary violence were relatively insignificant; a total of about 5,000 dead in all thirty-two counties in 1916–23. Far more people (about 23,000) had died on the island in the influenza epidemic of 1918–19,[743] and another 30,000 or so in the British armed forces in the First World War. However, the Civil War in particular, limited though it was in terms of lives lost, did very serious short-term economic damage. The anti-Treaty IRA had wrecked infrastructure such as roads, railways and government buildings in order to try to bring down the civilian administration. Where there was sustained armed resistance to the state in, for example, Kerry, Tipperary and parts of Cork, taxes could not be collected at all. County Clare alone, for instance, had a tax shortfall of £200,000. By 1926, it was calculated that the cost of the war, including reconstruction, compensation and financing the Army, came to £47 million, or roughly 170 per cent of the state's annual income.[744]

Out of a total expenditure in 1923–24 of about £30 million, £10.5 million was spent on the National Army. From a high of 58,000 men during the Civil War, gobbling up some 30 per cent of the new state's expenditure, it was reduced to 14,000 men in 1924, and by the 1930s was down to fewer than 10,000. The cuts had the added bonus for the government of getting rid of former IRA elements in the Dublin Guard and Army Intelligence, who had been behind some of the Civil War's worst atrocities. Paddy Daly, the man responsible for the massacre of anti-Treaty prisoners at Ballyseedy, was pressured into resigning – not for that incident, but for an assault on a woman at Kenmare. The CID was also stood down, and only a small number of detectives were retained in the Garda Special Branch.[745]

The demobilisation process almost provoked a mutiny among the former IRA officers in the National Army, who saw in the cuts preference being given to ex-British soldiers and a retreat from progress – Collins' 'stepping stone' – towards an all-Ireland Republic. Two men in particular, ousted intelligence chiefs Liam Tobin and Charlie Dalton, canvassed for support amongst both Army officers and anti-Treaty prisoners for a coup that would take power in the south and then attack Northern Ireland to end partition. Dublin IRA prisoner Joe O'Connor recalled how 'One morning I was called out to the camp office, to be faced by a Free State Intelligence Officer in uniform. I did not know his name and he did not tell me. He came straight to the point by asking what my attitude would be to a march on the North'.[746] O'Connor responded positively, but nothing came of the proposed *putsch*.

The main conspirators – around 40 men, including Tobin and Dalton – were arrested by armed troops in March 1924 on Parnell Street in Dublin. The resulting scandal also marked the sidelining of Richard Mulcahy, who (somewhat unfairly, given that he was the one who ordered the plotters' arrest) was forced to resign both from the Cabinet and as head of the Army by a faction in the Cabinet led by Kevin O'Higgins and Eoin O'Duffy.[747]

What sidelining Mulcahy meant for his Cabinet colleagues, however, was removing his IRB clique from the Army and government, and thereby removing the Army's ability to exert an influence on politics. It was a particularly inglorious end for the Brotherhood, the organisation that had in many respects been behind the Irish revolutionary process from day one. It was wound up soon after the failed Army coup.

A conservative state

Socially and economically speaking, the new state was highly conservative. The new government inherited intact a British-trained civil service, schooled in fiscal rectitude. One of the terms of the Treaty was that this be retained and the pensions of its staff paid. A senior British civil servant, C. J. Gregg, was loaned to the Free State to oversee the setting up of the Irish Department of Finance, emphasising the need to 'impress on people that one Minister holds the purse strings and... it is very difficult to get anything out of that purse'.[748]

The first Minister for Finance was Ernest Blythe, who in the early 1910s as a newly recruited IRB man had been spewing socialistic rhetoric in *Irish Freedom* about the need to transform Irish society. In 1923–24, however, he exemplified the pro-Treatyite nationalists' rapprochement with the propertied classes, whose taxes were desperately needed to keep the new state afloat. One of his first actions as a minister was to cut the pay of civil servants and reduce government expenditure from £42 million in 1923 to £28 million by 1926. At the same time, the Free State courted its wealthier citizens; income tax was reduced from 25 per cent to 15 per cent, which was lower than the rate in England.[749]

Blythe, along with his colleagues and senior civil servants such as James MacElligott, saw their role as running a tight financial ship and facilitating trade; not intervening in the economy. The Minister for Labour Patrick McGilligan stated in 1924 that 'It is not the function of the government to provide work'.[750] Taxation remained low, as did spending. This attitude would endure in the Department of Finance well into the 1950s.

The Irish banks, most of which then had their headquarters in London, were reluctant to loan money to the Free State until they were sure it would survive. W.T. Cosgrave, the new President of the Executive Council (effectively, Prime Minister), had to exploit a personal relationship with the Bank of Ireland to rescue the finances of the new state. The bank's large (though undisclosed) loan to the exchequer staved off bankruptcy in 1923–24. It was the second time the Irish banking establishment had bailed out the independence movement, and Cosgrave in particular. They had also provided emergency loans for local government in mid-1920.[751] Not until the late 1940s did Ireland found its own Central Bank, and while Irish notes and coins were minted, they remained interchangeable with sterling until 1980.[752]

The Irish state, therefore, while in theory still wedded to nationalist goals such as Irish reunification and economic and cultural transformation, placed a real priority on its own survival. Nowhere was this more obvious than in relation to partition. Ernest Blythe again illustrated the headlong retreat from radicalism on the part of the Irish Government with regard to Northern Ireland. Blythe, an Ulster Protestant himself, had never been comfortable with Collins' aggressive northern policies of early 1922. In August 1923, at an election meeting along the border, he told his listeners that 'the union of Ireland must be brought about by good government. The people of the six counties could never be brought in by force'.[753]

In 1925, the Boundary Commission in which Michael Collins had placed so much hope recommended no significant changes to the border between north and south. The Free State Government declined to have the embarrassing report published, and agreed to waive its claim to some Catholic areas along the border, in return for being freed from its share of Britain's imperial debt.

The Free State was therefore vulnerable from the first to the charge that it had betrayed the nationalist revolution, but so complete was the Republicans' defeat and disillusion after the Civil War that no serious attempt was again made to overthrow the Treaty settlement by force of arms. Instead, led by a chastened de Valera, most of the anti-Treatyites left Sinn Féin to the Republican purists and formed Fianna Fáil ('The Republican Party') in 1926, entered the political system and tried to reform it from within. The IRA remained ambiguous, some supporting de Valera while others remained sceptical.

Perhaps the Civil War's final reprisal killing came in 1927, when Kevin O'Higgins, whom Republicans had never forgiven for his role in the Civil War executions, was gunned down by three IRA men on his way to Mass. However, by then most of the 'Irregulars' of 1922 were already on their way to respectability in Fianna Fáil. De Valera said that the killing was 'murder', and 'a crime that cuts at the root of representative government'.[754]

In 1931, diplomacy by the Free State was instrumental in the passing of the Statute of Westminster, by which Britain gave up the right to legislate for members of the Commonwealth, including Ireland. In 1932, Fianna Fáil, the party constructed by de Valera from the ashes of the anti-Treatyites of the Civil War, entered power peacefully by election and dismantled many aspects of the Treaty. The democratic process in Ireland was therfore ultimately upheld against the claims of men with guns who claimed that they alone represented 'the people'. De Valera's own journey and that of his colleagues is often represented as one away from elitist militarism and towards peaceful democratic politics. There is much truth in this, but it is hazardous to characterise the Civil War division as being between pro-Treaty democrats on one side and anti-Treaty militarists on the other. Authoritarian and anti-democratic attitudes existed on both sides of the Treaty divide; clearly among the anti-Treaty IRA, who refused to accept the Dáil's endorsement of the Treaty settlement, but also among the National Army troops, who threatened to mutiny in 1924, and in Eoin O'Duffy, who set up a fascist-style movement, the Blueshirts, in the 1930s and who contemplated a military coup in 1932 to stop Fianna Fáil from coming to power.[755]

It is to the credit of Cosgrave – and also Mulcahy, who told one of the 1932 pro-Treaty military conspirators 'not to be an ass' – that the Civil War was not re-fought in the 1930s, as their Cumann na nGaedheal party handed over power peacefully to Fianna Fáil after the victory of the latter in a general election, and instructed the organs of the state to obey the new government. Fianna Fáil, for their part, banned both the Blueshirts and the IRA in the 1930s, effectively severing the link between the major political parties and paramilitarism.

The revolution betrayed or the revolution triumphant?

If the pro-Treatyites considered the revolution to have ended in 1922, for Fianna Fáil its end came in the 1930s. While some would scoff that this simply meant political power for their party, there is some validity in seeing in the first Fianna Fáil Government an attempt to achieve the goals of the revolution left unfinished in 1922.

First of all, the constitutional limits on the Irish state's independence were removed one by one. The Senate, intended to be a voice for the southern Unionist minority, which the IRA had tried to burn out of existence in 1923, was abolished, as was the office of Governor-General, the King's representative in Ireland (although the post had in fact been always filled since 1923 by a nationalist). The Oath of Allegiance to the King, the symbol of all that Republicans professed to hate about the Free State, was also removed. Finally, de Valera passed a new constitution in 1937, which made Ireland a 'Republic in all but name', he claimed.[756] In 1939 the British agreed to return to Ireland the naval ports they had retained under the Treaty, making possible Irish neutrality in the Second World War.

Fine Gael, the descendants of the pro-Treaty side, in a coalition government with the Republicans of Clann na Poblachta after the war, left the British Commonwealth in 1948 and formally declared the Republic of Ireland.[757]

De Valera, in his 1937 constitution, stated that the national territory was the whole island of Ireland, but with the proviso that until reunification took place, the effective territory of his 'all but Republic' was the same as that of the Free State. Little more than lip service was ever done to advance the territorial claim to the six counties, which was formally dropped in 1998.

The dreams of Irish nationalist revolutionaries in the early twentieth century had gone beyond simply political independence and Irish unity, however. Many in Sinn Féin, the IRB and the nascent Labour movement had also dreamed of an Ireland that would be prosperous, self-reliant, culturally Gaelic and more equal than before. And the first Fianna Fáil governments did try to realise some of these dreams.

On the land, where the pro-Treatyites had bought out the remaining landlords in 1923, Fianna Fáil went a step further in 1933 with another Land Act, making concerted efforts at redistribution of land. This had the tangible benefit of rewarding their supporters, but was also an attempt to, as nationalists saw it, reverse the process of colonisation and give the land back to 'the people'. This policy even went so far as instituting internal colonies of small farmers and landless men, often IRA veterans, from the west into the rich lands of Meath and Kildare. At least one of these, at Rathcairn in County Meath, was also Irish-speaking – which, for those disposed to see the revolution as kind of correction of history, conjured up images of the Gaels reconquering the old English Pale.[758]

In the first five years of Fianna Fáil's term in office, they divided 353,000 acres of land, which had been compulsorily purchased from graziers, and allotted it between nearly 26,000 applicants. This amounted to a very significant redistribution of wealth.[759] Like land reform elsewhere, though, while Fianna Fáil's land policy was good politics, it made little enough economic sense. It was in consolidating larger farms, not breaking them up, that agriculture became efficient – a practice that Irish Governments began to encourage from the 1940s onwards.

In 1933 de Valera withheld the Land Annuities, the loans that had been used to buy tenants' estates under the 1908 Land Act, and that the Free State had to pay back to Britain under the Treaty. Britain in return placed heavy tariffs on imported Irish beef – hurting the strong farmers who had been the mainstay of pro-Treaty politics since 1922. When the Fianna Fáil Government seized unsold cattle and distributed the meat to the poor, the Blueshirt movement led violent resistance by cattle farmers to the seizures – an echo of the social conflict of 1923. However, de Valera carried the day. In 1935 he worked out a deal with Britain to lower tariffs, and in 1938 agreed to pay off the remaining annuities, and the trade in cattle was resumed as before.

Fianna Fáil created a host of new state-run companies, and also passed laws stating that there had to be a certain number of Irish members on the board of every company. Small-scale Irish manufacturers were protected from foreign competition by high tariffs. In contrast to the first Irish Government, the anti-Treatyites introduced large-scale house-building schemes and some social welfare programmes. All of these factors meant that the descendants of the anti-Treatyites of 1922 secured for themselves the status of the 'real' nationalist and populist party.

However, in terms of realising, as *Irish Freedom* had wistfully predicted in 1910, an Ireland that would be 'a garden for 20 million people', the Irish revolution manifestly failed. Emigration remained perilously high: some 75,000 people emigrated, mostly to the UK, every year in the late 1930s. By the 1950s, veteran Republican and now Fianna Fáil Taoiseach Seán Lemass voiced a widespread fear that the Irish state might simply become unviable. Whether this economic failure was due to the failure to break the stranglehold of relatively unproductive elites such as cattle exporters on the Irish economy, as some argue, or the stifling consequences of inward-looking economic nationalism, as others maintain, it was clear that Irish independence alone was not a panacea for the ills of Irish society.

Minorities

One of the clearest results of the revolutionary period was the partition of Ireland between the predominantly Catholic Free State and the Protestant and Unionist-dominated Northern Ireland. Such an apparently clear-cut separation of two antagonistic national identities has been used to argue that the Irish revolution was essentially an ethnic conflict, part of the 'un-mixing of peoples' after the First World War and comparable in character, if not in scale, with the apocalyptic contemporary wars and population displacement in such places as Silesia, Greece, Turkey and Armenia, where hundreds of thousands of people were killed or uprooted from their homes.[760]

How did minorities fare in the two new polities in Ireland? In 1921–22, some 41,000 Protestants left the nascent Irish Free State for Britain or Northern Ireland, contributing to a fall of the Protestant population of the twenty-six counties of 106,000 people between the 1911 and 1926 censuses. Protestants went from being 10.4 per cent of the population in the territory of the Free State in 1911 to 7.4 per cent in 1926.[761]

On the face of it, this appears to show a very grim fate for the southern minority. However, recent research by historical demographer Andy Bielenberg calculates that no more than 16,000 and perhaps as few as 2,000 southern Protestants were forced to leave by violence. This violence killed about 100 Protestant civilians in the territory of the Free State but, especially in the anarchy of the truce and Civil War, threatened many more with robbery, intimidation and non-lethal attacks. A total of 20,000 'southern loyalists' sought refuge in Britain after 1922; a considerable population displacement, although many of these were Catholics, including former RIC men.

The greater part of Protestant flight, however, was accounted for by the withdrawal from Ireland of the British Army and civilian administration, who amounted to 30,000 people, plus an unspecified number of secondary workers. First World War deaths accounted for the disappearance of 5,000 more southern Protestants, and voluntary migration, estimated at around 40–50,000, based on a 10 per cent share of total emigration in those fifteen years, made up the rest. Some of the Protestant migration was also caused by a dislike of Irish independence and by accelerated land reform taking away the remaining estates of the gentry and associated jobs. However, it was not caused, as is sometimes alleged, by systematic campaigns of ethnic cleansing or murder on anything like a large scale.[762]

The Free State authorities promised to protect minorities, and by and large, once order had been restored after the Civil War, succeeded in doing so. Non-sectarian ideals aside, the fact was that the Free State needed its Protestant minority, who still at this date comprised a disproportionate section of the business community and paid much-needed taxes. Though some southern Protestants expressed regret at leaving the Union, most reconciled themselves to the new order. In Cavan, for example, a former Unionist. J. J. Cole, was elected as a TD in the general election of 1923. In one of his election rallies, an Orangeman by the name of Knight told Cole's supporters that 'we are under a constitution which is not of our choice', but, he asked rhetorically, 'Are we to disappear as a party in this country? No. We form a considerable minority and have substantial interests at stake. The Free State Government has promised to respect the liberties and rights of minorities and I for one am in favour of us taking our proper place in the community'.[763]

North of the border, the 420,000-strong Catholic nationalist minority suffered some 330 civilian deaths and over 800 wounded in 1920–22. Hundreds of Catholic houses were burnt out and Catholic families expelled, especially in Belfast. So, in human terms, northern Catholics fared considerably worse than their southern Protestant counterparts.[764] Moreover, while sectarian violence in the south tended to be carried out by maverick elements, much anti-Catholic violence in the north was perpetrated by members of the security forces, and many Unionist leaders and activists, including Edward Carson and James Craig, encouraged violence and discrimination.[765]

As against this, though, discrimination was not so bad as to cause a mass flight of Catholics from the north. The stronger northern economy meant that many Catholic refugees returned there after the conflict was over. Whereas the Protestant population of County Cork dropped by 34 per cent, Belfast Catholic numbers fell by only 2 per cent in the revolutionary period.[766]

Unlike southern Protestants, northern Catholics were a big enough minority to be a potential threat to the northern state, and as a result they suffered from considerably worse discrimination once the violence of the revolutionary period had died down. The Northern Ireland Government diluted the votes of its Catholic and nationalist minority by 'gerrymandering', where nationalists were grouped into constituencies for elections, under-representing their voting strength, and by franchise restrictions in local government, where, like the Free State in the same period, rate-payers had votes calculated according to their property. However, in the north this had the added discriminatory effect that the mainly Protestant and Unionist business community dominated local government, even where Catholics were in a majority.

Protestant political domination also tended to mean systematic discrimination in the allocation of jobs, public resources and housing, all of which eventually contributed to Catholic revolt and a long-running, low-intensity conflict in the north from 1969 to the late 1990s.

A new moral order?

It is often assumed in hindsight that the intention of the Irish revolution was to empower the Irish Roman Catholic Church, which had consolidated its position throughout the nineteenth century. This is an exaggeration. The purpose of the revolution was to secure independence for Ireland, and while for historical reasons Catholics formed the majority of nationalists, Protestant activists were too common and too prominent to ignore.

However, the Catholic Church, though at all times highly critical of the Republican use of violence, was perhaps the main social victor of the revolution. It warned that the violence of the War of Independence, and especially the Civil War, was a result of 'moral anarchy',[767] and it redoubled its efforts to reclaim moral hegemony as the Irish state was being established. Despite the fact that many Catholic Republicans had ignored and even wilfully disobeyed the Church during the revolution, many of them were fully in favour of the assertion of Catholic social mores in the independent Irish state.

Even so, those who had hoped for a new enlightened Ireland based on a flowering of Gaelic Irish culture were disappointed by a regime that censored heavily, especially with regards to matters of sexuality. Disillusioned former IRA man and writer Seán O'Faoláin wrote that the combination of a native 'acquisitive and uncultivated middle class and a rigorous and uncultivated Church meant that the fight for a republic as I now understand it – that is, a republic in the shape of France or the United States – had ended in total defeat'.[768]

Feminists such as Helena Molony also voiced their disappointment with the results of the revolution. There were some gains for women, all of whom over the age of 21 got the right to vote in 1923, four years ahead of women in Britain. However, the economic and social conservatism that took hold after the Civil War also affected women's rights. In the United Kingdom in 1923, women gained the right to petition for divorce on certain grounds. In the Free State, by contrast, divorce was technically legal under the 1922 Constituion, but the Dáil declined to legislate for its implementation in 1925, and it was made unconstitutional in 1937. It was not legalised until a referendum in 1996. Contraception, legalised in the late 1920s in Britain, remained illegal in Ireland until 1980, condemning many women to having huge families.

The consensus in the new Irish state was that women's role was in the home. In 1927, Kevin O'Higgins passed a bill excluding women from jury service on the basis that he did not want them exposed to disturbing cases.[769] De Valera's 1937 constitution stated that 'by her life within the home, woman gives to the State a support without which the common good cannot be achieved... The State shall, therefore, endeavour to ensure that mothers shall not be obliged by economic necessity to engage in labour to the neglect of their duties in the home'.[770] There was certainly to be no revolution in women's social status in the early decades of independent Ireland.

Was there really a new moral order in independent Ireland, freed, as some Catholic nationalists like to imagine, from corrupting British influences? Certainly the appearance was there. 'The Monto', for instance, the red-light district of Dublin, was closed down in 1925 by the police after a popular campaign led by lay Catholic activists in the Legion of Mary. Often, though, official piety hid a sordid reality. In 1930 the Free State set up a committee under a retired senior counsel, Carrigan, into sexual offences in Ireland. What they found was profoundly shocking to a new state that prided itself on its Catholic morality. From 1927 to 1929, Garda Commissioner Eoin O'Duffy told them, sexual assaults on females had risen by 63 per cent and on males by 43 per cent. O'Duffy believed that around 6,000 children had been sexually abused in this three-year period alone.[771]

The Cumann na nGaedheal Government decided to bury the report. It might, they concluded, embarrass important people to discover that 'ordinary feelings of decency and the influence of religion has failed and the only remedy is police action'. As a result, 'it is clearly undesirable', the Cabinet was told, 'that such a view of conditions in the Saorstát should be given wide circulation.[772] And even darker than such figures is the fact that we now know that much of this abuse was taking place inside facilities such as industrial schools and Magdalene Laundries paid for by the state but operated by the Roman Catholic Church.

According to one historian, the 'Irish democratic process was tinged by theocracy... opinions expressing contrary views were downplayed or even censored'. Whatever the dark face of clerical power was, however, it was not unpopular until much later in the twentieth century. As late as the 1960s, over 90 per cent of Catholics in Dublin thought that their Church was the greatest force for good in the country, and some 87 per cent would have backed the Catholic Church in any confrontation with the Irish state.[773]

Memory

The Irish Free State, therefore, by most measures fell far short of the dreams of the 1916 leaders. Despite efforts to promote the use of Irish, it would be almost entirely English-speaking. Partition and membership of the British Commonwealth, and the conservative and capitalistic character of the Free State, would not have been acceptable to many of the conspirators of 1916, such as James Connolly. It was an Irish state, it was true, a Catholic and nationalist one, yes, but one led by the older and more moderate men (and they were virtually all men) of the independence movement.

As a result of this, the immediate reaction to independence was not exhilaration but disillusion and depression. 'What was it all for?' many Republican activists would ask. It would be many years before they would be able to look back without a sense of rancour and betrayal at the independence struggle.

Joe O'Connor, for instance – a Dublin IRA man who had been through the whole struggle in the Volunteers from 1913, through the insurrection of 1916 and the guerrilla warfare of 1920–23, until his release from internment in 1924 – emerged from imprisonment a wreck of a man.

He, along with many other veterans, was displaying clear signs of what is now called post-traumatic stress disorder:

> My nerves were completely gone. For the next eighteen months I had the awful experience of being afraid, and it was my first acquaintance with fear... one day I was crossing Dame Street when I took a seizure and when I came to I was standing in front of a tramcar with the driver jumping on the bell and bellowing at me. I had just time to get out of the way. Frequently I had to ask my wife to accompany me home from the office in the evening. At night when asleep, if a motor car stopped within hearing distance I would spring onto the floor.[774]

For him, as for many others, the aftermath of revolution was deeply disheartening: 'I took an active part in all efforts to keep the Republican ideal before the people, but on the whole I was very downhearted'. It was not until some years later, in 1929, that during the commemoration of Catholic Emancipation he noticed the tricolour flying over Collins [formerly Royal] Barracks: 'The thought suddenly came to me that all our efforts were not in vain, and I was much happier in mind thereafter'.[775]

For all that, far beyond Ireland itself, the Irish independence struggle caused ripples throughout the British Empire. In India, one revolutionary 'read [IRA man] Dan Breen's *My Fight for Irish Freedom*. Dan Breen was Maserda's ideal. He named his organisation the "Indian Republican Army" after the Irish Republican Army'.[776] It was one of the first times that a guerrilla movement had defeated an imperial power and forced from it a political settlement. Nationalist revolutionaries as diverse as the Zionist *Irgun* and the Vietnamese Communists tried to absorb its lessons. For this reason, its lessons are still studied and cited by writers on counter-insurgency.[777]

In Ireland, the Easter Rising in particular became the touchstone of post-independence national identity. As its enactors had intended, the symbolism of the Rising – the brave fight, the noble martyrs – was perfect as a founding myth of the Irish state. Since the 1970s, against a background of a new armed Republican campaign in Northern Ireland, the un-mandated insurrection of 1916 was viewed more nervously, and its questionable democratic credentials opened to more scrutiny by historians. However, all the indications are that in the early twenty-first century the Rising is generally viewed positively by the Irish public.

The memory of the 'Tan War' in nationalist Ireland today is similarly largely one of heroic struggle, of the triumph of Irish democracy over the Empire, and of ambushes and barracks attacks. In some parts of the country – especially in Cork, where the war was most intense – there are annual commemorations of the ambushes, such as those at Kilmichael and Crossbarry. In 2009, 2,000 people attended a ceremony to celebrate an ambush at Dromkeen in rural Limerick, where eleven RIC men were killed in 1921. Marching bands, speeches from TDs and a parade marked the anniversary of the Burgery ambush in Waterford, where one Black and Tan and two IRA men lost their lives. In 2001, the Irish Government had the remains of ten IRA Volunteers, who had been executed during the war, exhumed and reinterred with military ceremony in Glasnevin Cemetery. Nationalist Ireland very much remembers the version of events that it prefers.

Yet the memory of the 1919–21 conflict too is to some degree disputed. Particularly raw is the idea that Catholic sectarianism lay behind the motivations of the IRA. This idea is so intolerable, even today, for many nationalists, that the suggestion of sectarian killings by the IRA – such as the execution of two Protestant brothers (the Pearsons) in Offaly as informers in June 1921, or the killing of thirteen Protestants in Dunmanway, Cork, in April 1922 – has raised a storm of debate in the Irish media in the first years of the twenty-first century over the justification and motivations of the killers.[778]

The Civil War, by contrast, was generally filtered out of collective memory. It remained for a long time a part of the present – Irish politics in the 1920s and 1930s was dominated by its immediate legacy. Fianna Fáil and Fine Gael (the successor to Cumann na nGaedhal) remain the two biggest parties in the Republic of Ireland. Republicans came out of the Civil War with a sense that they alone had stood by the national ideal, betrayed on all sides by cowards, by the Anglicised middle class, by the Church that had refused them sacraments, by the press that had vilified them. Their sense of togetherness and populism – that the 'real people of Ireland' had never betrayed them – would sustain them and eventually turn them into the country's ruling party.

Fianna Fáil made their peace with the upper echelons of Irish society after they came to power in the 1930s. More radical Republicans continued to flirt with ideas of social revolution. The most radical wing of the Republican movement, the IRA post-1923, would never accept either Irish state born out of the Treaty. But from the 1950s onwards, it would focus its armed attacks solely on Northern Ireland.

The Free State side would always feel that they had saved the country from lawlessness, radicalism and chaos, and that they represented the true party of government. To some extent they also provided a home for those alienated by the Republican revolution: former Unionists and constitutional nationalists who disliked the physical force tradition.

If the partisan rhetoric of the Civil War had a long afterlife, the conflict itself, however, fell into a kind of collective amnesia. Few but the most bitter or the most fanatical wanted to remember the horrors of 1922–23. It was easier to remember a glorified version of the struggle with the British. It had had a clear point: independence, the honour of standing up to a vastly stronger opponent and, to some extent, victory. The civil war had none of these things. Todd Andrews wrote, 'In civil war there is no glory, no monuments to victory or the victors, only to the dead'.[779]

Even the memorials to the Civil War were themselves allowed to decay. The post-Civil War Free State Government built a massive obelisk in honour of Griffith, Collins and the pro-Treaty dead outside the Dáil in Leinster House, but by the late 1930s it was in such bad condition it had to be taken down. No one wanted such an obtrusive reminder of internecine strife.[780] Republican memorials dot the countryside, recording their fighters who died in ones and twos – shot in the head, executed, killed in abortive ambushes; only a tiny minority of purist Republicans still guard their memory. No guided tours show visitors around the sites of Civil War skirmishes. Few ballads were ever sung or composed about the clash of rival Irish nationalists. The bloody and depressing conclusion of the Irish revolution in 1922–24 was therefore almost wilfully forgotten in the public discourse.

The Irish Revolution in perspective

Revolutions were once seen as mechanisms of human progress, dismantling the barriers in the way of a better future. The twentieth century, however, which unleashed the full horrors of utopian revolution, has tended to put paid to this notion. Revolutions may or may not solve the problems that bring them about. They may be less efficient at solving problems than gradual reform would have been. They may also create new ones.

More realistic is to see revolution as a social phenomenon – a period of radical popular mobilisation and political change. As such, it has been proposed that revolutions tend to occur at a time when things are generally improving, but when raised expectations are dashed.[781] This is certainly true in the Irish case, where the blocking of the long-promised Home Rule in 1912–14 incensed moderate Irish nationalists and compromised the legitimacy of the British state in Ireland. War is often a common factor in revolution – as in France in 1791† and in Russia in 1917 – and so it was in Ireland. The demands posed by the Great War,

---

† In 1789, the French revolutionaries had, during peacetime, agreed on a constitutional monarchy. It was the outbreak of war with the 'reactionary powers' in 1791 that led to the execution of the king and the declaration of a republic.

especially conscription, forced people to choose sides, and in many cases to reject loyalty to the British Empire.

The next stage is radicalisation, whereby a committed minority attacks the state, and in doing so draws in a large number of people to a utopian ideology of a new order. How utopian Irish Republicans were may be argued about (they did dream of a new national and cultural order, but only a minority imagined that they would create a whole new society), but radicalisation – an intense collective commitment – certainly occurred in Ireland, primarily among a generation of young people, from 1916 through the election of 1918 into 1921, until the signing of the Treaty. By this point there was a sizable constituency who were prepared to fight and to die for an Irish Republic.

A situation of 'dual power' is often said then to develop in revolutions, whereby the revolutionaries fight the state and, either through force or popular mobilisation, take on its institutions and replace them, in whole or in part, with their own. Again, this quite clearly occurred in Ireland in 1919 and 1920, not so much through the IRA guerrillas' force of arms – as they were never in a position to hold or administer territory – as through the Sinn-Féin-controlled local government and the Dáil Courts. These institutions existed side by side, and competed for popular support, with their British counterparts into late 1921.

It is posited that, in most revolutions, either the existing state wins back its monopoly over the functions of state and puts down the revolt, or the revolutionaries win and the old state collapses, to be replaced by new, revolutionary organs. Neither of these outcomes really happened in Ireland. Unusually for revolutions, even national-separatist ones, the end of the Irish revolution was negotiated. Under the Treaty, the institutions of the Republican 'counter-state' (with the exception of the police and Army, which were replaced) basically merged into the existing ones. In early 1922, for instance, the Dáil Courts were wound up and the system of district courts was re-established, though under Irish management.

The Civil War of 1922–23 seems in many ways baffling, but taken in the context of revolutionary history, it does not seem so surprising. After the high point of radicalisation many revolutions experience 'Thermidor',‡ in which revolutionary fatigue sets in and the more moderate revolutionaries put down the more radical in an effort to restore stability and consolidate what they consider the aims of the revolution to have been. The intra-nationalist conflict is probably best understood in these terms rather than as 'treachery' and 'imperialism', as Republicans had it at the time, or 'counter-revolution', as a more refined thesis would have it. The pro-Treatyites did not want to turn back the clock to either 1912, or even 1920, and to restore British rule. Rather, as they saw it, they were out to complete the nationalist revolution by getting the Free State up and running. Moreover, in strictly Irish terms, it is arguable that some element of conflict between moderate nationalists and Republicans had always been present. In 1916, rival Volunteers (Irish and National) very nearly came to blows during the Easter Rising, and the rise of Sinn Féin was marked by extensive rioting between their supporters and Irish Party or Hibernian street fighters.

Finally, we can also observe a final phase in revolutions in which, after popular mobilisation has died down, an attempt is made to institutionalise the achievements of the revolution. In the 1930s the Soviet Communists, who had retreated from their more radical aims in the 1920s,

---

‡   The analogy is taken from the French revolutionary month in which Robespierre and the radical Jacobins were deposed and executed.

embarked on a traumatic period of collectivisation and industrialisation to create a socialist society. In Mexico in the same decade, the aptly named Institutional Revolutionary Party (PRI) nationalised a swathe of industries, conducted extensive land redistribution and separated Church and State in an effort to make some social gains from the revolutionary turmoil of 1910–20. And so, also in the 1930s, did Fianna Fáil make a considerable effort to accomplish the national and social aims of the Irish nationalist revolution. The 'Soldiers of Destiny' did their best to break the remaining links with Britain, to 'break up the ranches' and give 'the land to the people'. They tried to create a protected Irish industrial base and to provide some social housing and welfare measures. If later generations, looking back at the jaded legacies of such policies in Ireland, saw in them little that was revolutionary, they were in good company. So too did later generations of, for instance, Russians, Mexicans and Algerians who looked at the legacy of their own revolutions.

'They only painted the post boxes green', goes a scornful remark commonly heard in Ireland at one point about the revolution of 1916–23.[782] This is not true. For better or for worse, whether it was worth the pain or not, whether its results were liberating or frustrating, the Irish Revolution marked a decisive end to the old order of British rule in Ireland, and was a true turning point in Irish history.

Acknowledgements

Thanks are due to many people on the publication of this book. First of all, thanks to Eoin Purcell, whose idea this book was, first of all in fragmented parts back in 2009 and in this more comprehensive shape in 2012. Thanks to Cathal Brennan and likewise to Eoghan Rice for constant comments and encouragement, and for reading early drafts of this book.

Similarly, my gratitude goes to Brian Hanley, who helped me along the way, suggested sources, and cleared up some misconceptions I had had about such things as IRA casualties in the Civil War. Eve Morrison also deserves an acknowledgement for pointing out to me the richness and some of the tropes found in the Bureau of Military History. Thanks to John Gibney for his work on the copy-editing.

Thanks also to Kevin Galligan, with whom I worked on a family history project of his own, on his grandfather Paul. This work gave me a whole different view of the Irish revolution as experienced by ordinary activists. Thanks to Kevin also for agreeing to let me use as a source his grandfather's correspondence with his father and brother in 1912–22.

Most of all, thanks to my immediate family, especially my mother and father, who allowed me to take over their study in order to write this book, and especially to my mother, who kindly proofread the document. Thanks to Mairead and Aisling for lightening my mood. There are more debts to my family, of course, which I can never repay.

Bibliography

Primary Sources
National Archives of the United Kingdom:

CAB/24/117: Intrigues Between Sinn Féin Leaders and the German Government.
WO 35/69/1: Daily Police Reports, 1916 Rebellion.
CO 904/109: County Inspector's Report, 1919.
CO 904: RIC Monthly and Annual reports
HO 45/10810/312350: Royal Commission on the Rebellion in Ireland (1916).

Military Archives, Cathal Brugha Barracks, Dublin:

Bureau of Military History: witness statements and contemporary documents (available online at http://www.bureauofmilitaryhistory.ie)

Ernest Blythe, WS 939
Bernard Brady, WS 1626
Francis Connell, WS 1,663

James Cullen, WS 1,343
Daniel Breen 1917–21, WS 1739
James Cahill, WS 503
Seamus Doyle, WS215 (Easter Rising), and WS 1,342 (Dartmoor)
Thomas Dwyer, WS 1198
Mary Flannery, WS 624
Patrick Fitzpatrick, WS 1,274
Peter Paul Galligan, WS 170
James Gleeson, WS 1,012
Hugh Maguire, WS1,387
Seamus McKenna, WS 1016
Seamus MacDiarmada, WS 768
Seán McLoughlin, WS 290
Peadar McMahon, WS 1730
Helena Molony, WS 391
Gilbert Morrissey, WS 874
Seán Murphy, WS 204
Fr. Patrick Murphy, WS 1216
William O'Brien, WS 1766
James J. O'Connor, WS 1,214
Joseph O'Connor: 1916, WS 157; On the Civil War, WS 544
John J. O'Reilly, WS 1,031
Patrick Ronan, WS 299
Seán Sheridan, WS 1613

Galligan Papers

Peter Paul Galligan, personal correspondence 1911–1922 (courtesy of Kevin Galligan, to whom I offer my thanks).

Peter Paul Galligan, official papers, at University College Dublin IE UCDA P25

Secondary sources

Andrews, Todd. (2002), *Dublin Made Me*, Dublin: Lilliput Press.

Augusteijn, Joost. (1996), *From Public Defiance to Guerrilla Warfare*, Dublin: Irish Academic Press

Barry, Tom. (1997), *Guerrilla Days in Ireland*, Dublin: Anvil Books

Bartlett, Thomas, and Jeffrey, Keith (eds.) (1997), *A Military History of Ireland*, Cambridge: Cambridge University Press

Bielenberg, Andy. (2013), 'Exodus, the Emigration of Southern Irish Protestants during the Irish War of Independence and Civil War', *Past and Present*, no. 218 (Feb. 2013)

Borgonovo, John. (2011), *The Battle for Cork, July–August 1922*, Cork: Mercier Press.

Boyce, D.G. and O'Day, Alan. (2001), *Defenders of the Union: A Survey of British and Irish Unionism since 1801*, London: Routledge.

Breen, Timothy Murphy. (2010), *The Government's Execution Policy during the Irish Civil War, 1922–23*, PhD thesis, Maynooth

Cahill, Liam. (1990), *Forgotten Revolution, The Limerick Soviet 1919, A Threat to British Rule in Ireland*, Dublin: The O'Brien Press

Campbell Fergus. (2009), *The Irish Establishment, 1879–1914*, Oxford: Oxford University Press

Campbell, Fergus. (2008), *Land and Revolution, Nationalist Politics in the West of Ireland 1891–1921*, Oxford: Oxford University Press

Campbell, Joseph. (2001), *As I was Among the Captives: Joseph Campbell's Prisoner Diary 1922–1923*. Eiléan Ní Chuilleanáin (ed.), Cork: University Press

Caulfield, Max. (1963), *The Easter Rebellion*, London: Four Square Books

Coakley, John, and Gallagher, Michael. (1999), *Politics in the Republic of Ireland*, 3rd edn, London: Routledge and PSAI Press

Coleman, Marie. (2006), *County Longford and the Irish Revolution 1910–1923*, Dublin: Irish Academic Press

Collins, M.E. (1993), *Ireland 1868–1968*, Dublin: The Educational Company of Ireland

Coogan, Tim Pat. (2005), *1916, The Easter Rising*, London: Phoenix

Coogan, Tim Pat. (1993), *De Valera: Long Fellow, Long Shadow*, London: Hutchinson

Coogan, Tim Pat. (1991), *Michael Collins*, London: Arrow Books

Corbett, Jim. (2008), *Not While I Have Ammo, The History of Connie Mackey, Defender of the Strand*, Dublin: Nonsuch

Corlett, Christian. (2008), *Robert L Chapman's Ireland, Photographs from the Chapman Collection, 1907–1957*, Cork: Collins Press

Deasy, Liam. (1998), *Brother against Brother*, Cork: Mercier Press

De Koster, Margo; Leuwers, Herve; Luyten, Dirk; Rousseaux, Xavier; Rijksarchief, lgemeen (eds) (2012), *Justice in Wartime and Revolutions*, Bruxelles: Archives générales du Royaume

Dillon, Paul. (2000), 'James Connolly and the Kerry Famine of 1898', *Saothar*, 25

Doherty, Gabriel, and Keogh, Dermot (eds.) (2007), *1916: The Long Revolution*, Cork: Mercier Press

Dolan, Anne. (2003), *Commemorating the Irish Civil War, 1923–2000*, Cambridge: Cambridge University Press

Donnelly, James S. (2009), *Captain Rock, The Irish Agrarian Rebellion 1821–1824*, Madison: University of Wisconsin Press

Dooley, Terence. (2004), *'The Land For the People': The Land Question in Independent Ireland*, Dublin: UCD Press

Dooley, Terence. (2001), *The Decline of the Big House in Ireland*, Dublin: Wolfhound Press

Doyle, Tom. (2008), *The Civil War in Kerry*, Cork: Mercier Press

Dunphy, Richard. (1995), *The Making of Fianna Fáil Power in Ireland 1923–1948*, Oxford: Oxford University Press

Durney, James. (2011), *The Civil War in Kildare*, Cork: Mercier Press

Durney, James. (2010), 'How Aungier Street became known as the Dardanelles', *The Irish Sword*, Summer 2010, vol. XXVII, p.245

Dwyer, T. Ryle. (2005), *The Squad and the Intelligence Operations of Michael Collins*, Cork: Mercier Press

Dwyer, T. Ryle. (2001), *Tans, Terror and Troubles: Kerry's Real Fighting Story*, Cork: Mercier Press

Dworkin, Dennis (ed.) (2012), *Ireland and Britain, 1798-1922: An Anthology of Sources*, Indianapolis: Hacket

English, Richard. (2006), *Irish Freedom: A History of Nationalism in Ireland*, London: Macmillan

English, Richard. (1998), *Ernie O'Malley: IRA Intellectual*, Oxford: Oxford University Press

Farry, Michael. (2012), *The Irish Revolution, 1912–1923, Sligo*, Dublin: Four Courts Press

Farry, Michael. (2000), *The Aftermath of Revolution, Sligo 1921–23*, Dublin: University College Dublin Press

Ferguson, Niall (ed.) (2011), *Virtual History, Alternatives and Counterfactuals*, London: Penguin

Ferriter, Diarmuid. (2007), *Judging Dev: A Reassessment of the Life and Legacy of Eamon de Valera*, Dublin: Royal Irish Academy

Ferriter, Diarmuid. (2005), *1900–2000, The Transformation of Ireland*, London: Profile Books

Figes, Orlando. (1996), *A People's Tragedy, The Russian Revolution*, London: Pimlico

Fitzgerald, Desmond. (1968), *The Memoirs of Desmond Fitzgerald*, London: Routledge & Keegan Paul

Fitzpatrick, David (ed.) (2012), *Terror in Ireland, 1913–23,* Dublin: Lilliput Press

Fitzpatrick, David. (1998), *Politics and Irish Life, 1913–1921: Provincial Experience of War and Revolution*, Cork: Cork University Press

Foy, Michael T. and Barton, Brian. (2011), *The Easter Rising*, Stroud: The History Press

Galligan, Kevin. (2012), *Peter Paul Galligan, One of the Most Dangerous Men in the Rebel Movement*, Dublin: Liffey Press

Gallimore, Andrew. (2007), *A Bloody Canvas: The Mike McTigue Story*, Cork: Mercier Press

Garvin, Tom. *The Evolution of Irish Nationalist Politics* , Gill & Macmillan Dublin, 1981.

Garvin, Tom. (2005), *The Birth of Irish Democracy*, Dublin: Gill & Macmillan

Geoghegan, Patrick. (2010), *Liberator: The Life and Death of Daniel O'Connell, 1830–1847*, Dublin: Gill & Macmillan

Geoghegan, Patrick. (2008), *King Dan: The Rise of Daniel O'Connell, 1775–1829*, Dublin: Gill & Macmillan

Gialanella Valiulis, Maryann. (1992), *Portrait of a Revolutionary: General Richard Mulcahy and the Founding of the Irish Free State*, Dublin: Irish Academic Press

Gillespie, Raymond (ed.) (2004), *Cavan: Essays on the History of an Irish County*, Dublin: Irish Academic Press

Glennon, Kieran. (2013), *From Pogrom to Civil War: Tom Glennon and the Belfast IRA*, Cork: Mercier Press

Hachey, Thomas E. (ed.) (2011), *Turning Points in Twentieth Century Irish History*, Dublin: Irish Academic Press

Harnden, Toby. (1999), *Bandit Country: The IRA and South Armagh*, London: Hodder & Stoughton

Harrington, Michael. (2009), *The Munster Republic: North Cork and the Irish Civil War*, Cork: Mercier Press

Harrington, Niall C. (1992), *Kerry Landing, August 1922: An Episode of the Irish Civil War*, Dublin: Anvil Books

Hartnett, Mossie. (2002), *Victory and Woe*, James H. Joy (ed.), Dublin: University College Dublin Press

Hart, Peter. (2006), *Mick: The Real Michael Collins*, London: Macmillan

Hart, Peter. (2005), *The IRA at War, 1916–1923*, Oxford: Oxford University Press

Hart, Peter. (1999), *The IRA and its Enemies, Violence and Community in Cork 1916–1923*, Oxford: Clarendon Press

Hegarty, Kathleen. (2007), *They Put the Flag A-Flyin': The Roscommon Volunteers, 1916–1923*, Eugene: Generation Organisation.

Hobsbawm, Eric. (1999), *The Age of Extremes: The Short Twentieth Century, 1914–1991,* London: Abacus

Hopkinson, Michael. (2004), *Green Against Green: The Irish Civil War*, Dublin: Gill & Macmillan

Hopkinson, Michael. (2004), *The Irish War of Independence*, Dublin: Gill & Macmillan

Jackson, Alvin. (2010), *Ireland, 1798–1998: War, Peace and Beyond*, London: John Wiley & Sons

Jackson, Alvin. (2003), *Home Rule: An Irish History, 1800–2000*, London: Phoenix

Kennerk, Barry. (2010), *Shadow of the Brotherhood: The Temple Bar Shootings,* Cork: Mercier Press

Kiberd, Declan (ed.) (1998), *1916 Rebellion Handbook*, Dublin: Mourne River Press

Kostick, Conor. (2009), *Revolution in Ireland: Popular Militancy, 1917–1923*, Cork: Cork University Press

Laffan, Michael. (2000), *The Resurrection of Ireland: The Sinn Féin Party, 1916–1923,* Cambridge: Cambridge University Press

Lawlor, Pearse. (2009), *The Burnings, 1920*, Cork: Mercier Press

Lee, Joseph. (2008), *The Modernisation of Irish Society 1848–1918* (1973), Dublin: Gill & Macmillan

Lee, Joseph. (2001), *Ireland 1912–1985, Politics and Society*, Cambridge: Cambridge University Press

Leeson, David. (2001), *The Black and Tans, British Police and Auxiliaries in the Irish War of Independence*, Oxford: Oxford University Press

Lenihan, Padraig. (2008), *Consolidating Conquest, Ireland 1603–1727*, Essex: Pearson

Litton, Helen. (2006), *The Irish Civil War: An Illustrated History*, Dublin: Wolfhound Press

Lynch, Robert. (2006), *Northern Divisions: The Northern IRA and the Early Years of Partition*, Dublin: Irish Academic Press

Lyons, F. S. L. and Hawkins, Richard (eds). (1980), *Ireland under the Union: Varieties of Tension*, Oxford: Clarendon Press

MacAtasney, Gerard. (2004), *Seán MacDiarmada: The Mind of a Revolution*, Manorhamilton: Drumlin

MacEoin, UinSeánn. (1980), *Survivors: The Story of Ireland's Struggle as Told Through Some of Her Outstanding Living People*, Dublin: Argenta

Maye, Brian. (1997), *Arthur Griffith*, Dublin: Griffith College Productions

McCabe, Conor. (2011), *Sins of the Father, Tracing the Decisions that Shaped the Irish Economy*, Dublin: The History Press Ireland

McCarthy, Cal. (2007), *Cumann na mBan and the Irish Revolution*, Cork: The Collins Press

McCarthy, John P. (2006), *Kevin O'Higgins, Builder of The Irish Free State*, Dublin: Irish Academic Press

McGarry, Fearghal. (2007), *Eoin O'Duffy: A Self-Made Hero*, Oxford: Oxford University Press

McGarry, Fearghal. (2010), *The Rising, Ireland, Easter 1916*, Oxford: Oxford University Press

McGuire, Charlie. (2006), *Roddy Connolly and the Struggle for Socialism in Ireland*, Cork: Cork University Press

McMahon, Paul. (2008), *British Spies and Irish Rebels, British Intelligence in Ireland 1916–1945*, London: Boydell

Murphy, James. (2003), *Ireland: A Social, Cultural and Literary History, 1791–1891*, Dublin: Four Courts Press

Murray, Peter. (1980), 'Electoral Politics and the Dublin Working Class before the First World War', *Saothar*, vol. 6

Nevin, Donal (ed.) (1998), *James Larkin: Lion of the Fold*, Dublin: Gill & Macmillan

Novick, Ben. (2001), *Conceiving Revolution: Irish Nationalist Propaganda during the First World War*, Dublin: Four Courts Press

O'Brien, Paul. (2008), *Blood on the Streets: 1916 and the Battle For Mount Street Bridge*, Cork: Mercier Press

O Bróin, Leon. (1969), *The Chief Secretary, Augustine Birrell in Ireland*, London: Chatto & Windus

O'Connor, Diarmuid and Connolly, Frank. (2011), *Sleep Soldier Sleep, The Life and Times of Padraig O'Connor*, Dublin: Miseab

O'Connor, Emmet. (1980), 'Agrarian Unrest and the Labour Movement in Waterford, 1917–1923', in *Saothar*, Labour History Journal, vol. 6 pp. 48–53

O'Connor, Frank. (1964), *An Only Child*, London: MacMillan & Co.

O'Donnell, Ruán. (2008), *The Impact of the 1916 Rising: Among the Nations*, Dublin: Irish Academic Press

Ó Faoláin Seán. (1993), *Vive Moi! An Autobiography*, London: Sinclair Stevenson

Ó Gádhra, Nollaig. (1999), *The Civil War in Connacht,* Cork: Mercier Press

Ó Gráda, Cormac. (2000), *Black '47 and Beyond, The Great Irish Famine in History, Economy, and Memory,* New Jersey: Princeton University Press

O'Grady, John and Newman, Carol (eds.) (2011), *The Economy of Ireland,* Dublin: Gill & Macmillan

O'Halpin, Eunan. (1999), *Defending Ireland: The Irish State and its Enemies since 1922,* Oxford: Oxford University Press

O'Malley, Cormac K. H. and Dolan, Anne (eds.) (2007), *No Surrender Here! The Civil War Papers of Ernie O'Malley,* Dublin: Lilliput Press

O'Malley, Ernie. (2002), *On Another Man's Wound,* Dublin: Anvil Books

O'Malley, Ernie. (1992), *The Singing Flame,* Dublin: Anvil Books

O'Malley, Ernie. (1982), *Raids and Rallies,* Dublin: Anvil Books

O'Reilly, Terence. (2009), *Rebel Heart: George Lennon, Flying Column Commander,* Cork: Mercier Press

Ó Ruairc, Padraig Óg. (2009), *Blood on the Banner: The Republican Struggle in Clare,* Cork: Mercier Press

Ó Ruairc, Padraig Óg. (2010), *The Battle For Limerick City,* Cork: Mercier Press

Ó Tuathaigh, Gearóid. (2007), *Ireland Before the Famine, 1798–1848,* Dublin: Gill & Macmillan

Packenham, Frank. (1972), *Peace By Ordeal, The Negotiations of the Anglo-Irish Treaty, 1921,* London: Sidwick & Jackson

Parkinson, Alan F. (2004), *Belfast's Unholy War,* Dublin: Four Courts Press

Pearse, Patrick. (2012), *The Coming Revolution,* Cork: Mercier Press

Philpin, Charles H.E. (2002), *Nationalism and Popular Protest in Ireland*, Cambridge: Cambridge University Press

Regan, John M. (1999), *The Irish Counter-Revolution 1921–1931: Treatyite Politics and Settlement in Independent Ireland*, Dublin: Gill & Macmillan

Ryan, Annie. (2007), *Comrades: Inside the War of Independence*, Dublin: Mercier Press

Ryan, Annie. (2005), *Witnesses: Inside the Easter Rising*, Dublin: Liberties Press

Ryan, Meda. (2005), *Liam Lynch, the Real Chief*, Cork: Mercier Press

Ryan, Meda. (2003), *Tom Barry, IRA Freedom Fighter*, Cork: Mercier Press

Ryan, Meda. (1989), *The Day Michael Collins was Shot*, Dublin: Poolbeg Press

Sheehan, William. (2011), *A Hard Local War, The British Army and the Guerrilla War in Cork, 1919–1921*, Gloucestershire: Spellmount

Sheehan, William. (2009), *Hearts and Mines: The British 5th Division in Ireland 1920–1922*, Cork: Collins Press

Sheehan, William. (2007), *British Voices from the Irish War of Independence, 1918–1921,* Cork: Collins Press

Sheehan, William. (2007), *Fighting for Dublin, The British Battle for Dublin 1919–1921*, Cork: Collins Press

Sherwin, Frank. (2007), *Independent and Unrepentant*, Dublin: Irish Academic Press

Stephens, James. (1992), *The Insurrection in Dublin (1916)*, Buckinghamshire: Colin Smythe

Townshend, Charles. (2006), *Easter 1916: The Irish Rebellion*, London: Penguin,

Walker, Brian M. (ed.) (1978), *Parliamentary election results in Ireland 1801–1922*, Dublin: Royal Irish Academy

Walsh, Maurice. (2008), *The News from Ireland, Foreign Correspondents and the Irish Revolution*, London: Taurus

White, Gerry and O'Shea, Brendan. (2006), *The Burning of Cork*, Cork: Mercier Press

Yeates, Padraig. (2000), *Lockout: Dublin 1913*, Dublin: Gill & Macmillan

Yeates, Padraig. (2011), *A City in Wartime, Dublin 1914–1918*, Dublin: Gill & Macmillan,

Yeates Padraig. (2012), *Dublin, A City in Turmoil, 1918–1921*, Dublin: Gill & Macmillan,

Online Articles

Brennan, Cathal. *The Postal Strike of 1922*, The Irish Story, June 2012, http://www.theirishstory.com/2012/06/08/the-postal-strike-of-1922/#.Ug-QeNK1HTo Accessed 17/08/2013

Byrne, Patricia. Achill 1912, *A Microcosm of Swirling of Political Movements*, The Irish Story, May 2012, http://www.theirishstory.com/2012/05/21/achill–island–1912-a-microcosm-of-swirling-political-movements/#.UTSEmKIqzTo Accessed 17/0813 Accessed 17/08/2013

Connolly, James. '*The Slums or the Trenches*, The Workers Republic, 26 February 1916, located at http://www.marxists.org/archive/connolly/1916/02/slums.htm Accessed 17/0813 Accessed 17/08/2013

Dorney, John. *Casualties of the Civil War in Dublin*, The Irish Story, June 2012, http://www.theirishstory.com/2012/06/19/casualties-of-the-irish-civil-war-in-dublin/#.UZlJNKK1HTo Accessed 17/0813 Accessed 17/08/2013

Fallon, Donal. Come Here to Me! Website, '*Severity for Suffragettes,*' Dublin 1912, http://comeheretome.com/2013/01/18/severity-for-suffragettes-dublin-1912/ Accessed 17/0813 Accessed 17/08/2013

Kenna, Shane. *'One Skilled Scientist is worth an Army'* – *The Fenian Dynamite Campaign, 1881-85*, The Irish Story, February, 2012 http://www.theirishstory. com/2012/02/13/one-skilled-scientist-is-worth-an-Army-the-fenian-dynamite-campaign-1881-85/#. USwLiaIqzTo Accessed 17/0813 Accessed 17/08/2013

Kenna, Shane. *Thomas Clarke, Treason Convict J464*, The Irish Story, May 2012, http://www.theirishstory. com/2012/05/04/thomas-clarke-treason-felony-convict-j464/#.UTchKqIqzTo Accessed 17/08/2013

McCabe, Conor, of the Labour History Society on the Railway strike of 1911, 9 March 2011, reported herehttp://www.theirishstory.com/2011/03/09/the-great-southern-railway-strike-of-1911/#. UVq4xhfvvTo. Accessed 17/0813

McConway, Phillip, *The Pearsons of Coolacrease*, www. offalyhistory.com/attachments/1_philip_mcconway_pearsons_coolacrease_1.pdf Accessed 17/08/2013

McConway, Phillip, Offaly and Civil War Executions www. offalyhistory.com Accessed 17/08/2013

Milne, Ida. Is History Repeating? The Spanish flu of 1918 http://puesoccurrences.com/2009/06/02/history-repeating-the-spanish-flu-of-1918/ Accessed 17/08/2013

O'Donovan, John. The All for Ireland League, 1909-1918, The Irish Story, 27 December 2012 http:// www.theirishstory.com/2012/12/27/the-all-for-ireland-league-1909-1918/#.UaOvPtK1HTo Accessed 17/08/2013

Peel, Henry. The Scourge of Conscription, St Martin de Porres magazine, a publication of the Irish Dominicans. http://www.catholicireland.net/the-scourge-of-conscription/30 November 1999 Accessed 17/0813

Sheppard, Barry. Rathcairn: Land and Language Reform in the Irish Free State, The Irish Story, July 2012, http://www.theirishstory.com/2012/07/13/rath-cairn-land-reform-language-politics-in-the-irish-free-state/#.UZ06jKK1HTo Accessed 17/0813

John, Shelley. A Short History of the Third Tipperary Brigade http://homepage.eircom.net/~150/page14.html Accessed 17/08/2013

Walsh, Paul V. *'The Irish Civil War 1922-23 -A Study of the Conventional Phase'*. A paper delivered to NYMAS at the CUNY Graduate Center, New York, N.Y. on 11 December 1998, http://bobrowen.com/nymas/irish-civilwar.html Accessed 17/0813

Walsh, Robert. *Dartmoor, the Prison that broke the body and then the Soul*, Crime Magazine, May 16, 2010. http://crimemagazine.dreamhosters.com/dartmoor-prison-broke-body-and-then-soul Accessed 17/0813

Newspapers

The Anglo Celt
Irish Freedom
The Irish Times
The New York Times
Dundalk Democrat
An Phoblacht/Republican News
The Workers Republic

Websites and online resources:

ARK Northern Ireland: http://www.ark.ac.uk/
Come here to me!: http://comeheretome.com

Elections Ireland: http://www.electionsireland.org/

Internet Archive: http://archive.org

Irish Labour Party: http://www.labour.ie/

The Irish Story:http://www.theirishstory.com

Multitext: http://multitext.ucc.ie/

National Archives of Ireland: 1901& 1911 census returns: http://www.census.nationalarchives.ie/

Offaly Historical and Archaelogical Society: http://www. offalyhistory.com

Parliamentary Debates of the United Kingdom: http:// hansard.millbanksystems.com/

Pues Occurrences: http://puesoccurrences.wordpress.com

National Census Archive 1901, http://www.census.nation-alarchives.ie/pages/1901/Cavan/Derrin/Drumnalaragh/

The 1918 Election results: elections/h1918.htm

Election results from 1922 and 1923

★http://www.electionsireland.org/results

Charter of the Gaelic League 1893

http://www.nli.ie/1916/pdf/3.4.2.pdf

The Home Rule Bill, by John Redmond M.P. (Gassell and company limited, London, New York, Toronto and Melbourne 1912.) Hosted by the Library of The University of Toronto at http://archive.org/stream/hom-erulebill00redmuoft/homerulebill00redmuoft_djvu.txt Accessed 17/08/13

Documentaries

RTÉ, *Ballyseedy*, Producer: Frank Hand, Script: Pat Butler, Broadcast 12/11/1997.

Double band Films for BBC Northern Ireland *The Ulster Covenant*, Broadcast 22/09/2012 Producer Anne Hegarty, Script: William Crawley.

Endnotes

1   *The Irish Times*, Thursday, 13 July 1911
2   *Irish Freedom*, January 1911
3   Dolan, Anne. *Commemorating the Irish Civil War, 1923–2000*, pp.17–19.
4   Campbell, Fergus. *The Irish Establishment, 1879–1914*, p.138
5   Ibid, p.56
6   *Irish Freedom*, October 1911
7   Townshend, Charles. *Easter 1916: The Irish Rebellion*, p.26
8   Murphy, James. *Ireland: A Social, Cultural and Literary History, 1791–1891*, p.24
9   Donnelly, James S. *Captain Rock, The Irish Agrarian Rebellion 1821–1824*, pp.323–324.
10 Ó Tuathaigh, Gearóid. *Ireland Before the Famine, 1798–1848*, p.148
11 Geoghegan, Patrick. *King Dan: The Rise of Daniel O'Connell, 1775–1829*, pp.268–269; Ó Tuathaigh, *Ireland Before the Famine*, p.66
12 Murphy, James. *Ireland: A Social, Cultural and Literary History, 1791–1891*, p.116
13 Hill, Jacqueline. *The Protestant Response to Repeal, the case of the Dublin working class in Ireland Under the Union* (Lyons and Hawkins eds), Clarendon 1980. pp.45–46
14 Peter Murray, *Electoral Politics and the Dublin Working Class before the First World War*
15 See Lee, Joseph, *The Modernisation of Irish Society*.
16 G. Moran, 'The Home Rule Movement in Cavan, 1870–1886', pp.159–160, in Cavan: *Essays on the History of an Irish County*, Irish Academic Press, 2004.
17 Campbell, *The Irish Establishment*, p.138
18 Townshend, *Easter 1916*, p.25
19 Yeates, Pádraig, *Lockout: Dublin 1913*, p.87
20 Campbell, *The Irish Establishment*, p.119
21 Ibid, p.113
22 Ibid, pp.100–104

23 Yeates, Pádraig. *Lockout, Dublin 1913*, pp.259–265
24 David George Boyce, Alan O'Day. *Defenders of the Union: A Survey of British and Irish Unionism Since 1801*, p.166
25 Campbell, *The Irish Establishment*, p.75
26 Ó Faoláin, Seán, *Vive Moi! An Autobiography*, p.25
27 English, Richard, *Ernie O'Malley: IRA Intellectual*, p.107
28 Haughton, Jonathan, 'Growth in Output and Living Standards'in John O'Grady, Carol Newman (eds.) *The Economy of Ireland*, pp.19–25
29 Dworkin, *Ireland and Britain, 1798–1922: An Anthology of Sources*, p.48
30 Ó Gráda, Cormac, *Black '47 and Beyond, The Great Irish Famine in History, Economy, and Memory*, p.124
31 Murphy, James. *Ireland, A Social, Cultural and Literary History, 1791–1891*, p.100
32 Campbell, *The Irish Establishment*, pp.16, 40
33 Seán Sheridan, BMH WS 1613, s2894
34 *Irish Freedom*, October 1911
35 Dillon, Paul. 'James Connolly and the Kerry Famine of 1898', p.29
36 McAtasney, Gerard. *Seán MacDiarmada, The Mind of the Revolution*, p.35.
37 See for instance: McCabe, Conor. *Sins of the Father*, chs. 2,3.
38 Talk by Conor McCabe of the Labour History Society on the Railway strike of 1911, 9 March 2011, reported here: http://www.theirishstory. com/2011/03/09/the-great-southern-railway-strike-of-1911/#. UVq4xhfvvTo.
39 Geoghegan, Patrick. *Liberator, The Life and Death of Daniel O'Connell, 1830–1847*, p.163
40 Walker, Brian M. (ed.) Parliamentary election results in Ireland 1801–1922. pp.164, 332–333.
41 Townshend, *Easter 1916*, p.10
42 John O'Donovan, 'The All for Ireland League, 1909–1918', *The Irish Story*, 27 December 2012
43 Murray, Peter. 'Electoral Politics and the Dublin Working Class before the First World War'
44 Yeates, *Lockout*, pp.501–502
45 Collins, *Ireland 1868–1968*
46 All details from: Ernest Blythe BMH WS 939.
47 Peter Paul Galligan, BMH WS 170
48 Gilbert Morrissey, BMH WS 874
49 McGee, Owen. 'Who were the Fenian Dead? The IRB and the Background to the 1916 Rising', in Doherty and Keogh (eds), *The Long Revolution*, p.103
50 Lee, Joseph, *The Modernisation of Irish Society 1848–1918*, p.56
51 *Irish Freedom*, December 1910
52 Ibid.
53 *Irish Freedom*, November 1910

54   James Cullen, BMH WS 1,343
55   MacAtasney, *Seán MacDiarmada*, pp.137, 146
56   *Irish Freedom*, March 1911
57   MacAtasney, ibid, p.51
58   James Cullen, BMH WS 1,343
59   Ernest Blythe, WS 939 BMH
60   Ryan, *Witnesses: Inside the Easter Rising*, p.133. Mass Rocks were illicit places of worship when public practice of Catholicism was banned. The Famine refers to the calamity in 1845–48, when over a million people died. Oliver Plunkett was a Catholic Bishop martyred in the seventeenth century. Wolfe Tone, Henry Joy McCracken and Sheares were Protestant leaders of the United Irishmen, who led the Republican insurrection against British rule in 1798. Robert Emmet was a (Protestant) nationalist revolutionary who led another failed rebellion in Dublin in 1803. All the four above were executed by the British.
61   Coogan, Tim Pat, *1916, The Easter Rising*, p.108
62   McGee, 'Who Were the Fenian Dead?' in *1916: The Long Revolution*, p.108
63   Campbell, Fergus, *Land and Revolution*, p.190; Ó Ruairc, Pádraig Óg, *Blood on the Banner*, pp. 27–29
64   *Irish Freedom*, February 1913
65   *Irish Freedom*, August 1911
66   McMahon, Paul. *British Spies and Irish Rebels*, p.14
67   Barry, Kennerk, *Shadow of the Brotherhood*
68   Lee, *The Modernisation of Irish Society*, p.74
69   Shane Kenna, 'One Skilled Scientist is worth an Army' – The Fenian Dynamite Campaign, 1881–85, *The Irish Story*, February, 2012
70   Ibid.
71   Ernest Blythe, BMH WS 939
72   Mary Flannery, BMH WS 624
73   *Irish Freedom*, April 1914
74   Paul Galligan, BMH WS 170
75   English, Richard, *Irish Freedom: A History of Nationalism in Ireland*, p.272
76   Kenna, Thomas Clarke, Treason Convict J464, *The Irish Story*, May 2012
77   Charter of the Gaelic League 1893
78   Garvin, Tom, *The Evolution of Irish Nationalist Politics*, p.118
79   Ibid, pp.75–76
80   Patricia Byrne, Achill 1912, A Microcosm of Swirling of Political Movements, *The Irish Story*, May 2012
81   O'Connor, Frank, *An Only Child*, p.144
82   Townshend, *Easter 1916*, p.13
83   Collins, *Ireland 1868–1968*, p.174
84   Lenihan, Padraig, *Consolidating Conquest, Ireland 1603–1727*, pp.238–239

85   Ernest Blythe, WS BMH 939

86   Paul Galligan to Monsignor Eugene Galligan, 4 May 1917 (Galligan personal papers, courtesy of the Galligan family).

87   Novick, Ben. *Conceiving Revolution, Irish Nationalist Propaganda during the First World War*, p.133

88   Helena Molony, BMH WS 391

89   Cited in McCarthy, Cal, *Cumann na mBan and the Irish Revolution*, p.100

90   *Come Here to Me!* website, 'Severity for Suffragettes,' Dublin 1912, http://comeheretome.com/2013/01/18/severity-for-suffragettes-dublin-1912/, *Irish Freedom*, October 1912

91   All above quotations from Helena Molony, BMH WS 391

92   Yeates, *Lockout, Dublin 1913*, pp.86–87. They briefly had one MP in 1908 when sitting MP in North Leitrim Charles Dolan resigned from the IPP and joined Sinn Féin, but he was subsequently defeated in a by-election.

93   Townshend *Easter 1916*, pp.11–12

94   *Irish Freedom*, October 1913

95   English, *Irish Freedom*, p.264

96   Ibid.

97   *Irish Freedom*, October 1911

98   Ibid.

99   Seán MacDermott to Joe MacGarritty, 12 December 1913 http://www.nli.ie/1916/pdf/4.2.pdf

100   *Irish Freedom*, February 1913

101   *Irish Freedom*, October 1913

102   *Irish Freedom*, November 1913

103   Jackson, Alvin. 'British Ireland – What if Home Rule had been enacted?' In Niall Ferguson (ed.), *Virtual History*, p.196

104   *The Home Rule Bill* By John Redmond, M.P., Gassell And Company, Limited, London, New York, Toronto And Melbourne 1912 Hosted By The Library '557713 University Of Toronto at http://archive.org/stream/homerulebill00redmuoft/homerulebill00redmuoft_djvu.txt

105   Jackson, 'British Ireland', in Ferguson (ed.), *Virtual History*, p.195

106   Ibid, p.175

107   For details of the Third Home Rule Bill, see: Redmond, *Home Rule Bill* and Jackson, 'British Ireland', pp.196–198

108   Redmond, *Home Rule Bill*.

109   Farry, Michael, *The Irish Revolution, 1912–1923*, p.11

110   *Irish Freedom*, April 1912

111   Seán MacDermott to Joe McGarrity, 20 December 1913 http://www.nli.ie/1916/pdf/4.2.pdf

112   Cited in *The Irish Times*, 25 April 2012.

113   Yeates, *A City in Wartime, Dublin 1914–1918*, p.11. The total population of 470,000 refers to the greater urban area in the county. Within city boundaries, Dublin's population was about 300,000.

114   *Irish Freedom*, February 1911
115   House of Commons Debate, 31 July 1912 vol 41 cc2088-149 http://hansard.millbanksystems.com/commons/1912/jul/31/belfast-riots
116   The total was about 470,000 signatures, split almost evenly between men and women. Women signed a separate 'Declaration'.
117   BBC Documentary *The Ulster Covenant*; directed by Brian Henry Martin, presented by William Crawley. Broadcast 30/9/12.
118   Jackson, *British Ireland*, p.220
119   McGarry, Fearghal, *The Rising, Ireland, Easter 1916*, p.51
120   Ibid, p.52
121   Two Addresses to the Protestants of Ireland, 6 September 1843. National Library of Ireland
122   *The Irish Times*, July 13 1911
123   *The Warder*, August 26, 1843
124   Redmond, *The Home Rule Bill*
125   Redmond, *The Home Rule Bill*
126   *Irish Freedom*, March 1914
127   Ernest Blythe, BMH WS 939
128   McGarry, *The Rising*, pp.28, 73
129   Townshend, *Easter 1916*, pp.52–53
130   MacAtasney, *Seán MacDiarmada*, p.69
131   Townshend, *Easter 1916*, p.45
132   *Irish Freedom*, March 1914
133   Paul Galligan, BMH WS 170
134   Ernest Blythe, BMH WS 939
135   Helena Molony, BMH WS 391; also McCarthy, *Cumann na mBan and the Irish Revolution*, pp.32–33
136   Townshend, *Easter 1916*, p.52
137   Pearse, Patrick, *The Coming Revolution*, p.84
138   *Irish Freedom*, July 1914
139   Paul Galligan, BMH WS 170
140   Ibid.
141   Townshend, *Easter 1916*, p.56
142   Ibid, p.55
143   Yeates, *A City in Wartime*, p.4
144   Paul Galligan, BMH WS 170
145   Yeates, *A City in Wartime*, p.5
146   *Irish Freedom*, August 1914
147   Ibid.
148   Jackson, *British Ireland*, p.222
149   MacAtasney, *Seán MacDiarmada*, p.72
150   Partial text of Redmond's speech is available here: http://multitext.ucc.ie/d/John_Redmond

151 Fitzpatrick, David, 'Militarism in Ireland 1912–1922', in *A Military History of Ireland*, p.397. The officially recorded total of Irish deaths was 27,405. Higher figures suggesting as many as 50,000 Irish war deaths have also been published, but Fitzpatrick suggests that this figure is taken from counting all casualties in nominally Irish units, as opposed to Irish-born soldiers.

152 Townshend, *Easter 1916*, pp.68–70

153 Ibid, p.68

154 Paul Galligan, BMH WS 170

155 MacAtasney, *Seán MacDiarmada*, p.74

156 *Irish Freedom*, September and October 1914

158 O'Malley, Ernie, *On Another Man's Wound*, p.29

159 Townshend, *Easter 1916*, p.73

160 Farry, *The Irish Revolution*, p.22

161 Fitzpatrick, 'Militiarism in Ireland' in *A Military History of Ireland*, p.388

162 Yeates, *A City in Wartime*, p.56

163 Ibid, p.47

164 Campbell, *Land and Revolution*, p.197

165 Barry, *Guerilla Days in Ireland*, p.2

166 Yeates, *A City in Wartime*, p.63

167 Hart, Peter, 'What did the Easter Rising Really Change?' in *Turning Points in Twentieth Century Irish History*, Thomas Hachey (ed.), p.10

168 Yeates, *A City in Wartime*, p.67

169 Townshend, *Easter 1916*, p.79

170 Ibid, p.75

171 Ibid.

172 McGarry, *The Rising*, pp.98–99

173 Townshend, *Easter 1916*, pp.94–95

174 Joseph O'Connor, BMH WS 157

175 *Irish Freedom*, September 194

176 MacAtasney, *Seán MacDiarmada*, p.146

177 *The Memoirs of Desmond Fitzgerald*, p.80

178 Paul Galligan to Monsignor Eugene Galligan, 29 November 1917. (Galligan personal papers)

179 Connolly, James, 'The Slums or the Trenches', *The Workers Republic*, 26 February 1916,

180 Farry, *The Irish Revolution*, pp.22–24

181 Townshend, *Easter 1916*, pp.70–71

182 Ryan, *Witnesses*, p.82

183 Townshend, *Easter 1916*, p.192

184 Helena Moloney, BMH WS 391

185 Seamus Doyle, BMH WS 768

186 Gialanella Valiulis, Maryann, *Portrait of a Revolutionary*, pp.11–13

187 Paul Galligan, BMH WS 170

188   McGarry, *The Rising, Ireland, Easter 1916*, p.92.
189   Ó Faoláin, *Vive Moi*, pp.100–101
190   Ernest Blythe, BMH WS 939
191   Townshend, *Easter 1916*, p.28
192   Gilbert Morrissey, BMH WS 874
193   Aan de Wiel, Jerome, 'Europe and the Irish Crisis, 1900–1917', in Doherty and Keogh (eds.) *1916, The Long Revolution*, pp.38–39
194   Ó Broin, Leon, *The Chief Secretary, Augustine Birrell in Ireland*, pp.160–168
195   Coogan, *The Easter Rising*, p.74
196   Aan de Wiel, 'Europe and the Irish Crisis', pp.39–40
197   Townshend, *Easter 1916*, p.126, 143. British military intelligence calculated they had 4,800 rifles, shotguns and revolvers in their possession, along with home-made grenades and bayonets.
198   Dwyer, T. Ryle, *Tans, Terror and Troubles: Kerry's Real Fighting Story*, pp.84–85; Townshend, *Easter 1916*, pp.129–130
199   Paul Galligan to Monsignor Eugene Galligan, 29 November, 1917 (Galligan personal papers)
200   Townshend, *Easter 1916*, pp.131–133
201   Ibid, pp.136–139
202   McGarry, *The Rising, Ireland, Easter 1916*, p.117
203   Ibid.
204   Ryan, *Witnesses*, pp.86–93; Townshend, *Easter 1916*, pp.221–224
205   Hart, *The IRA and its Enemies*, pp.47–49
206   Townshend, p.123
207   Stephens, James, *The Insurrection in Dublin*, pp.3–7
208   O'Malley, *On Another Man's Wound*, pp.34–35
209   Ibid.
210   Ibid, pp.37–38
211   Ibid, pp.39
212   Ryan, *Witnesses*, p.121
213   Townshend, p.174
214   Stephens, *The Insurrection in Dublin*, p.18
215   Townshend, p.183
216   Coogan, *The Easter Rising*, p107
217   Ibid.
218   O'Brien, Paul, *Blood on the Streets: 1916 and the Battle For Mount Street Bridge*, pp.22–23
219   Townshend, p.163
220   Ibid, p.177
221   Coogan, *The Easter Rising*, pp.103–104
222   O'Malley, *On Another Man's Wound*, pp.40–41
223   Townshend, pp.263–264
224   William O'Brien, BMH WS 1766
225   Townshend, pp.263–264

226   Ibid, p.191
227   Stephens, *The Insurrection in Dublin*, p.26
228   Ibid, p.53
229   Coogan, *Easter Rising*, pp.130–131
230   Ryan, *Witnesses*, p.158
231   Foy, Michael T. and Barton, Brian, *The Easter Rising*, pp.196–198
232   Seán McLoughlin, BMH WS 290
233   Seán McLoughlin, BMH WS 290
234   Coogan, *The Easter Rising*, pp.124–125
235   Ibid, p.122
236   O'Brien, *Blood on the Streets*, p.36
237   Townshend, p.195
238   O'Brien, *Blood on the Streets*, p.43
239   Caulfield, Max, *The Easter Rebellion*; Doherty, Gabriel, and Dermot Keogh, (eds.), *1916: The Long Revolution*, p.251
240   O'Brien, *Blood on the Streets*, p.69
241   Ibid; Declan Kiberd, *1916, Rebellion Handbook*, pp.50–55
242   O'Brien, *Blood on the Streets*, p.83; Declan Kiberd, *1916, Rebellion Handbook*, pp.50–55
243   McGarry, *The Rising, Ireland, Easter 1916*, p.173.
244   Caulfield, *The Easter Rebellion*, pp.287–292
245   Ryan, *Witnesses*, pp.128–133
246   Caulfield, *The Easter Rebellion*, p.342,
247   Coogan, *The Easter Rising*, pp.152–155
248   Caulfield, *The Easter Rebellion*, pp.338–340
249   Coogan, *The Easter Rising*, p.155
250   Townshend, p.245: the recollection is that of Volunteer Medical Officer James Ryan.
251   Foy and Barton, *The Easter Rising*, p.204
252   Townshend, p.205
253   Seán McLoughlin, BMH WS 290
254   Townshend, p.246
255   Townshend, p.250
256   Stephens, *The Insurrection in Dublin*, p.67
257   Townshend, pp.246–250
258   Townshend, p.252
259   Ryan, *Witnesses*, p.135
260   Townshend, pp.250–251
261   O'Malley, *On Another Man's Wound*, pp.40–47
262   Yeates, *A City in Wartime*, p.122. The figure refers to the amount of compensation paid, but the chief fire officer of Dublin thought that the real damages were no more than one million pounds.
263   NLI image: http://www.nli.ie/blog/wp-content/uploads/2012/05/Prevention-of-Epidemic.jpg

264 O'Connor, Diarmuid, and Connolly, Frank, *Sleep Soldier Sleep: The Life and Times of Padraig O'Connor*, pp.14–15

265 McGarry, *The Rising*, p.253

266 Caulfield, *The Easter Rebellion*, p.355

267 Ryan, *Witnesses*, p.135

268 Stephens, *The Insurrection in Dublin*, p.39

269 Ibid, p.57

270 Townshend, p.267

271 O'Donnell, Ruán (ed.), *The Impact of the 1916 Rising: Among the Nations*, pp.196–97

272 O'Malley *On Another Man's Wound*, pp.43–47

273 McGarry, *The Rising*, p.281

274 Seamus Doyle, BMH WS 215

275 Paul Galligan, BMH WS 170

276 Father Patrick Murphy, BMH WS 204,

277 Seamus Doyle, BMH WS 215

278 Ibid.

279 RIC Report on the Sinn Féin or Irish Volunteer Rebellion in HO 45/10810/312350 Royal Commission on the Rebellion in Ireland (1916)

280 Campbell, *Land and Revolution*, p.218

281 Gilbert Morrissey, BMH WS 874

282 Campbell, *Land and Revolution*, p.217. See also Fearghal McGarry, *The Rising*, p.243

283 Gilbert Morrissey, BMH WS 874

284 Seamus Doyle, BMH WS 215

285 Campbell, *Land and Revolution*, p.215

286 McGarry, *The Rising*, p.243

287 John O'Reilly, BMH WS 1,301

288 Farry, *The Irish Revolution*, p.29

289 Townshend, p.393

290 O'Halpin, Eunan, 'Counting Terror', in David Fitzpatrick (ed.) *Terror in Ireland*, p.150

291 Coogan, *The Easter Rising*, pp.145–46

292 Ibid, p.168

293 Ibid, p.155

294 Townshend, pp.293–294

295 Caulfield, *The Easter Rebellion*, p.198

296 Ibid, p.240

297 Townshend, p.293

298 Caulfield, *The Easter Rebellion*, p.279

299 Ibid, p.305

300 Wheatley, Michael, '"Irreconcilable Enemies" or "Flesh and Blood"? The Irish Party and the Easter Rebels, 1914–16' in Keogh, Dermot and Doherty, Gabriel (eds.) *1916: The Long Revolution*, p.65

301   Townshend, pp.280–282

302   Townshend, p.306

303   McGarry, *The Rising*, p.276

304   Seán Murphy, BMH WS 204

305   MacAtasney, *Seán MacDiarmada*, p.137

306   Seán McLoughlin, BMH WS 290

307   Townshend, p.274

308   Wheatley, '"Irreconcilable Enemies" or "Flesh and Blood", The Irish Party and the Easter Rebels', in Keogh, Dermot and Doherty, Gabriel (eds) *1916, the Long Revolution*, p.74

309   Seamus MacDiarmada, BMH WS 768

310   Campbell, *Land and Revolution*, p.222

311   Walsh, Maurice, *The News from Ireland, Foreign Correspondents and the Irish Revolution*, p.54

312   Keogh, Dermot, 'The Catholic Church, the Holy See and the 1916 Rising', in *1916: The Long Revolution*, p.283

313   Townshend, p.269

314   Above quotes from provincial newspapers, cited in Wheatley's 'Irreconcilable Enemies' in *1916: The Long Revolution*, pp.61–74

315   RIC Yearly report 1916 (UK National Archives). CO 904 RIC Monthly and Annual reports

316   Figes, Orlando, *A People's Tragedy: The Russian Revolution*, p.201

317   Yeates, *A City in Wartime*, p.128

318   Farry, *The Irish Revolution*, p.32

319   Yeates, *A City in Wartime*, pp.191–192

320   William O'Brien, BMH WS1766

321   Paul Galligan to Eugene Galligan, 29 November 1917 (Galligan personal papers)

322   Gilbert Morrissey, BMH WS 874

323   Ernest Blythe, BMH WS 939

324   Walsh, Robert, 'Dartmoor: The Prison That Broke the Body and then the Soul', *Crime Magazine*, May 16 , 2010.

325   Paul Galligan to Monsignor Eugene Galligan, October 1917. (Galligan personal papers)

326   Paul Galligan to Monsignor Eugene Galligan, 4 May 1917 (Galligan personal papers)

327   Coogan, Tim Pat, *De Valera, Long Fellow, Long Shadow*, p.80

328   Paul Galligan, BMH WS 170

329   Caulfield, *The Easter Rebellion*, p.219

330   Ferriter, Diarmaid, *Judging Dev: A Reassessment of the Life and Legacy of Eamon de Valera*, p.30

331   Paul Galligan, BMH WS 170

332   Coogan, *De Valera*, p.80

333   Seamus Doyle, BMH WS 1,342

334 Coogan, *De Valera*, p.80

335 Paul Galligan, BMH WS 170

336 Coogan, *De Valera*, p.81

337 Paul Galligan, BMH WS 170

338 Laffan, Michael, *The Resurrection of Ireland, The Sinn Féin Party, 1916–1923*, p.55

339 McCarthy, John, *P. Kevin O'Higgins, Builder of The Irish Free State*, p.4

340 Hart, *The IRA and its Enemies*, p.205; McGarry, *The Rising*, p.281

341 McGarry, *Eoin O'Duffy*, p.26

342 Hartnett, Mossie, *Victory and Woe*, p.23

343 O'Malley, *On Another Man's Wound*, p.11

344 RIC Yearly report, 1917 (UK National Archive) CO 904

345 Laffan, *The Resurrection of Ireland*, p.98

346 Ibid, p.118

347 Paul Galligan to Monsignor Eugene Galligan, 15 November 1917 (Galligan personal papers)

348 Dwyer, T. Ryle, *Tans, Terror and Troubles, Kerry's Real Fighting Story*, p.116. See also *The Irish Times*, June 16, 1917

349 Paul Galligan to Monsignor Eugene Galligan, 15 November 1917 (Galligan personal papers)

350 *The Irish Times*, 27 September 1917

351 Hopkinson, Michael, *The Irish War of Independence*, p.98

352 Hart, Peter, *Mick, The Real Michael Collins*, pp.142–143

353 Ibid, p.71

354 Valiulis, *Richard Mulcahy, Portrait of a Revolutionary*, p.8

355 O'Malley, *The Singing Flame*, p.34

356 Fitzpatrick, David, *Politics and Irish Life, 1913–1921: Provincial Experiences of War and Revolution*, p.132

357 Dooley, Terence, '*The Land For the People': The Land Question in Independent Ireland*, p.32

358 Ibid.

359 Hart, Peter, *The IRA at War 1916–1923*, p.53

360 Yeates, *A City in Wartime*, p.227

361 Kostick, Conor, *Revolution in Ireland, Popular Militancy, 1917–1923*, p.35

362 Paul Galligan to Monsignor Eugene Galligan, 17 October 1917 (Galligan personal papers)

363 Campbell, *Land and Revolution*, p.197

364 Jackson, *Home Rule, An Irish History, 1800–2000*, pp.206–214

365 James Cahill, BMH WS 503

366 Full text of Sheehan's speech available here: http://en.wikisource.org/wiki/Irish_Anti-Conscription_Crisis.

367 Peel, Henry, 'The Scourge of Conscription', *St Martin de Porres magazine*, a publication of the Irish Dominicans.http://www.catholicireland.net/the-scourge-of-conscription/

368 Walsh, *The News from Ireland*, p.56
369 Collins, Ireland 1868–1968, pp.241–242
370 Townshend, pp.341–342
371 Ernest Blythe, BMH WS 939
372 Townshend, p.340
373 Hart, Mick, *The Real Michael Collins*, p.203
374 Laffan, *The Resurrection of Ireland*, p.164
375 Dwyer, *Tans, Terror and Troubles*, pp.152–153
376 Philpin, Charles H. E., *Nationalism and Popular Protest in Ireland*, p.415
377 http://www.ark.ac.uk/elections/h1918.htm
378 Ryan, *Comrades: Inside the War of Independence*, p.222
379 Ó Ruairc, *Blood on the Banner: The Republican Struggle in Clare*, p.63
380 Hart, *The IRA and its Enemies*, p.47
381 Ryan, Meda, *Liam Lynch, the Real Chief*, p.13
382 Witness Statements: Seán Sheridan WS 1613, Hugh Maguire WS 1387 , Francis Connell, WS 1663 BMH
383 Dwyer, *Tans, Terror and Troubles*, p.16
384 Hopkinson, *The Irish War of Independence*, p.115,. Richard Mulcahy, head of the Volunteers, said it was 'tantamount to murder'.
385 Daniel Breen, BMH WS 1739
386 Hart, *The IRA at War*, p.71
387 Dwyer, *The Squad*, p.46
388 Ibid, pp.47–48
389 Ernest Blythe, BMH WS 939
390 Valiulis, *Richard Mulcahy, Portrait of a Revolutionary*, p.48
391 Cahill, Liam, *Forgotten Revolution, The Limerick Soviet 1919, A threat to British Rule in Ireland*, pp.21–22
392 The text of the Democratic Programme is available here: http://www.labour.ie/download/pdf/dem_pr3.pdf
393 Ernest Blythe, BMH WS 939
394 Borgonovo, John, 'Republican Courts, Ordinary Crime and the Irish Revolution 1919–21' in De Koster, Margo; Leuwers, Herve; Luyten, Dirk; Rousseaux, Xavier (eds.) *Justice in Wartime and Revolutions*, p. 54
395 Ryan, *Comrades*, p.139
396 Borgonovo, 'Republican Courts, Ordinary Crime and Irish Revolution' in *Justice in Wartime and Revolutions*, p.53
397 Seán Sheridan, WS 1613; Francis Connell WS 1663 BMH
398 Francis Connell, BMH WS 1663
399 Borgonovo, 'Republican Courts, Ordinary Crime and Irish Revolution' in *Justice in Wartime and Revolutions*, p56
400 Dwyer, *Tans, Terror and Troubles*, pp.176–177
401 Borgonovo, 'Republican Courts, Ordinary Crime and Irish Revolution' in *Justice in Wartime and Revolutions*, p.59

402   Fitzpatrick, David, *Politics and Irish Life, 1913–1921: Provincial Experiences of War and Revolution*, p.132

403   Campbell, *Land and Revolution*, p.281

404   Sheehan, William, *Hearts and Mines: The British 5th Division in Ireland 1920–1922*, p.107.

405   Borgonovo, 'Republican Courts, Ordinary Crime and Irish Revolution' in *Justice in Wartime and Revolutions*, p.62

406   Hopkinson, *The Irish War of Independence*, pp.43–44

407   Yeates, *A City in Turmoil*, pp.106–107

408   Ryan, *Comrades*, p.133

409   Cahill, *The Forgotten Revolution*, pp.160–161

410   O'Malley, *On Another Man's Wound*, p.122

411   Dwyer, *Tans, Terror and Troubles*, p.160

412   Hopkinson, *The Irish War of Independence*, p.55

413   Ibid, p.119

414   O'Malley, *On Another Man's Wound*, pp.170–172

415   Hart, *The IRA and its Enemies*, p.1

416   Dwyer, *Tans, Terror and Troubles*, p.182

417   Sheehan, *Hearts and Mines*, pp.36–37

418   Yeates, *A City in Turmoil*, p.112

419   Kostick, *Revolution in Ireland*, pp.132–135

420   Ibid, p.141

421   Dwyer, *Tans, Terror and Troubles*, pp.219–220

422   Hart, *The IRA and its Enemies*, p.77

423   Ibid, p.78

424   Dwyer, *Tans, Terror and Troubles*, pp.210–212

425   Lawlor, Pearse, *The Burnings, 1920*, pp.75–81

426   Lynch, Robert, *Northern Divisions: The Northern IRA and the Early Years of Partition*, pp.25–26

427   Parkinson, Alan F., *Belfast's Unholy War*, pp.33–36

428   Lynch, *Northern Divisions*, p.34

429   Parkinson, Alan F., *Belfast's Unholy War*, p.317

430   Maye, Brian, *Arthur Griffith*, p.148; Hart, *Mick*, p.268

431   Hopkinson, *The Irish War of Independence*, p.65

432   Ó Ruairc, *Blood on the Banner*, pp.332–333. In County Clare alone, 15 locals joined the Auxiliaries and 46 joined the Black and Tans.

433   Peter Galligan to Monsignor Eugene Galligan, 9 September 1920. (Galligan personal papers)

434   Ó Ruairc, *Blood on the Banner*, p.123

435   Hart, *Mick*, p.268

436   Barry, *Guerilla Days in Ireland*, p.41

437   Hopkinson, *The Irish War of Independence*, p.146

438   Dwyer, *Tans, Terror and Troubles*, p.220

439 Leeson, David, *The Black and Tans, British Police and Auxiliaries in the Irish War of Independence*, pp.176–177

440 *The Anglo-Celt,* January 21 1922

441 Leeson, *Black and Tans*, p.137

442 Coleman, Marie, *County Longford and the Irish Revolution 1910–1923*, pp.226–236, 124

443 Hart, *The IRA and its Enemies*, p.86

444 Ó Ruairc, *Blood on the Banner*, pp.162–166; O'Malley, Ernie, *Raids and Rallies*, pp.72–77

445 Ó Ruairc, *Blood on The Banner*, pp.167–171; O'Malley, *On Another Man's Wound*, pp.77–87

446 Ryan, *Comrades*, p.132

447 Ibid, p.203

448 Dwyer, *Tans, Terror and Troubles*, pp.228–253

449 Leonard, Jane, "'English Dogs or Poor Devils?" The Dead of Bloody Sunday Morning' in *Terror in Ireland*, p.130

450 See Hopkinson, *The Irish War of Independence*, pp.89–90; Dwyer, *The Squad*, pp.190–192

451 Hopkinson, *The Irish War of Independence*, p.88

452 Ibid.

453 Barry, *Guerilla Days In Ireland*, p.41

454 Peter Hart, in *The IRA and it Enemies* maintains the Auxiliaries were 'exterminated'. Meda Ryan, in her biography of Tom Barry, sticks to Barry's contention that there was a false surrender which forfeited the British right to be taken prisoner. See Hart, The IRA and its Enemies, pp.21–27 and Ryan, *Tom Barry IRA Freedom Fighter*, pp.43–47.

455 Hopkinson, *The Irish War of Independence*, p.139

456 White, Gerry and O'Shea, Brendan, *The Burning of Cork*

457 Maye, *Arthur Griffith*, p.149

458 Collins, *Ireland 1868–1968*, p.265

459 Dwyer, *Tans, Terror and Troubles*, pp.289–295

460 Ryan, *Comrades*, p.87; Hart, *The IRA and its Enemies*, p.97

461 Barry, *Guerilla Days in Ireland*, pp.96–98

462 Sheehan William, *A Hard Local War, The British Army and the Guerrilla War in Cork, 1919–1921*, p.142

463 O'Malley, *On Another Man's Wound*, p.316

464 James Durney, 'How Aungier Street became known as the Dardanelles', *The Irish Sword*, Summer 2010, vol. XXVII p.245

465 Sheehan, William, *Fighting for Dublin, The British battle for Dublin 1919–1921*, p.125

466 *The Irish Times*, 13 May 1921

467 *The Irish Times*, May 1921

468 Doyle, Tom, *The Civil War in Kerry*, p.43

469 Augusteijn, Joost, *From Public Defiance to Guerrilla Warfare*, pp.170–171

470 Defence Forces Review 2007, Lecture on the Customs House attack delivered by Captain M. O. Kelly, Infantry School, Millitary College, June 1935

471 Corlett, Christian, *Robert L Chapman's Ireland. Photographs from the Chapman Collection, 1907–1957*, Collins Press, Cork 2008, p 57

472 *Irish Bulletin*, reported in *The Irish Times*, 28 May 1921

473 Hopkinson, *The Irish War of Independence*, p.102

474 Harnden, Toby, *Bandit Country: The IRA and South Armagh*, pp.93–94

475 McGarry, *Eoin O'Duffy, A Self-Made Hero*, pp.59–61

476 Ó Ruairc, *Blood on the Banner*, p.231

477 Hart, *The IRA and its Enemies*, p.99

478 O'Malley, *On Another Man's Wound*, pp.371–373

479 Dwyer, *Tans, Terror and Troubles*, p.287

480 *The Anglo-Celt*, 18 June 1921

481 McMahon, The Anglo-Celt, p.46

482 Ó Ruairc, *Blood on the Banner*, p.267

483 *The Anglo-Celt*, 16 July 1921

484 Valiulis, *Richard Mulcahy*, p.68

485 Augusteijn, *From Public Defiance to Guerrilla Warfare*, pp.170–17

486 Coleman, *Longford and the Irish Revolution*, p.154

487 Hart, *The IRA and its Enemies*, pp.293–296

488 Ryan, Meda, *Tom Barry: IRA Freedom Fighter*, p.164

489 Barry, *Guerilla Days in Ireland*, p.113

490 Fitzgerald, Thomas Earls, 'The Execution of Spies and Informers', in Fitzpatrick (ed.), *Terror in Ireland*, pp.184–185

491 Barry, *Guerilla Days in Ireland*, p.214

492 Valiulis, *Richard Mulcahy*, p.69

493 *The Anglo-Celt*, 18 June 1921

494 Lynch, Robert, *Northern Divisions*, pp.65–86; McGarry, *Eoin O'Duffy*, pp.53–55

495 O'Malley, *On Another Man's Wound*, p.370

496 Valiulis, *Richard Mulcahy*, p.70

497 McMahon, *British Spies and Irish Rebels*, p.46

498 Sheehan, William, *Fighting for Dublin*, p.60

499 McMahon, *British Spies and Irish Rebels*, p.53; Hart, *The IRA and its Enemies*, p.110

500 O'Malley, *On Another Man's Wound*, pp.380–381

501 Francis Connell, BMH WS 1,663

502 Hart, *The IRA and its Enemies*, p.109

503 Dwyer, *Tans, Terror and Troubles*, p.320

504 Parkinson, Alan F., *Belfast's Unholy War*, p.154

505 O'Malley, *On Another Man's Wound*, p.381

506 O'Halpin, Eunan, 'Counting Terror', in *Terror in Ireland*, p.153

507   Ibid., and Hart, *IRA and its Enemies*, p.87. Hart gives a higher total of 523 killed.

508   O'Halpin, 'Counting Terror', in *Terror in Ireland*, p.153

509   Ibid.

510   Ibid. and Ó Ruairc, *Blood on the Banner*, p.259

511   Ibid.

512   Sheehan, William, *British Voices from the Irish War of Independence*, p.89

513   Hopkinson, Michael, *Green Against Green, The Irish Civil War*, p.12

514   *The Anglo-Celt*, 12 November 1921

515   McGarry, *Eoin O'Duffy*, p.72

516   Ibid, pp.76–77

517   Regan, John M., *The Irish Counter-Revolution 1921–1931: Treatyite Politics and Settlement in Independent Ireland*, p.12

518   Hopkinson, *Green against Green*, pp.19–22, 27–28, 31

519   Ibid, p.279

520   Coogan, Tim Pat, *Michael Collins*, p.263.

521   Pakenham, Frank, *Peace by Ordeal, The Negotiations of the Anglo Irish Treaty, 1921*, pp.209–211

522   Hopkinson, *Green Against Green*, pp.30–32; Pakenham, *Peace by Ordeal*, pp.245–247

523   Coogan, *Michael Collins*, p.276

524   Regan, John M., *The Irish Counter-Revolution*, p.10

525   Ibid, p.41

526   Ibid

527   Ibid, p.44

528   Hopkinson, *Green Against Green*, p.37

529   *The Anglo-Celt*, 10 December, 1921

530   Hopkinson, *Green Against Green*, pp.44–45

531   Seamus McKenna, BMH WS 1,016,

532   O'Malley, *The Singing Flame*, p.41

533   Andrews, Todd, *Dublin Made Me*, p.217

534   O'Malley, *The Singing Flame*, p.285

535   Regan, *The Irish Counter-Revolution*, p.42

536   Hopkinson, *Green Against Green*, p.131

537   Ibid, p.67

538   See, for instance: Tom Garvin, *1922, The Birth of Irish Democracy*

539   Peter Hart, in *The IRA at War* (p.97) has written, 'The Volunteers were democratic, not anti-democratic. They typically felt themselves to be above the political process, but they never sought to change it or to end it in the name of a fascist, communist or militarist alternative, or even in the name of a national emergency',

540   Andrews, *Dublin Made Me*, p.233

541   O'Malley, *The Singing Flame*, p.25

542   Hart, *The IRA and its Enemies*, p.112

543   Ó Ruairc, *Blood on the Banner*, p.291

544   Dwyer, *Tans, Terror and Troubles*, pp.342–343

545   Hart, *The IRA and its Enemies*, pp.274–278

546   MacMahon, Paul, *British Spies and Irish Rebels, British Intelligence in Ireland*, p.71

547   *The New York Times*, 29 April 1922 http://query.nytimes.com/mem/archive-free/pdf?res=9C06E4D71E3CE533A2575AC2A9629C946395D6CF

548   Harrington, Niall C., *Kerry Landing, August 1922: An Episode of the Irish Civil War*, p.21

549   Andrews, *Dublin Made Me*, pp.241–242

550   *The Anglo-Celt*, November 1921–March 1922

551   *The Anglo-Celt*, December 24 1921 and January 3 1922

552   *The Anglo-Celt*, April 25 1922

553   *The Anglo-Celt*, January 28 1922

554   Harrington, *Kerry Landing*, p.21

555   McMahon, *British Spies and Irish Rebels*, p.75

556   McLure, Charlie, *Roddy Connolly and the Struggle for Socialism in Ireland*, Cork University Press 2006, p.52

557   Corbett, Jim, *Not While I Have Ammo, A History of Captain Connie Mackey, Defender of the Strand*, p.77

558   Hopkinson, *Green Against Green*, p.74

559   Hartnett, Mossie, *Victory and Woe*, p.127

560   *The Irish Times*, April 29, 1922

561   Hopkinson, *Green Against Green*, p.75

562   Harrington, *Kerry Landing*, p.22

563   Coogan, *Michael Collins*, p.319

564   Ernest Blythe, BMH WS 939

565   Lynch Robert, *Northern Divisions*, p.136

566   Ibid, p.127

567   Parkinson, *Belfast's Unholy War*, p.318

568   *The Anglo-Celt*, April 15 and 29, 1922

569   Parkinson, *Belfast's Unholy War*, pp.229–231

570   Ibid, pp 229–235, 245–246; Lynch, *Northern Divisions*, p.122

571   Parkinson, *Belfast's Unholy War*, pp.170–172

572   Lynch, *Northern Divisions*, p.148

573   Hopkinson, *Green against Green*, pp.83–87. See also: Glennon, Kieran, *From Pogrom to Civil War*, pp.179–181

574   Litton, Helen, *The Irish Civil War, an Illustrated History*, p.63

575   Hopkinson, *Green against Green* p.107

576   Walsh, *The Irish Civil War – A study of the Conventional Phase*,

577   Borgonovo, John, *The Battle for Cork, July–August 1922*

578   Hopkinson, *Green Against Green*, p.116

579   Ibid, p.112; Collins, *Ireland 1868–1966*, p.229; Hartigan, Niall C., *The Kerry Landings*, p.29

580 Harrington, *Kerry Landings*, p.26

581 O'Malley, *The Singing Flame*, p.75

582 Ryan, *Tom Barry*, pp.172–173

583 O'Malley, *The Singing Flame*, p.91

584 Walsh, Paul V., *The Irish Civil War – a Study of the Conventional phase*

585 O'Malley, *The Singing Flame*, p.101

586 Walsh, Paul V., *The Irish Civil War 1922–23 -A Study of the Conventional Phase*

587 *An Phoblacht*, 3 July 1997, http://www.anphoblacht.com/news/detail/28711

588 O'Malley, *The Singing Flame*, p.126

589 Walsh, *The Irish Civil War 1922–23 -A Study of the Conventional Phase.*

590 Walsh, Paul V., *The Irish Civil War 1922–23 -A Study of the Conventional Phase*; Hopkinson, *Green Against Green*, p.126.

591 Hopkinson, *Green Against Green*, p.126

592 Harrington, *Kerry Landings*, p.167; Doyle, Tom, *The Civil War in Kerry*, p.105

593 Andrews, *Dublin Made Me*, p.247

594 O'Malley, *The Singing Flame*, p.129

595 Andrews, *Dublin Made Me*, p.246

596 Hartnett, *Victory and Woe*, p.140

597 Sherwin, Frank, *Independent and Unrepentant*, p.15

598 Harrington, *Kerry Landings*, pp.35–36

599 O'Malley, Cormac K.H., and Dolan, Anne (eds.) *No Surrender Here! The Civil War Papers of Ernie O'Malley*, pp.152–153

600 McLure, Roddy Connolly and Struggle for Socialism in Ireland, pp.62–65

601 Hegarty, Kathleen, *They Put the Flag A-Flyin': The Roscommon Volunteers, 1916–1923*, p.317

602 Hopkinson, *Green Against Green*, p.157

603 Corbett, *Not While I Have Ammo, The History of Connie Mackey, Defender of the Strand*, p.84

604 *The New York Times*, July 16 1922; Harrington, Kerry Landings, p.167; Corbett, *Not While I Have Ammo*, p.87.

605 Corbett, *Not While I Have Ammo*, p.93

606 Ibid, p.94

607 Ibid, p.95

608 Ibid, p.99

609 Ibid, p.99; Ó Ruairc, *The Battle For Limerick City*, pp.140–141

610 Ibid, pp.99–100

611 Hopkinson, *Green Against Green*, p.165

612 O'Reilly, Terence, *Rebel Heart: George Lennon, Flying Column Commander*, p.175

613 Ibid, p.173

614 Ibid, p.205

615 Ibid, p.181

616 Ibid, pp.175–188

617 Ibid, p.195

618 Ibid, p.191

619 Hopkinson, *Green Against Green*, p.152

620 Hart, *The IRA and its Enemies*, p.117

621 Hopkinson, *Green Against Green*, p.152

622 Harrington, *Kerry Landings*, p.167; *The New York Times*, 1 July 1922

623 Campbell, Joseph, *As I was Among the Captives, Joseph Campbell's Prison Diary 1922–1923*

624 Harrington, *Kerry Landings*, p.91

625 Ibid, pp.130–131

626 Hopkinson, *Green Against Green*, p.164

627 Walsh, Paul V., *The Irish Civil War, A study of the Conventional Phase*

628 Hopkinson, *Green Against Green*, p.164

629 Hart, *The IRA and its Enemies*, p.119

630 Hopkinson, *Green Against Green*, p.164

631 Ibid, p.177

632 Harrington, Michael, *The Munster Republic: North Cork and the Irish Civil War*, p.77

633 Dooley, Terence, *The Decline of the Big House in Ireland*, p.192

634 Regan, *The Irish Counter-Revolution*, p.104

635 Andrews, *Dublin Made Me*, p.147, 264

636 O'Malley and Dolan (eds.), *No Surrender Here!* p.134

637 McMahon, *British Spies and Irish Rebels*, p.90

638 Ryan, *Tom Barry*, p.179

639 Ryan, Meda, *The Day Michael Collins was Shot*, p.125

640 *The New York Times*, 22 August 1922

641 O'Malley and Dolan (eds.), *No Surrender Here!* p.135

642 Deasy, Liam, *Brother Against Brother*, p.81

643 Regan, *The Irish Counter-Revolution*, p.97

644 Ibid.

645 All above quotes taken from: Cathal Brennan, 'The Postal Strike of 1922', *The Irish Story*, June 2012, http://www.theirishstory.com/2012/06/08/the-postal-strike-of-1922/#.UZlN8KK1HTo Accessed 12/08/13

646 Hopkinson, *Green Against Green*, p.171

647 Doyle, *The Civil War in Kerry*, pp.181–185; Hart, *The IRA and its Enemies*, p.119; Hopkinson, *Green Against Green*, p.203

648 *The Irish Times*, August 31, 1922

649 Doyle, *The Civil War in Kerry*, p.181

650 Hopkinson, *Green Against Green*, p.215

651 Ibid.

652 Ibid, p.164

653 O'Malley, *The Singing Flame*, p.171

654 Harrington, *Kerry Landings*, p.140

655 Doyle, *The Civil War in Kerry*, p.167

656 Hopkinson, *Green Against Green*, p.215

657 O'Halpin, *Defending Ireland, the Irish State and its Enemies since 1922*, pp.13–14; Hart, Mick, p.412

658 Regan, *The Irish Counter-Revolution*, p.105

659 Ernest Blythe, BMH WS 939

660 Dwyer, *Tans, Terror and Troubles*, p.359

661 O'Malley, Dolan, *No Surrender Here!* p.185

662 Doyle, *The Civil War in Kerry*, p.187

663 Regan, *The Irish Counter-Revolution*, pp.107–108

664 Hopkinson, *Green Against Green*, p.138; O'Halpin, Defending Ireland, pp.13–14

665 O'Halpin, *Defending Ireland*, p.13

666 O'Malley, Dolan, *No Surrender Here!* p.214

667 O'Halpin, *Defending Ireland*, p.14

668 Sherwin, *Independent and Unrepentant*, pp.20–21

669 O'Halpin, *Defending Ireland*, p.13

670 Hopkinson, *Green Against Green*, p.145

671 Ibid; O'Malley, *The Singing Flame*, pp.181–188

672 Hopkinson, *Green Against Green*, p.158

673 Farry, *The Aftermath of Revolution*, p.110

674 Hopkinson, *Green Against Green*, pp.215–218

675 Coogan, *De Valera*, p.344

676 O'Malley, *The Singing Flame*, pp.176–177

677 McGarry, *Eoin O'Duffy*, pp.120–124

678 Garvin, *Tom, 1922, The Birth of Irish Democracy*, p.111

679 Hopkinson, *Green Against Green*, p.188

680 Ibid, p.222

681 Coogan, *De Valera*, p.354

682 Breen, Timothy Murphy, PhD Thesis, *The Government's Execution Policy during the Irish Civil War, 1922–23*, Maynooth, 2010

683 Hopkinson, *Green Against Green*, p.181

684 *The Irish Times*, December 16, 1922

685 Hopkinson, *Green Against Green*, p.191

686 Ibid, p.222

687 O'Connor, Diarmuid and Connolly, Frank, *Sleep Soldier Sleep*, p.131

688 Andrews, Todd, *Dublin Made Me*, p.269

689 Hopkinson, *Green Against Green*, p.190; Litton, Helen, *The Irish Civil War, an Illustrated History*, p.113

690 Andrews, *Dublin Made Me*, pp.270–272

691 Dooley, *The Decline of the Big House*, p.189

692 Dooley, *The Decline of the Big House*, pp.174, 196

693   *The Anglo-Celt*, February 3, 1923

694   Ernest Blythe, WS 939 BMH

695   Litton, *Illustrated History of the Irish Civil War*, p.113

696   Hopkinson, *Green Against Green*, p.199

697   Doyle, *The Civil War in Kerry*, p.248

698   Hart, *The IRA and its Enemies*, p.125

699   MacEoin, UinSeánn, *Survivors: The Story of Ireland's Struggle as Told Through Some of Her Outstanding Living People*, p.141

700   Deasy, *Brother Against Brother*, p.98

701   Ibid, pp.110–111

702   Hopkinson, *Green Against Green*, pp.235–6

703   Ibid, p.241; Doyle, *The Civil War in Kerry*, pp.324–6

704   Doyle, *The Civil War in Kerry*, p.269

705   According to Niall Harrington, cited in the RTÉ documentary Ballyseedy, 1997.

706   Doyle, *The Civil War in Kerry*, pp.273–274

707   Harrington, *Kerry Landings*, p.241

708   Doyle, *The Civil War in Kerry*, pp.270–80

709   Hopkinson, p.241

710   *The Irish Times*, December 31, 2008

711   Hopkinson, p.246

712   *An Phoblacht*, March 13, 2003

713   Gallimore, Andrew, *A Bloody Canvass, The Mike McTigue Story*, pp.122–134

714   *The Irish Times*, March 24 1923

715   Ryan, *Tom Barry*, p.193

716   John Shelley, *A Short History of the Third Tipperary Brigade*

717   Doyle, *The Civil War in Kerry*, p.299

718   O'Halpin, *Defending Ireland*, p.44

719   MacEoin, UinSeánn, *Survivors*, p.5

720   Kostick, *Revolution in Ireland*, pp.205–207. See also Emmet O'Connor, 'Agrarian Unrest and the Labour Movement in Waterford, 1917–1923', in *Saothar*, Labour History Journal, 1980, vol. 6, pp.48–53

721   Dooley, *The Land for the People*, p.51

722   *The Anglo-Celt*, March 17, 1923

723   *The Anglo-Celt*, June 2, 1923

724   Hopkinson, *Green Against Green*, pp,272–273

725   Hart, *The IRA and its Enemies*, p.121

726   Doyle, *The Civil War in Kerry*, pp.323–331

727   Dorney, John, 'Casualties of the Civil War in Dublin', *The Irish Story*, June 2012, http://www.theirishstory.com/2012/06/19/casualties-of-the-irish-civil-war-in-dublin/#.UZlJNKK1HTo Accessed 17/08/13

728   Farry, *The Irish Revolution*, p.110

729   Durney, James, The Civil War in Kildare, pp.14–15

730   Phillip McConway, *Offaly and the Civil War Executions*, www.offalyhistory. com

731   Coleman, Marie, *County Longford and the Irish Revolution 1919–1923*, p.144

732   Andrews, *Dublin Made Me*, p.312

733   Durney, *The Civil War in Kildare*, p.159

734   http://electionsireland.org/results/general/04Dáil.cfm | 4th Dáil 1923 General Election

735   MacEoin, *Survivors*, pp.49–50

736   *The Anglo-Celt*, May 12, 1922

737   *The Anglo-Celt*, August 4, 1923

738   *The Anglo-Celt,* September 1, 1923

739   O'Malley, *The Singing Flame*, p.238

740   *The Anglo-Celt*, August 18, 1923

741   *Dundalk Democrat*, October 18 1924

742   Garvin, *The Evolution of Nationalist Politics*, p.159

743   Milne, Ida. 'Is History Repeating? The Spanish flu of 1918' http:// puesoccurrences.com/2009/06/02/history-repeating-the-spanish-flu-of-1918/ Accessed 17/08/13

744   Information on the financial impact of the Civil War is taken from Michael Hopkinson, *Green Against Green, The Irish Civil War*, p.273

745   Ibid; O'Halpin, *Defending Ireland*, pp.45–51; McCarthy, *Kevin O'Higgins*, pp.122–123

746   Joseph O'Connor, BMH WS 544

747   Valiulis, *General Richard Mulcahy*, pp.214–215

748   Lee, *Ireland 1912–1985*, p.106

749   Collins, *Ireland 1866–1966*, p.342

750   Lee, *Ireland 1912–1985*, p.127

751   Hopkinson, p.273

752   McCabe, *Sins of the Father*, p.133

753   *The Anglo-Celt*, August 11,1923

754   Coogan, *De Valera*, pp.400–401

755   McGarry, *Eoin O'Duffy*, p.189

756   Jackson, *Ireland, 1798–1998, War, Peace and Beyond*, p.293

757   Coakley & Gallagher, *Politics in the Republic of Ireland*, pp.73–75

758   Sheppard, Barry, 'Rathcairn: Land and Language Reform in the Irish Free State', *The Irish Story*, July 2012, http://www.theirishstory. com/2012/07/13/rath-cairn-land-reform-language-politics-in-the-irish-free-state/#.UZ06jKK1HTo Accessed 17/09/13

759   Dooley, *The Land for the People*, p.107

760   Hart, *The IRA at War*, p.240

761   Hopkinson, p.195.

762 Bielenberg, Andy, 'Exodus, the Emigration of Southern Irish Protestants during the Irish War of Independence and Civil War', *Past and Present*, no.218, February 2013.

763 Reported in *The Anglo-Celt*, July 21, 1923

764 Lynch, Northern Divisions, p.227; Hart, *The IRA at War*, p.245

765 Hart, *The IRA at War*, p.252

766 Ibid, pp.249–50

767 *The Anglo-Celt*, October 14, 1922, reporting on the Catholic Truth Society Convention

768 Ó Faoláin, *Vive Moi!* p.176

769 McCarthy, *Kevin O'Higgins*, pp.265–266

770 https://www.constitution.ie/AttachmentDownload.ashx?mid= ee219062-2178-e211-a5a0-005056a32ee4

771 McGarry, *Eoin O'Duffy, a Self-Made Hero*, p.157

772 Ibid, p.158

773 Garvin, Tom, 'Turmoil in a Sea of Faith, The Secularisation of Irish Social Culture, 1960–2007', *Turning Points in Twentieth Century Irish History*, pp.156–157

774 Joseph O'Connor, BMH WS 544

775 Ibid.

776 Hobsbawm, *The Age of Extremes, The Short Twentieth Century*, p.199

777 Ahmed Hashim, *Insurgency and Counter Insurgency in Iraq* for example, has a chapter comparing Ireland to contemporary Iraq. A More direct example is William Kaut's *Ambushes and Armour*.

778 Peter Hart, in *The IRA and its Enemies*, writes of the Dunmanway incident: 'the religion of the men is inescapable, they were shot because they were Protestants'. Nationalist author Meda Ryan, in *Tom Barry, IRA Freedom Fighter*, wrote a riposte, claiming stridently that they were shot for informing on 'Fight for freedom activities'. Hart, p.291; Ryan, p.209

779 Andrews, *Dublin Made Me*, p.254

780 Dolan, *Commemorating the Irish Civil War*, p.50

781 The classic text on revolutionary sociology is Crane Brinton, *The Anatomy of Revolution*, (1965).

782 The post box remark was, according to historian Diarmuid Ferriter, 'a favourite sneer of Republicans in the 1920s'. *The Transformation of Ireland*, pp.304–305.

Index Terms